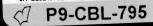

REWILD ™

BERGER BOOKS

AN IMPRINT OF
DARK HORSE COMICS

Devin Grayson

writer

Yana Adamovic

artist

Sal Cipriano

letterer

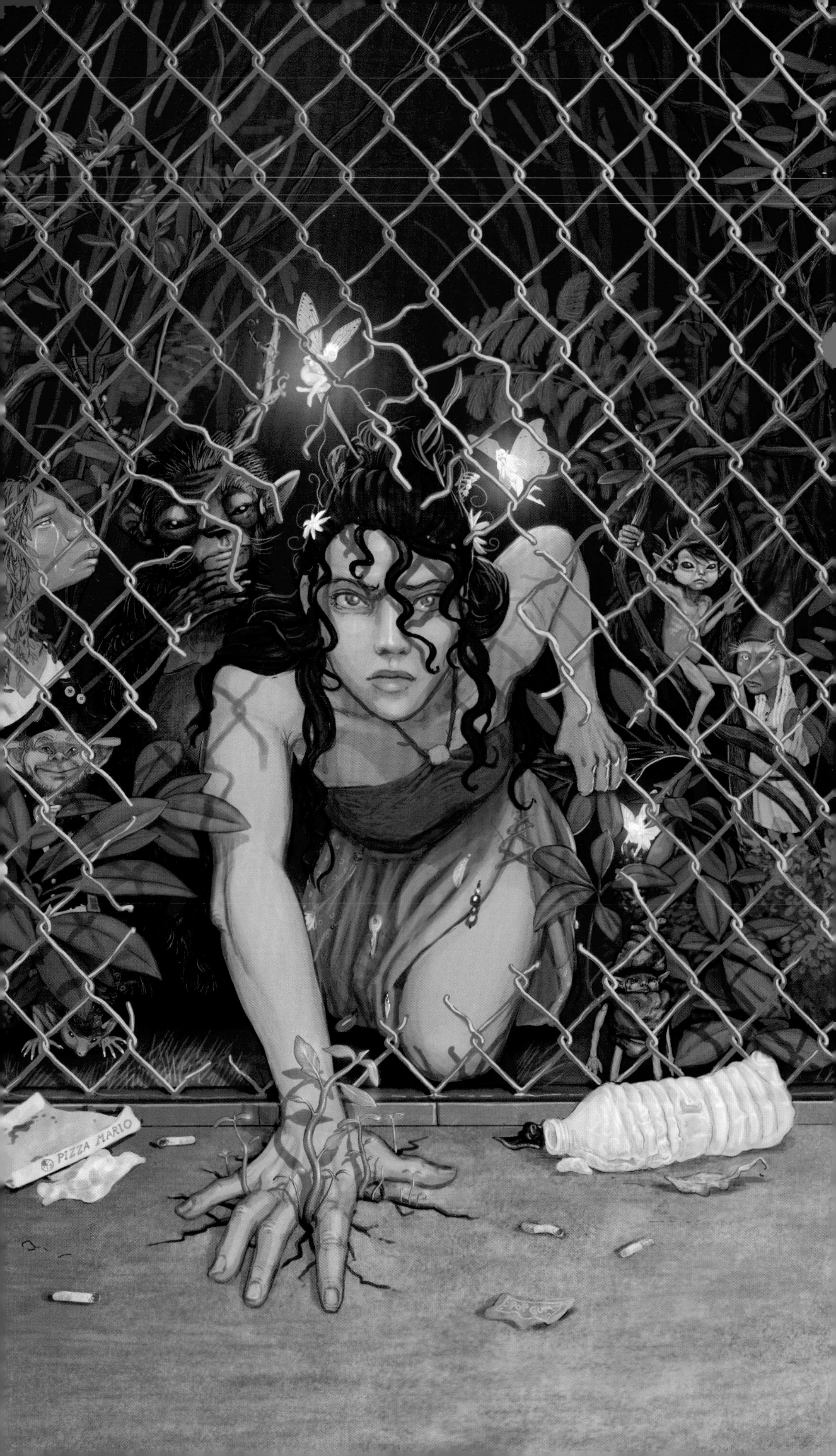
PIZZA MARIO

To my mom, who never stopped trying
to make this world a better place.
– Devin Grayson

To my son, Taras, along with my dreams
of a better future for you.
– Yana Adamovic

Chapter I

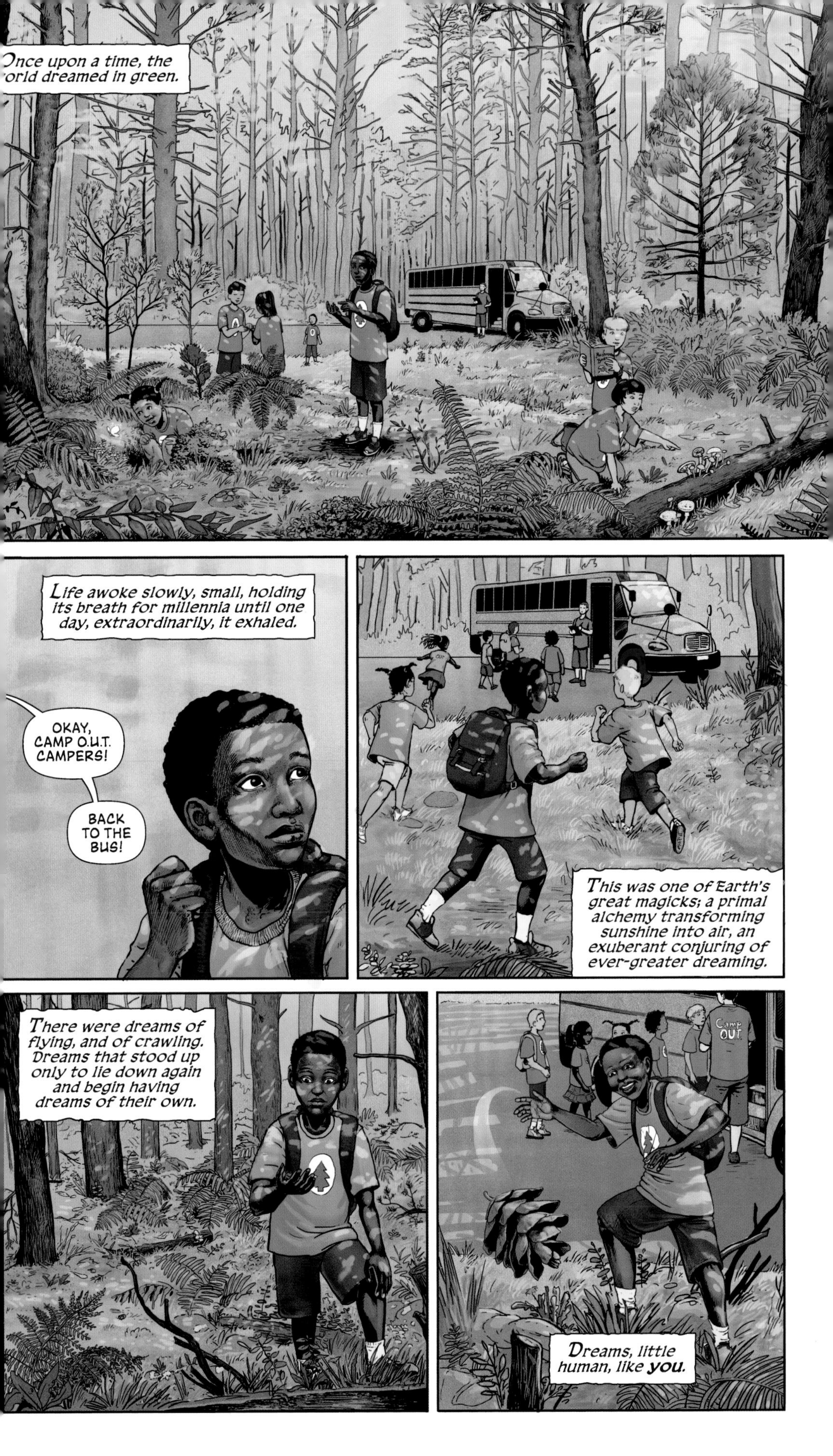
Once upon a time, the
orld dreamed in green.
Life awoke slowly, small, holding its breath for millennia until one day, extraordinarily, it exhaled.
OKAY, CAMP O.U.T. CAMPERS!
BACK TO THE BUS!
This was one of Earth's great magicks; a primal alchemy transforming sunshine into air, an exuberant conjuring of ever-greater dreaming.
There were dreams of flying, and of crawling. Dreams that stood up only to lie down again and begin having dreams of their own.
Camp OUT
Dreams, little human, like **you**.

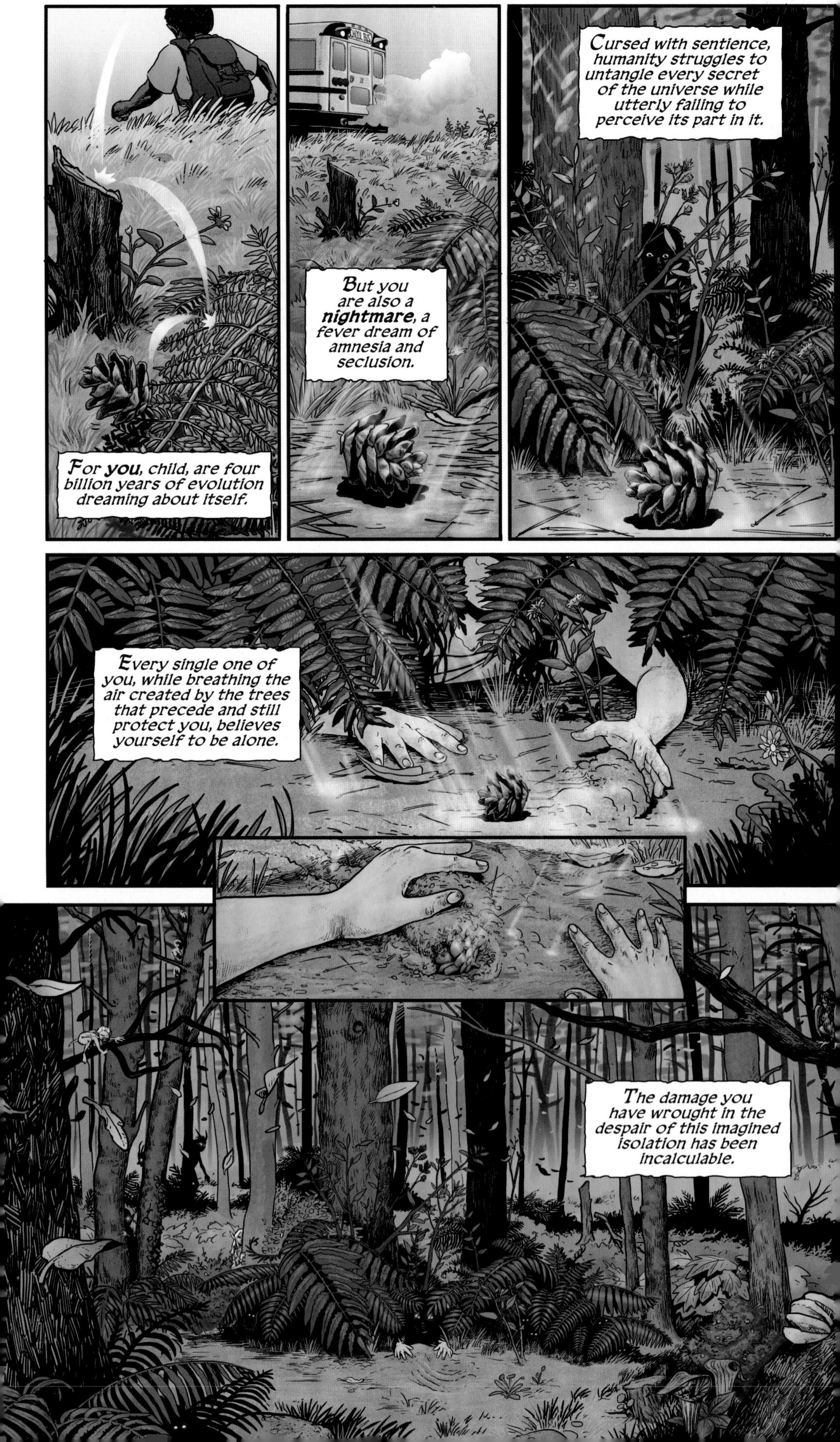
For you, child, are four billion years of evolution dreaming about itself.
But you are also a nightmare, a fever dream of amnesia and seclusion.
Cursed with sentience, humanity struggles to untangle every secret of the universe while utterly failing to perceive its part in it.
Every single one of you, while breathing the air created by the trees that precede and still protect you, believes yourself to be alone.
The damage you have wrought in the despair of this imagined isolation has been incalculable.
SCHOOL BUS

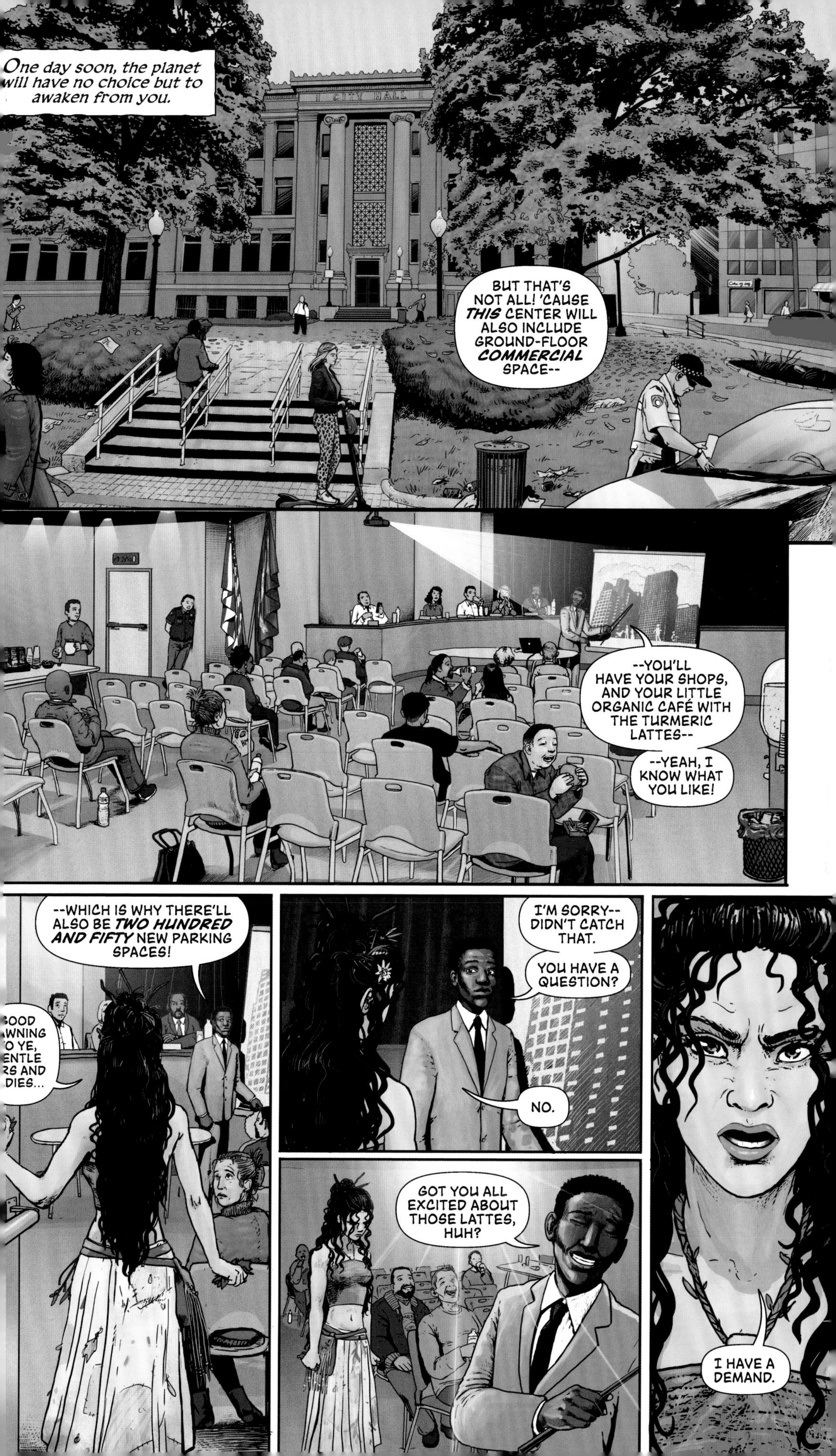
One day soon, the planet will have no choice but to awaken from you.
CITY HALL
BUT THAT'S NOT ALL! 'CAUSE *THIS* CENTER WILL ALSO INCLUDE GROUND-FLOOR *COMMERCIAL* SPACE--
--YOU'LL HAVE YOUR SHOPS, AND YOUR LITTLE ORGANIC CAFÉ WITH THE TURMERIC LATTES--
--YEAH, I KNOW WHAT YOU LIKE!
--WHICH IS WHY THERE'LL ALSO BE *TWO HUNDRED AND FIFTY* NEW PARKING SPACES!
GOOD
WNING
O YE,
ENTLE
RS AND
DIES...
I'M SORRY-- DIDN'T CATCH THAT.
YOU HAVE A QUESTION?
NO.
GOT YOU ALL EXCITED ABOUT THOSE LATTES, HUH?
I HAVE A DEMAND.

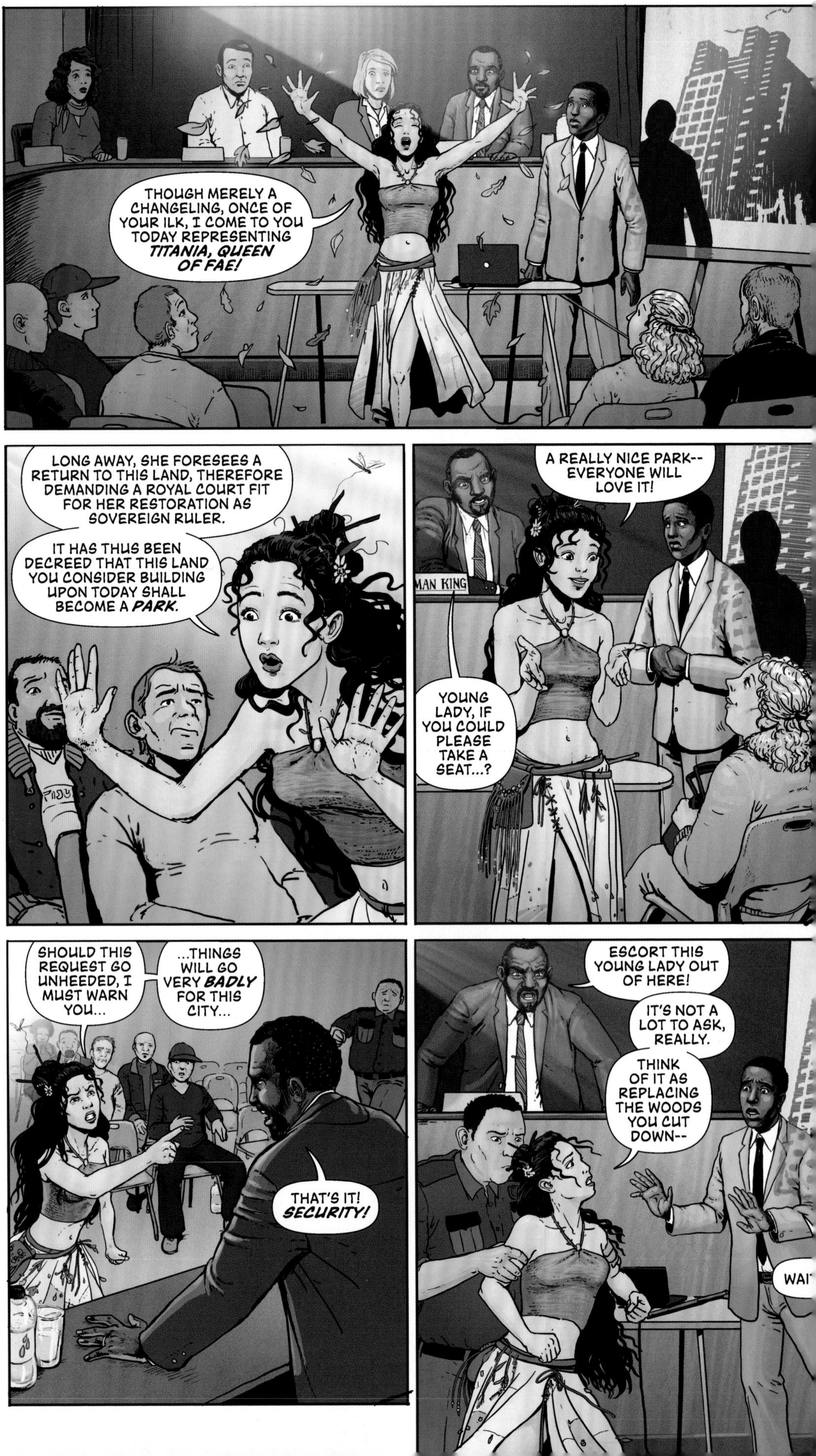

THOUGH MERELY A CHANGELING, ONCE OF YOUR ILK, I COME TO YOU TODAY REPRESENTING *TITANIA, QUEEN OF FAE!*
LONG AWAY, SHE FORESEES A RETURN TO THIS LAND, THEREFORE DEMANDING A ROYAL COURT FIT FOR HER RESTORATION AS SOVEREIGN RULER.
IT HAS THUS BEEN DECREED THAT THIS LAND YOU CONSIDER BUILDING UPON TODAY SHALL BECOME A *PARK*.
A REALLY NICE PARK-- EVERYONE WILL LOVE IT!
MAN KING
YOUNG LADY, IF YOU COULD PLEASE TAKE A SEAT...?
SHOULD THIS REQUEST GO UNHEEDED, I MUST WARN YOU...
...THINGS WILL GO VERY *BADLY* FOR THIS CITY...
THAT'S IT! *SECURITY!*
ESCORT THIS YOUNG LADY OUT OF HERE!
IT'S NOT A LOT TO ASK, REALLY.
THINK OF IT AS REPLACING THE WOODS YOU CUT DOWN--
WAI

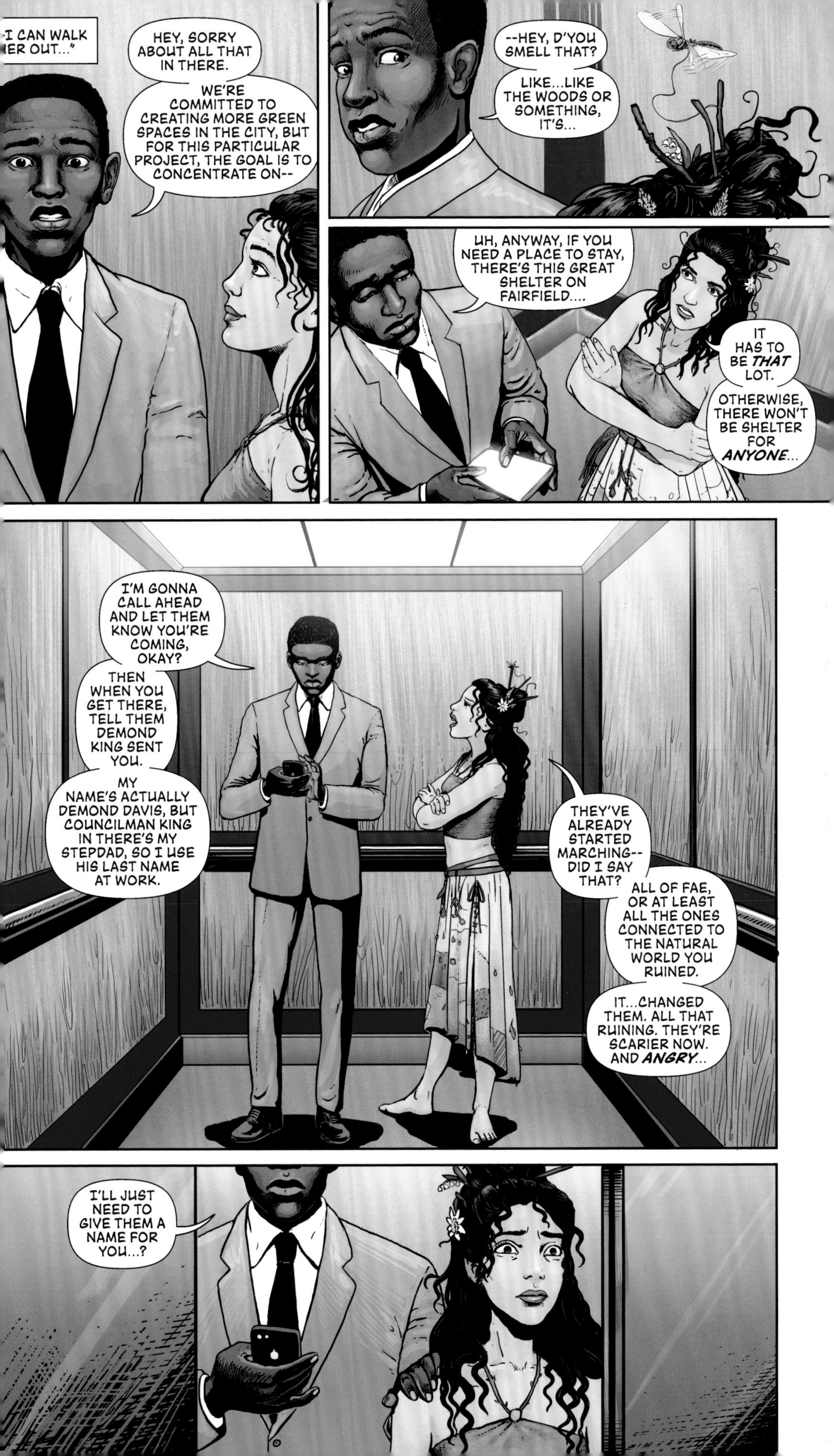
"I CAN WALK
ER OUT..."
HEY, SORRY ABOUT ALL THAT IN THERE.
WE'RE COMMITTED TO CREATING MORE GREEN SPACES IN THE CITY, BUT FOR THIS PARTICULAR PROJECT, THE GOAL IS TO CONCENTRATE ON--
--HEY, D'YOU SMELL THAT?
LIKE...LIKE THE WOODS OR SOMETHING, IT'S...
UH, ANYWAY, IF YOU NEED A PLACE TO STAY, THERE'S THIS GREAT SHELTER ON FAIRFIELD....
IT HAS TO BE *THAT* LOT.
OTHERWISE, THERE WON'T BE SHELTER FOR ***ANYONE***...
I'M GONNA CALL AHEAD AND LET THEM KNOW YOU'RE COMING, OKAY?
THEN WHEN YOU GET THERE, TELL THEM DEMOND KING SENT YOU.
MY NAME'S ACTUALLY DEMOND DAVIS, BUT COUNCILMAN KING IN THERE'S MY STEPDAD, SO I USE HIS LAST NAME AT WORK.
THEY'VE ALREADY STARTED MARCHING-- DID I SAY THAT?
ALL OF FAE, OR AT LEAST ALL THE ONES CONNECTED TO THE NATURAL WORLD YOU RUINED.
IT...CHANGED THEM. ALL THAT RUINING. THEY'RE SCARIER NOW. AND ***ANGRY***...
I'LL JUST NEED TO GIVE THEM A NAME FOR YOU...?

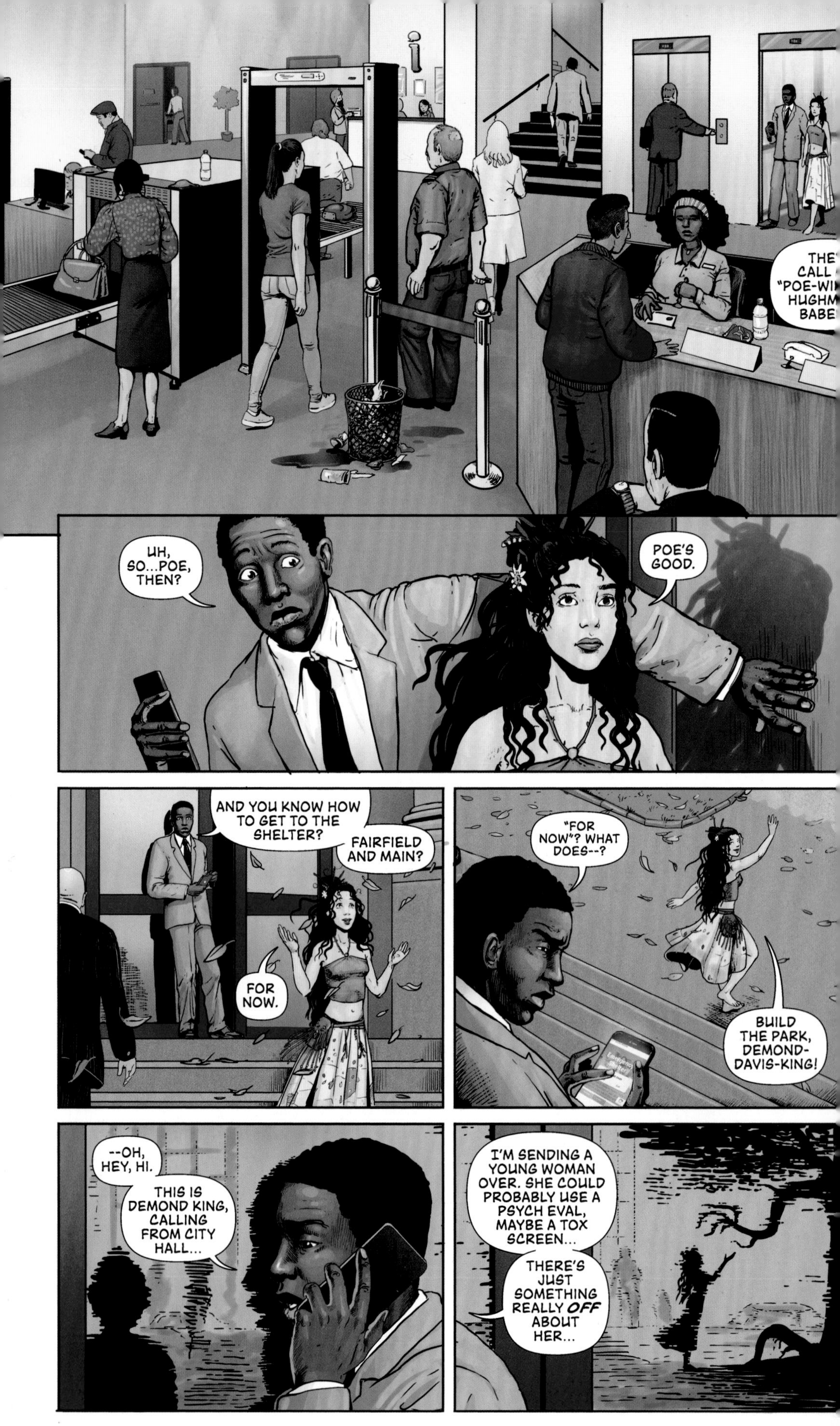
THE CALL "POE-WI HUGHM BABE
UH, SO...POE, THEN?
POE'S GOOD.
AND YOU KNOW HOW TO GET TO THE SHELTER?
FAIRFIELD AND MAIN?
FOR NOW.
"FOR NOW"? WHAT DOES--?
BUILD THE PARK, DEMOND-DAVIS-KING!
--OH, HEY, HI.
THIS IS DEMOND KING, CALLING FROM CITY HALL...
I'M SENDING A YOUNG WOMAN OVER. SHE COULD PROBABLY USE A PSYCH EVAL, MAYBE A TOX SCREEN...
THERE'S JUST SOMETHING REALLY *OFF* ABOUT HER...

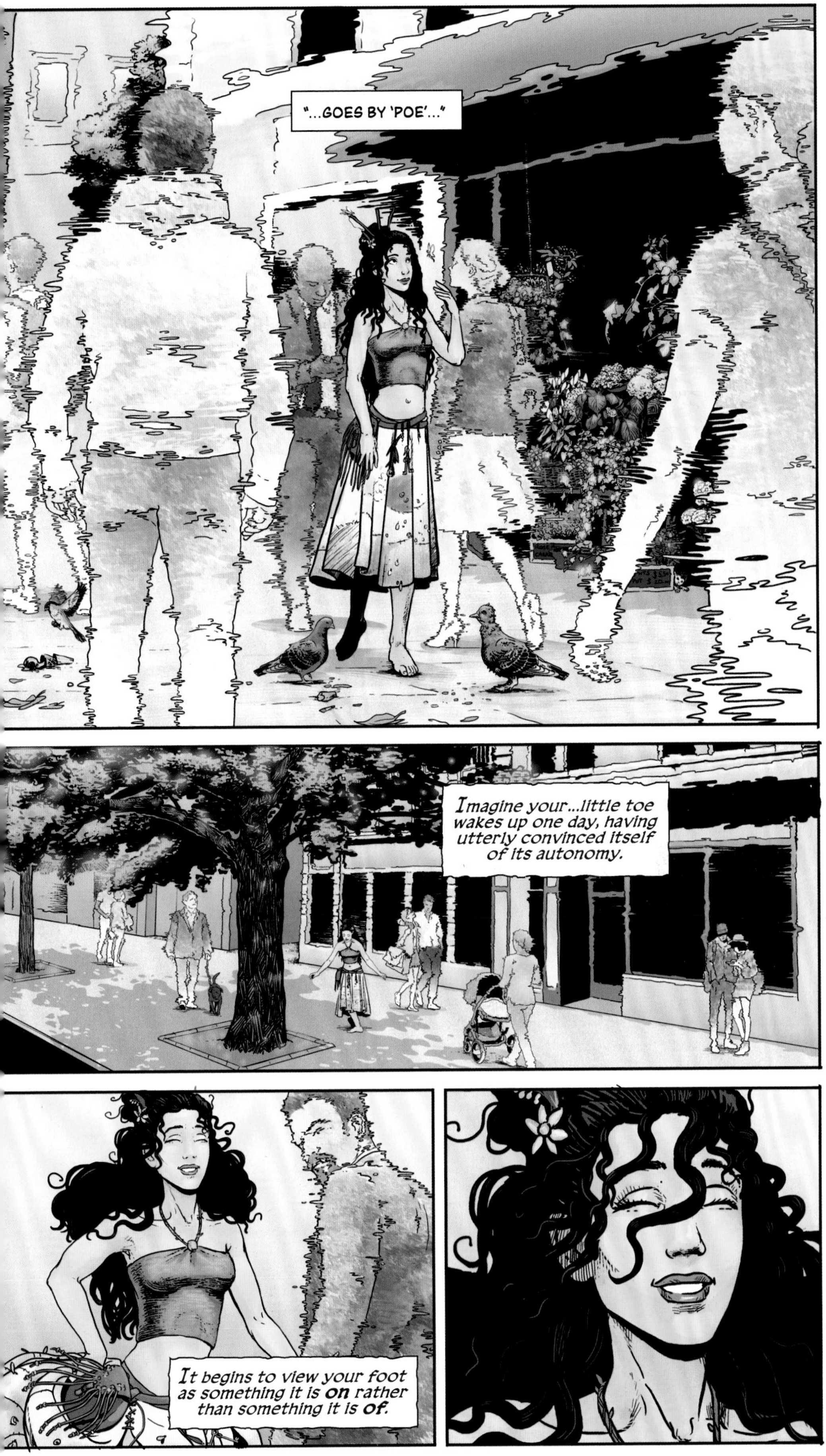
"...GOES BY 'POE'..."
Imagine your...little toe wakes up one day, having utterly convinced itself of its autonomy.
It begins to view your foot as something it is **on** rather than something it is **of**.

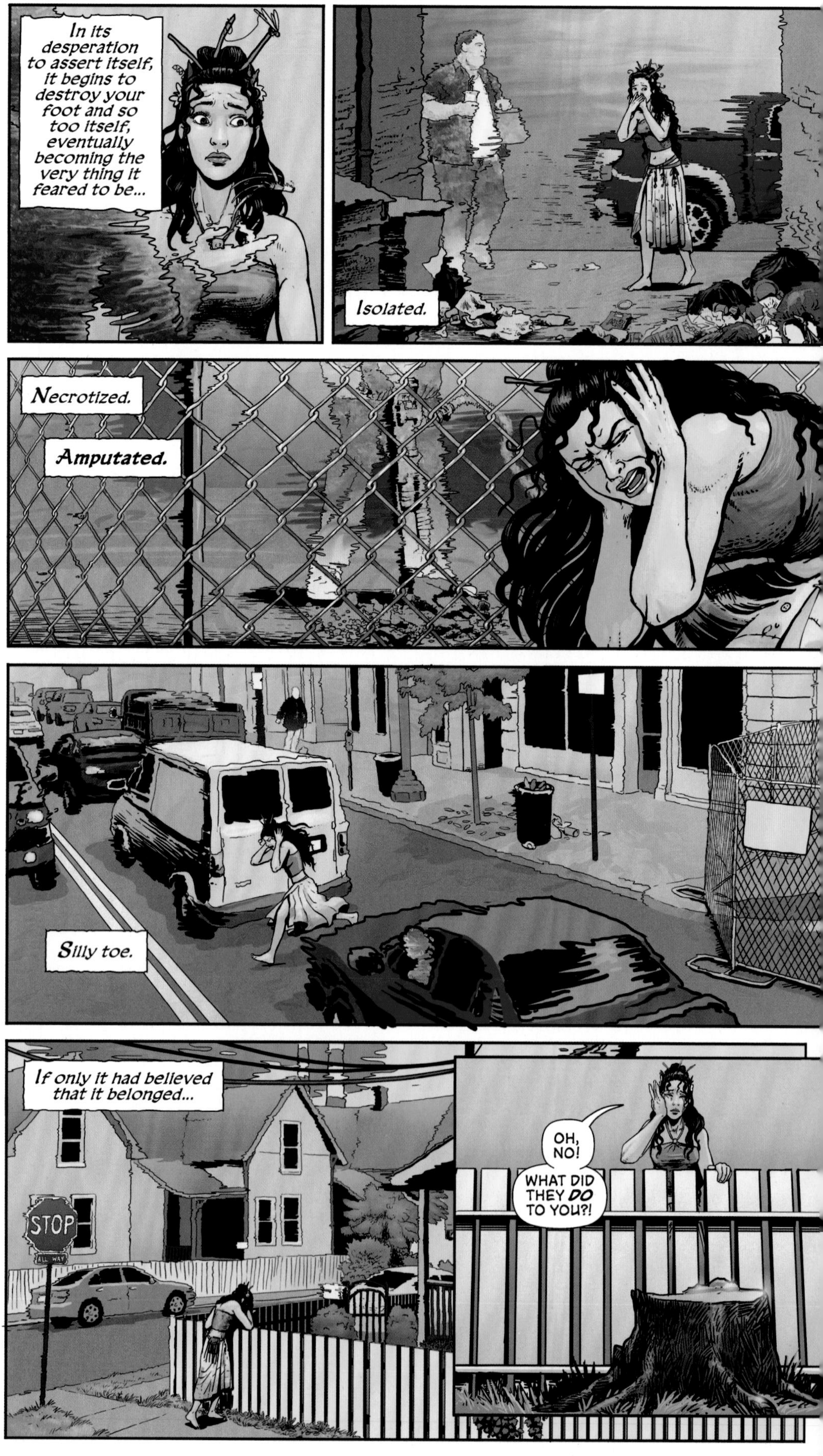

In its desperation to assert itself, it begins to destroy your foot and so too itself, eventually becoming the very thing it feared to be...
Isolated.
Necrotized.
Amputated.
Silly toe.
If only it had believed that it belonged...
STOP
OH, NO!
WHAT DID THEY DO TO YOU?!

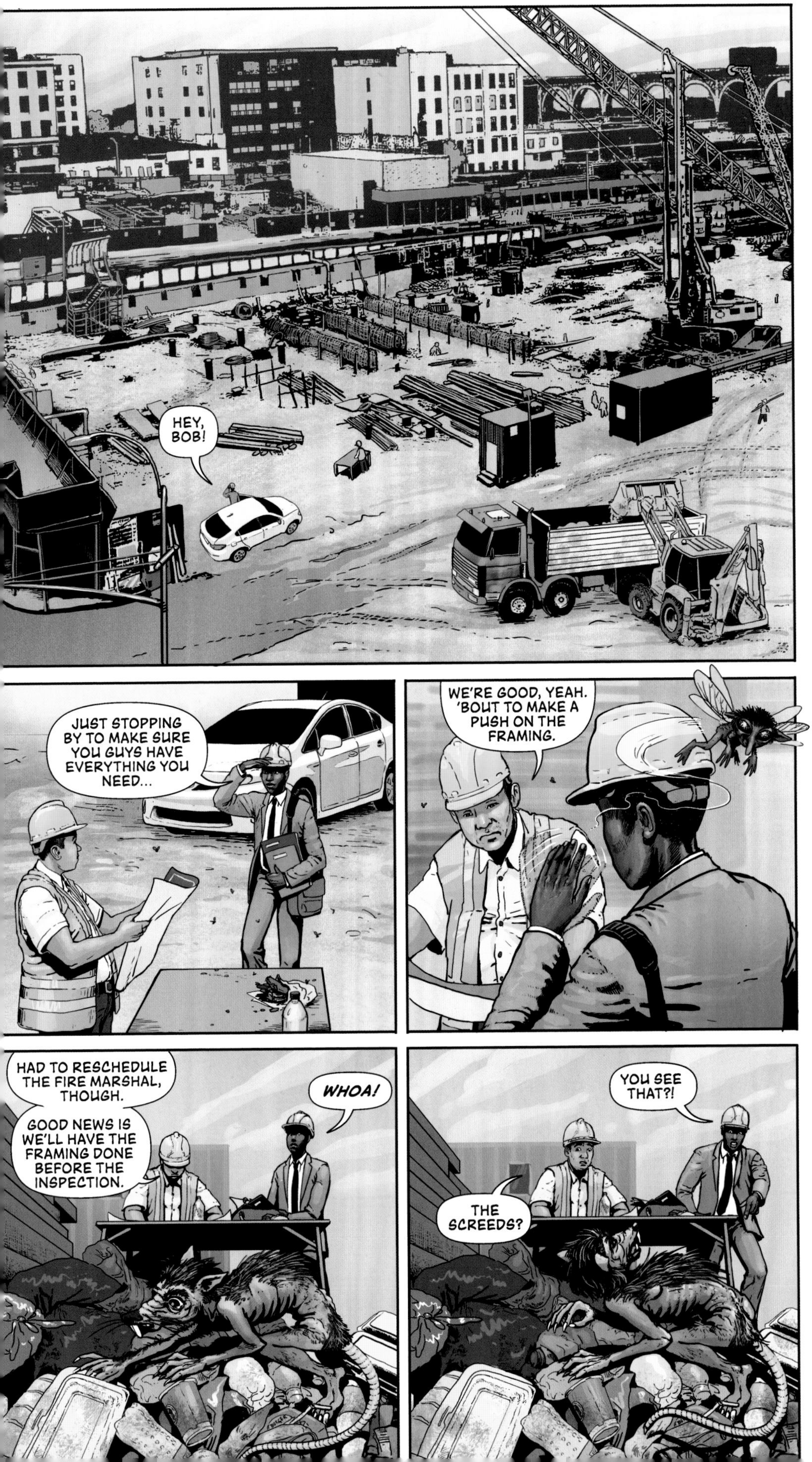
HEY, BOB!
JUST STOPPING BY TO MAKE SURE YOU GUYS HAVE EVERYTHING YOU NEED...
WE'RE GOOD, YEAH. 'BOUT TO MAKE A PUSH ON THE FRAMING.
HAD TO RESCHEDULE THE FIRE MARSHAL, THOUGH.
GOOD NEWS IS WE'LL HAVE THE FRAMING DONE BEFORE THE INSPECTION.
WHOA!
YOU SEE THAT?!
THE SCREEDS?

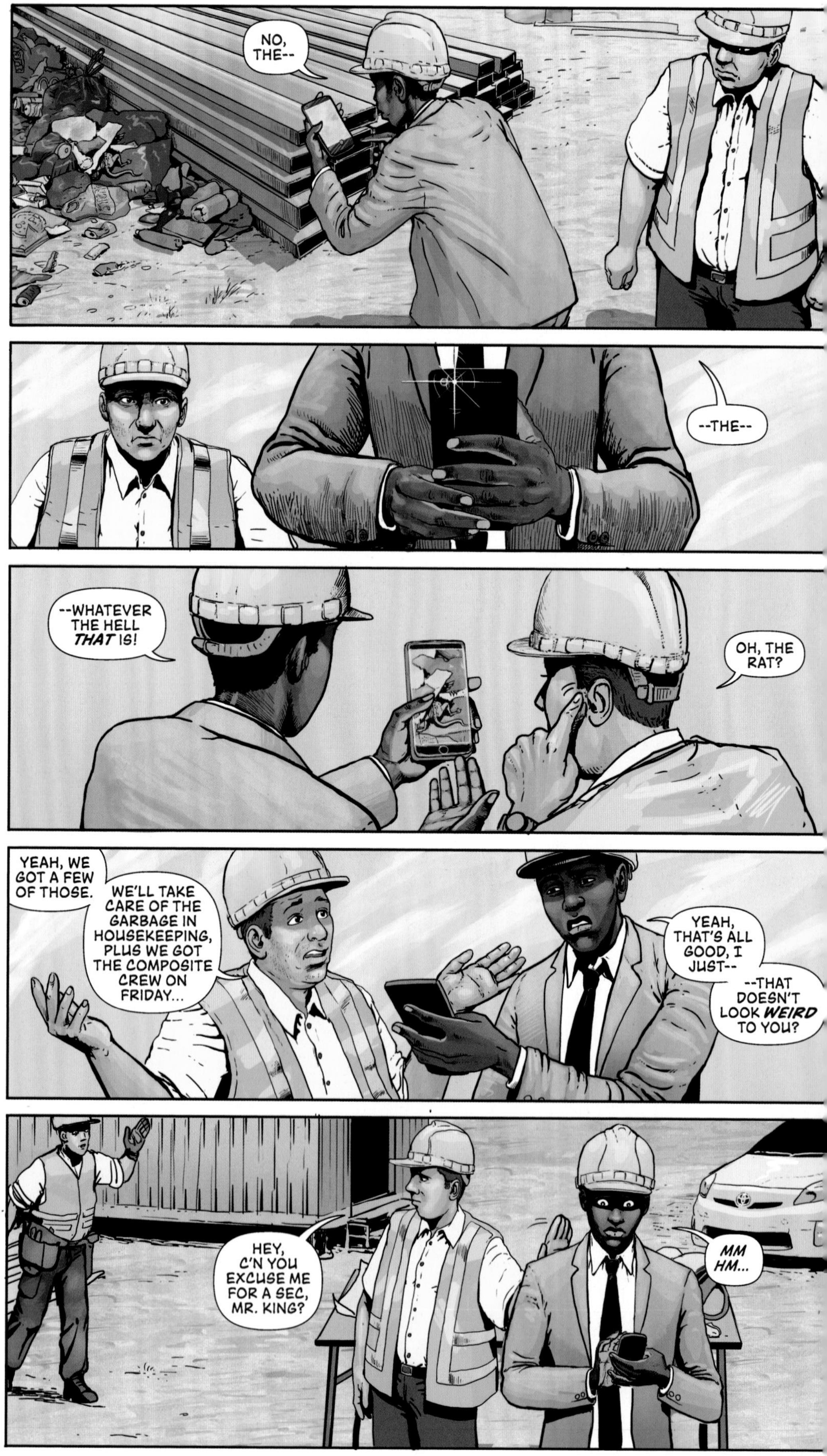
NO, THE--
--THE--
--WHATEVER THE HELL *THAT* IS!
OH, THE RAT?
YEAH, WE GOT A FEW OF THOSE.
WE'LL TAKE CARE OF THE GARBAGE IN HOUSEKEEPING, PLUS WE GOT THE COMPOSITE CREW ON FRIDAY...
YEAH, THAT'S ALL GOOD, I JUST--
--THAT DOESN'T LOOK *WEIRD* TO YOU?
HEY, C'N YOU EXCUSE ME FOR A SEC, MR. KING?
MM HM...

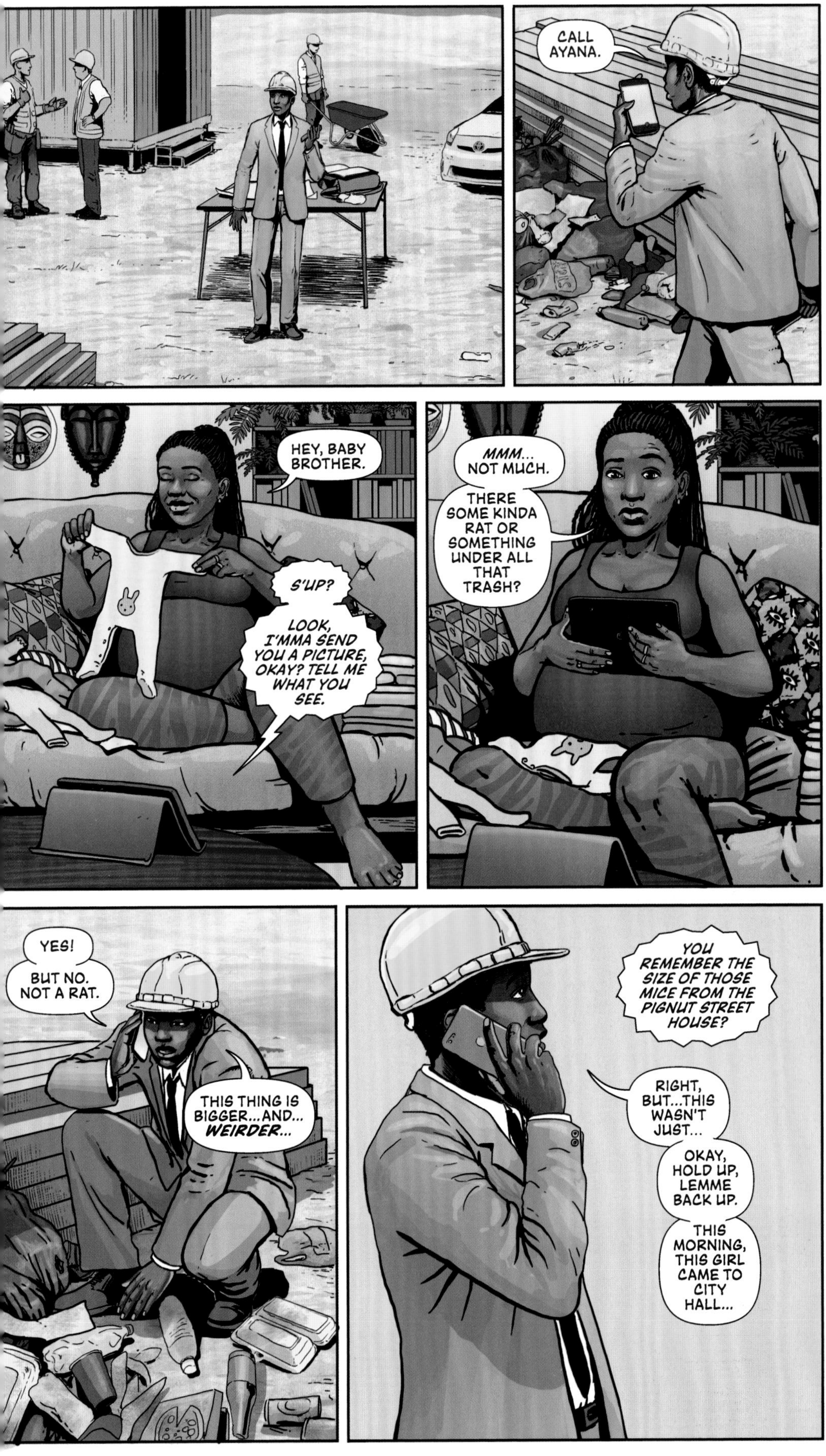
CALL AYANA.
HEY, BABY BROTHER.
S'UP?
LOOK, I'MMA SEND YOU A PICTURE, OKAY? TELL ME WHAT YOU SEE.
MMM... NOT MUCH.
THERE SOME KINDA RAT OR SOMETHING UNDER ALL THAT TRASH?
YES!
BUT NO. NOT A RAT.
THIS THING IS BIGGER...AND... WEIRDER...
YOU REMEMBER THE SIZE OF THOSE MICE FROM THE PIGNUT STREET HOUSE?
RIGHT, BUT...THIS WASN'T JUST...
OKAY, HOLD UP, LEMME BACK UP.
THIS MORNING, THIS GIRL CAME TO CITY HALL...

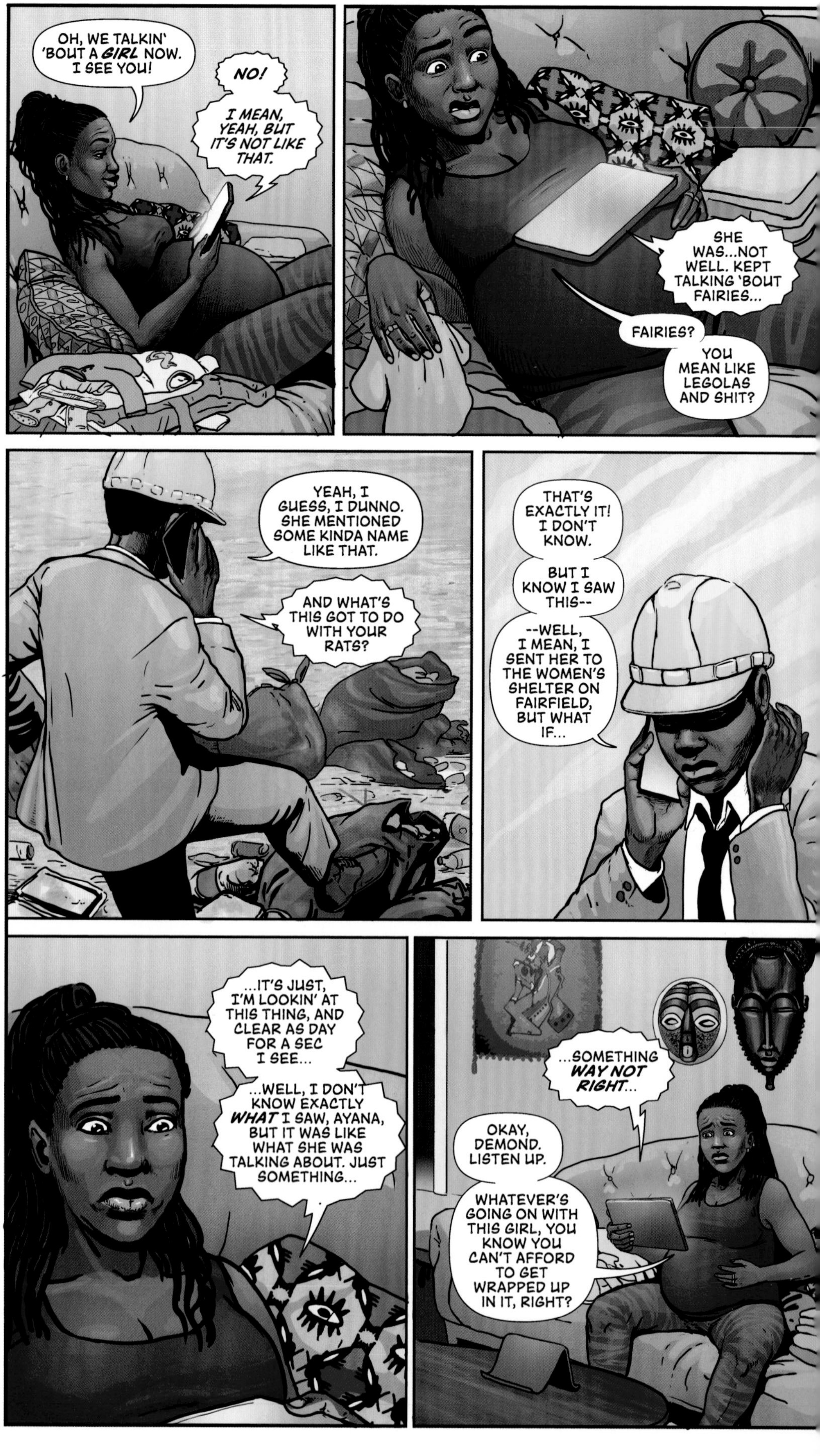

OH, WE TALKIN' 'BOUT A *GIRL* NOW. I SEE YOU!
NO!
I MEAN, YEAH, BUT IT'S NOT LIKE THAT.
SHE WAS...NOT WELL. KEPT TALKING 'BOUT FAIRIES...
FAIRIES?
YOU MEAN LIKE LEGOLAS AND SHIT?
YEAH, I GUESS, I DUNNO. SHE MENTIONED SOME KINDA NAME LIKE THAT.
AND WHAT'S THIS GOT TO DO WITH YOUR RATS?
THAT'S EXACTLY IT! I DON'T KNOW.
BUT I KNOW I SAW THIS--
--WELL, I MEAN, I SENT HER TO THE WOMEN'S SHELTER ON FAIRFIELD, BUT WHAT IF...
...IT'S JUST, I'M LOOKIN' AT THIS THING, AND CLEAR AS DAY FOR A SEC I SEE...
...WELL, I DON'T KNOW EXACTLY *WHAT* I SAW, AYANA, BUT IT WAS LIKE WHAT SHE WAS TALKING ABOUT. JUST SOMETHING...
...SOMETHING *WAY NOT RIGHT*...
OKAY, DEMOND. LISTEN UP.
WHATEVER'S GOING ON WITH THIS GIRL, YOU KNOW YOU CAN'T AFFORD TO GET WRAPPED UP IN IT, RIGHT?

"YOU GOT WAY TOO MUCH ON YOUR SHOULDERS JUST NOW..."

...though the root grows old in the earth and the stock dies in the ground...

POE?

...at the scent of water it will bud and bring forth boughs. But man...

POE, WHAT ARE YOU DOING?

WHAT ARE YOU DOING?

OH, I UH--JUST CLEARING MY HEAD, YOU KNOW-- LITTLE WALK OR WHATEVER.

I SHOULD PROBABLY GO AHEAD AND...GET BACK, BUT, UH...

...WELL, LOOK, WHILE I'VE GOT YOU, LET ME GET YOUR THOUGHTS ON THIS PICTURE I TOOK AT THE CONSTRUCTION SITE...

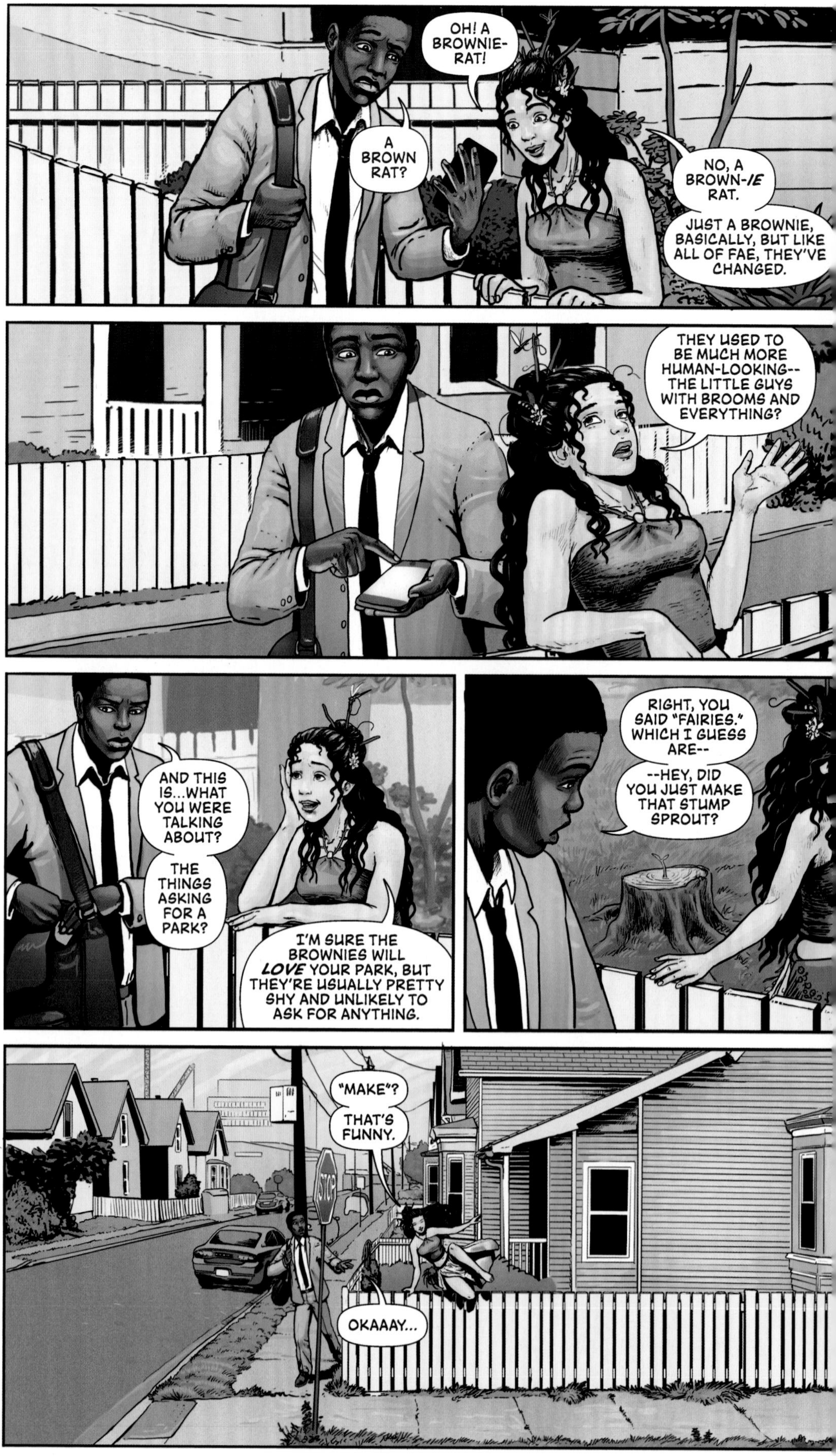
OH! A BROWNIE-RAT!
A BROWN RAT?
NO, A BROWN-*IE* RAT.
JUST A BROWNIE, BASICALLY, BUT LIKE ALL OF FAE, THEY'VE CHANGED.
THEY USED TO BE MUCH MORE HUMAN-LOOKING-- THE LITTLE GUYS WITH BROOMS AND EVERYTHING?
AND THIS IS...WHAT YOU WERE TALKING ABOUT?
THE THINGS ASKING FOR A PARK?
I'M SURE THE BROWNIES WILL *LOVE* YOUR PARK, BUT THEY'RE USUALLY PRETTY SHY AND UNLIKELY TO ASK FOR ANYTHING.
RIGHT, YOU SAID "FAIRIES." WHICH I GUESS ARE--
--HEY, DID YOU JUST MAKE THAT STUMP SPROUT?
"MAKE"?
THAT'S FUNNY.
STOP
OKAAAY...

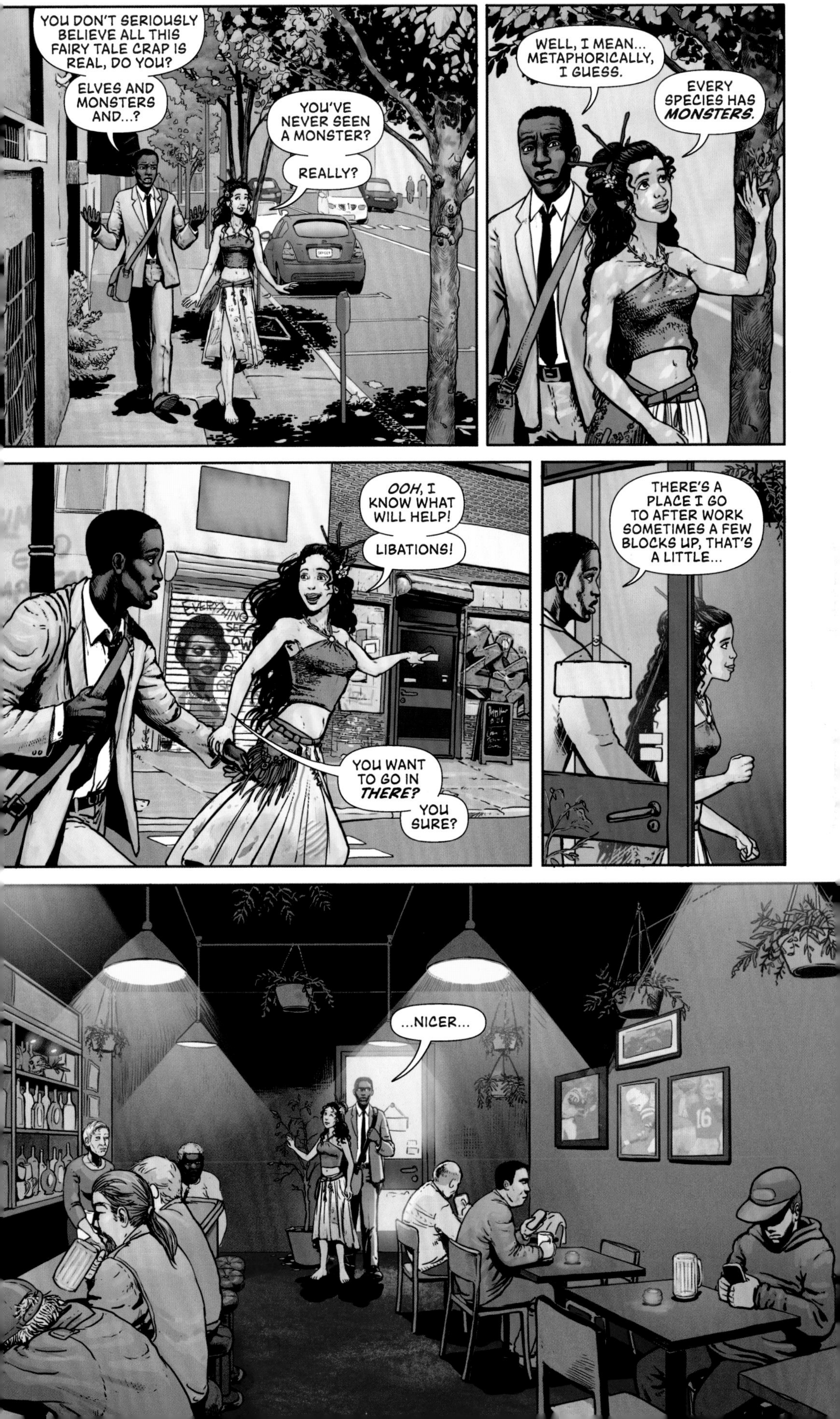
YOU DON'T SERIOUSLY BELIEVE ALL THIS FAIRY TALE CRAP IS REAL, DO YOU?
ELVES AND MONSTERS AND...?
YOU'VE NEVER SEEN A MONSTER?
REALLY?
WELL, I MEAN... METAPHORICALLY, I GUESS.
EVERY SPECIES HAS *MONSTERS*.
OOH, I KNOW WHAT WILL HELP!
LIBATIONS!
YOU WANT TO GO IN *THERE?*
YOU SURE?
THERE'S A PLACE I GO TO AFTER WORK SOMETIMES A FEW BLOCKS UP, THAT'S A LITTLE...
...NICER...

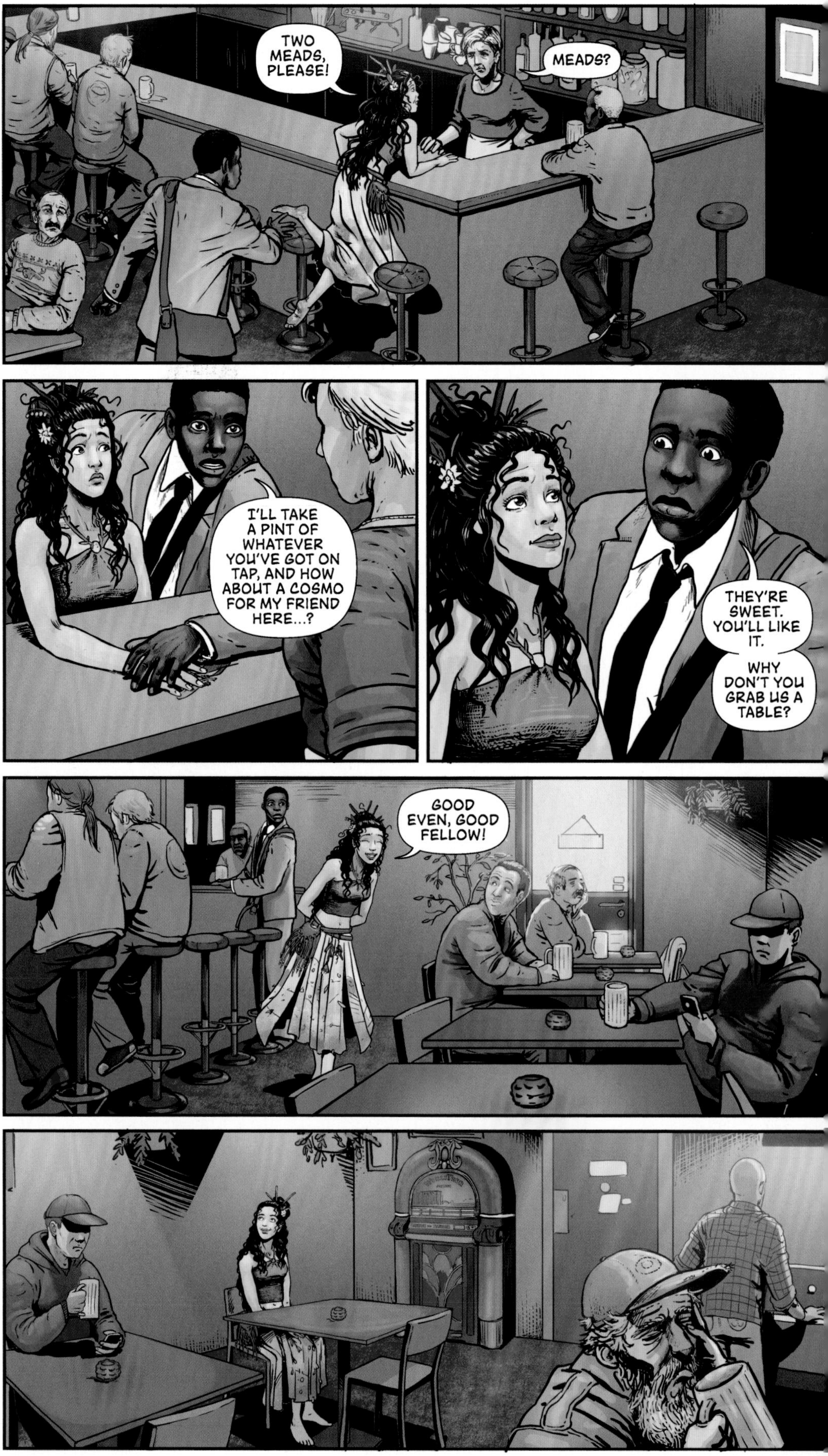
TWO MEADS, PLEASE!
MEADS?
I'LL TAKE A PINT OF WHATEVER YOU'VE GOT ON TAP, AND HOW ABOUT A COSMO FOR MY FRIEND HERE...?
THEY'RE SWEET. YOU'LL LIKE IT.
WHY DON'T YOU GRAB US A TABLE?
GOOD EVEN, GOOD FELLOW!

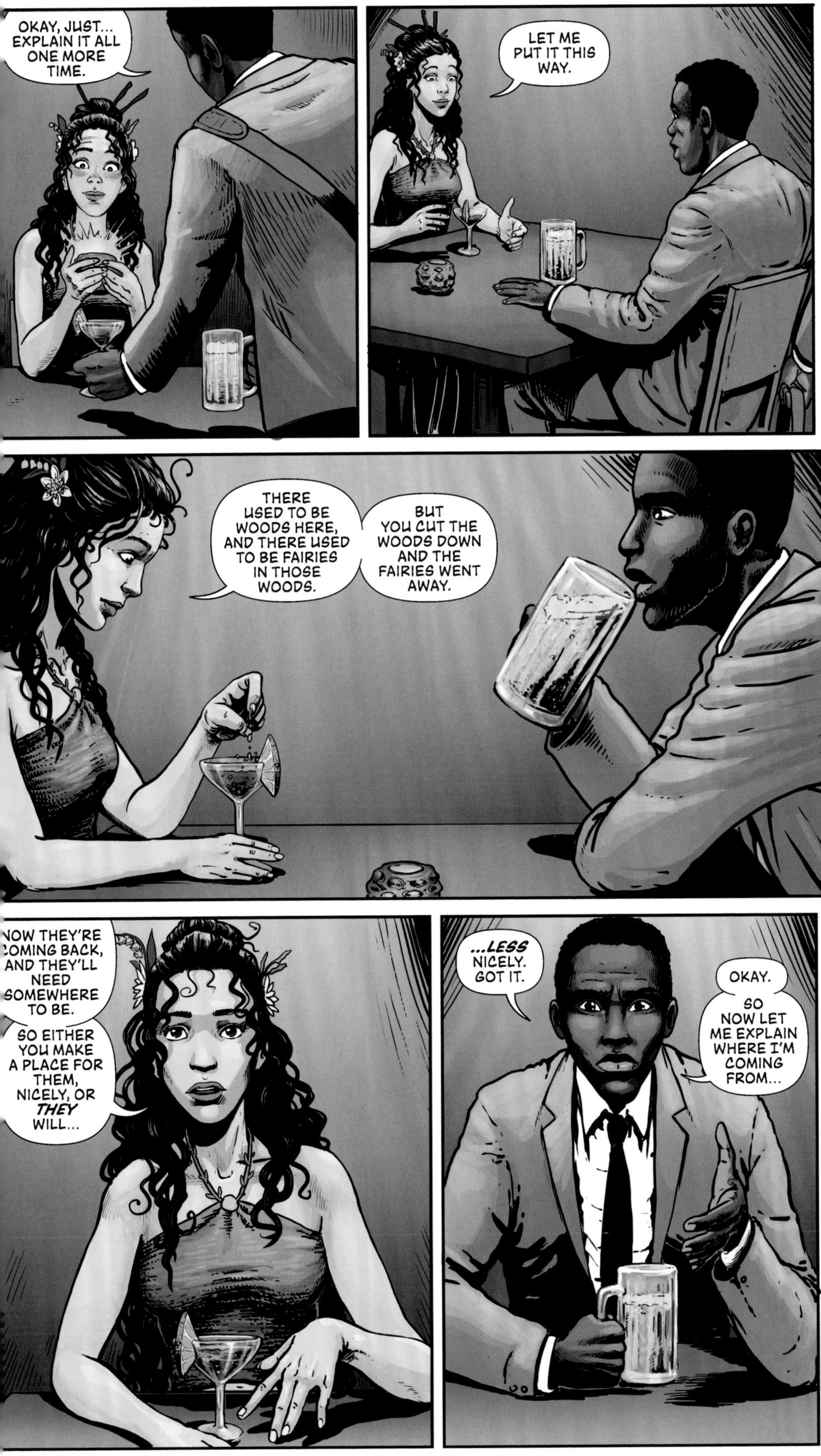
OKAY, JUST... EXPLAIN IT ALL ONE MORE TIME.
LET ME PUT IT THIS WAY.
THERE USED TO BE WOODS HERE, AND THERE USED TO BE FAIRIES IN THOSE WOODS.
BUT YOU CUT THE WOODS DOWN AND THE FAIRIES WENT AWAY.
NOW THEY'RE COMING BACK, AND THEY'LL NEED SOMEWHERE TO BE.
SO EITHER YOU MAKE A PLACE FOR THEM, NICELY, OR *THEY* WILL...
...*LESS* NICELY. GOT IT.
OKAY.
SO NOW LET ME EXPLAIN WHERE I'M COMING FROM...

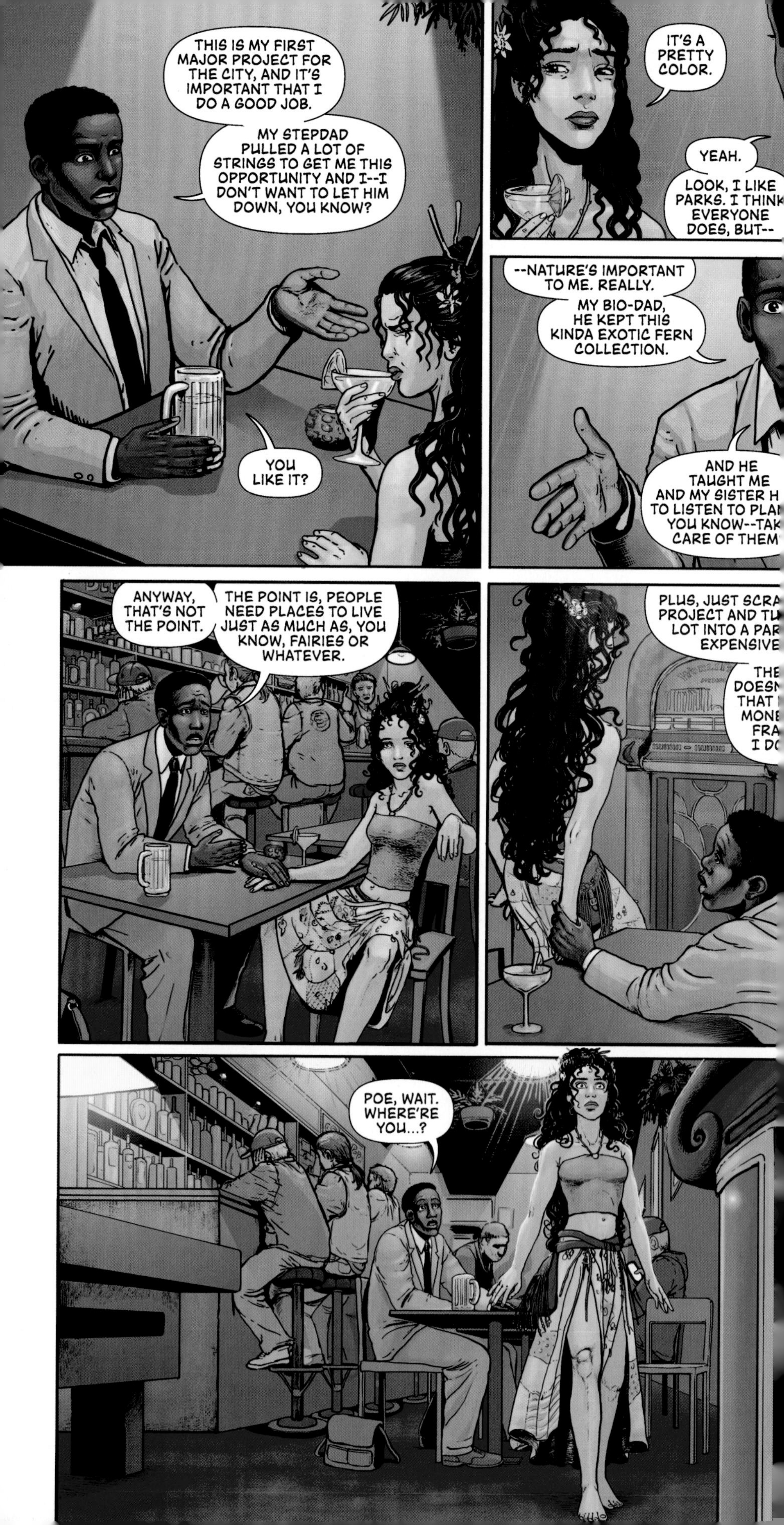
THIS IS MY FIRST MAJOR PROJECT FOR THE CITY, AND IT'S IMPORTANT THAT I DO A GOOD JOB.
MY STEPDAD PULLED A LOT OF STRINGS TO GET ME THIS OPPORTUNITY AND I--I DON'T WANT TO LET HIM DOWN, YOU KNOW?
YOU LIKE IT?
IT'S A PRETTY COLOR.
YEAH.
LOOK, I LIKE PARKS. I THINK EVERYONE DOES, BUT--
--NATURE'S IMPORTANT TO ME. REALLY.
MY BIO-DAD, HE KEPT THIS KINDA EXOTIC FERN COLLECTION.
AND HE TAUGHT ME AND MY SISTER H TO LISTEN TO PLAN YOU KNOW--TAK CARE OF THEM
ANYWAY, THAT'S NOT THE POINT.
THE POINT IS, PEOPLE NEED PLACES TO LIVE JUST AS MUCH AS, YOU KNOW, FAIRIES OR WHATEVER.
PLUS, JUST SCRA PROJECT AND TU LOT INTO A PAR EXPENSIVE
THE DOESN THAT MONE FRA I DO
POE, WAIT. WHERE'RE YOU...?

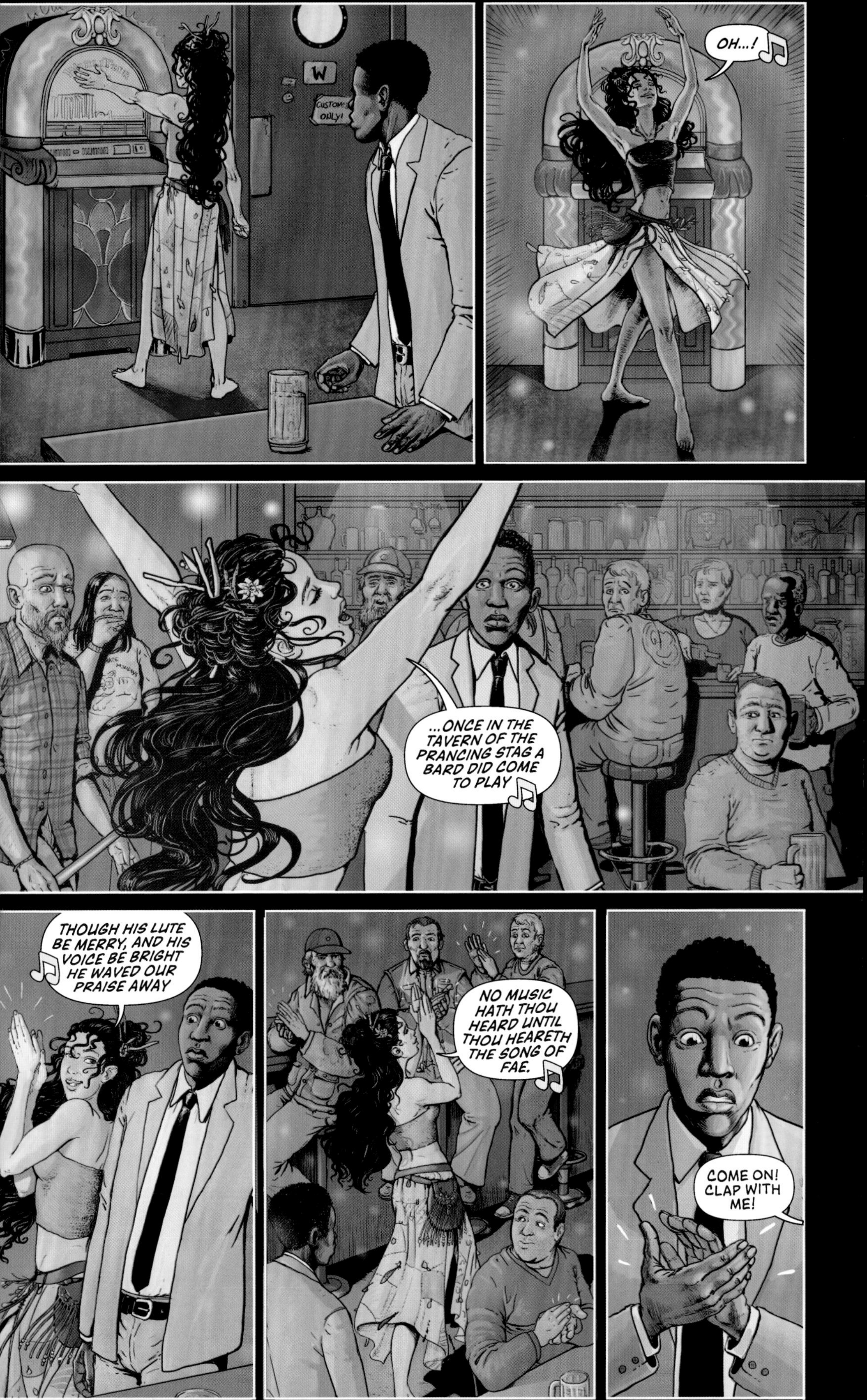
W
OH...!
...ONCE IN THE TAVERN OF THE PRANCING STAG A BARD DID COME TO PLAY
THOUGH HIS LUTE BE MERRY, AND HIS VOICE BE BRIGHT HE WAVED OUR PRAISE AWAY
NO MUSIC HATH THOU HEARD UNTIL THOU HEARETH THE SONG OF FAE.
COME ON! CLAP WITH ME!

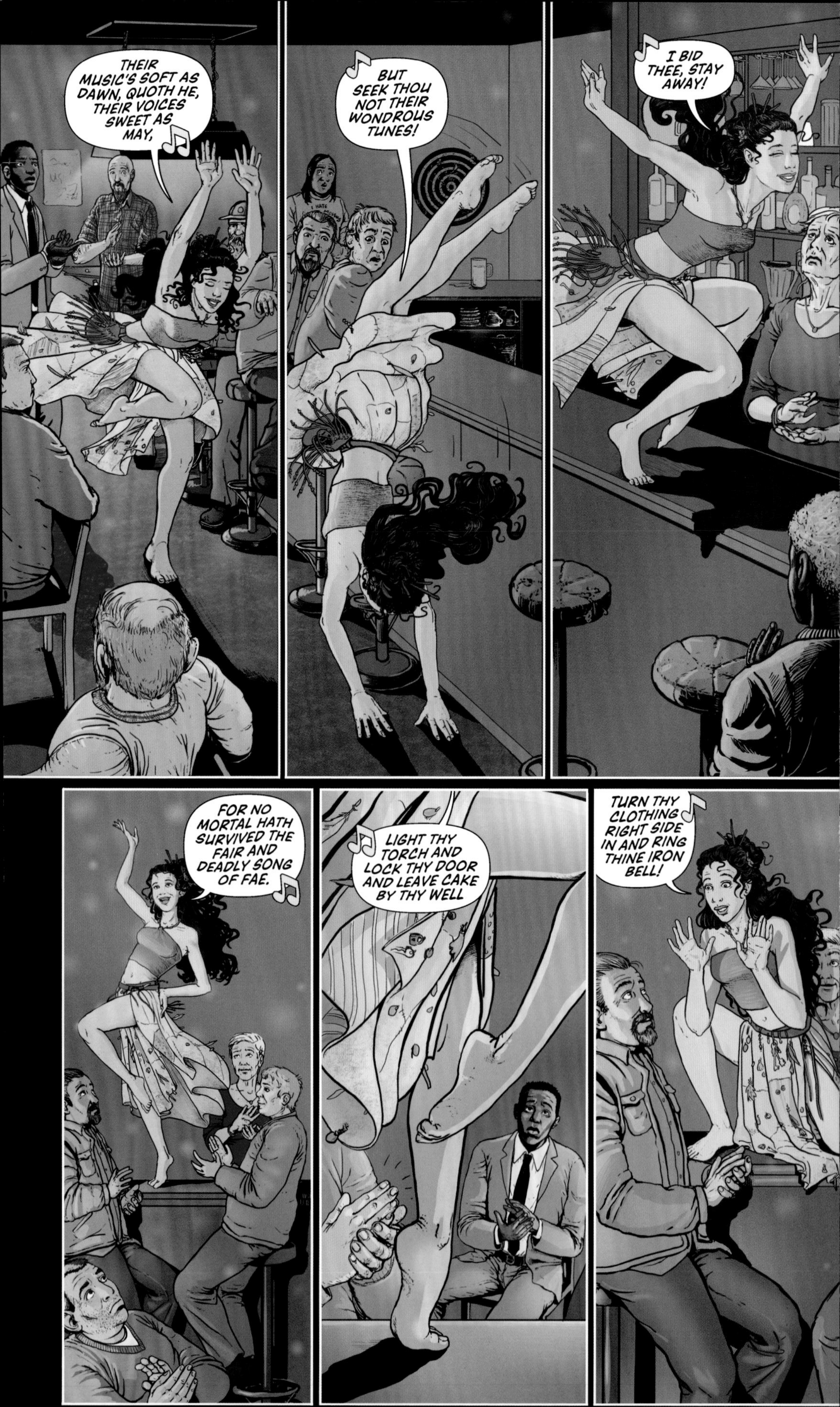
THEIR MUSIC'S SOFT AS DAWN, QUOTH HE, THEIR VOICES SWEET AS MAY,
BUT SEEK THOU NOT THEIR WONDROUS TUNES!
I BID THEE, STAY AWAY!
FOR NO MORTAL HATH SURVIVED THE FAIR AND DEADLY SONG OF FAE.
LIGHT THY TORCH AND LOCK THY DOOR AND LEAVE CAKE BY THY WELL
TURN THY CLOTHING RIGHT SIDE IN AND RING THINE IRON BELL!

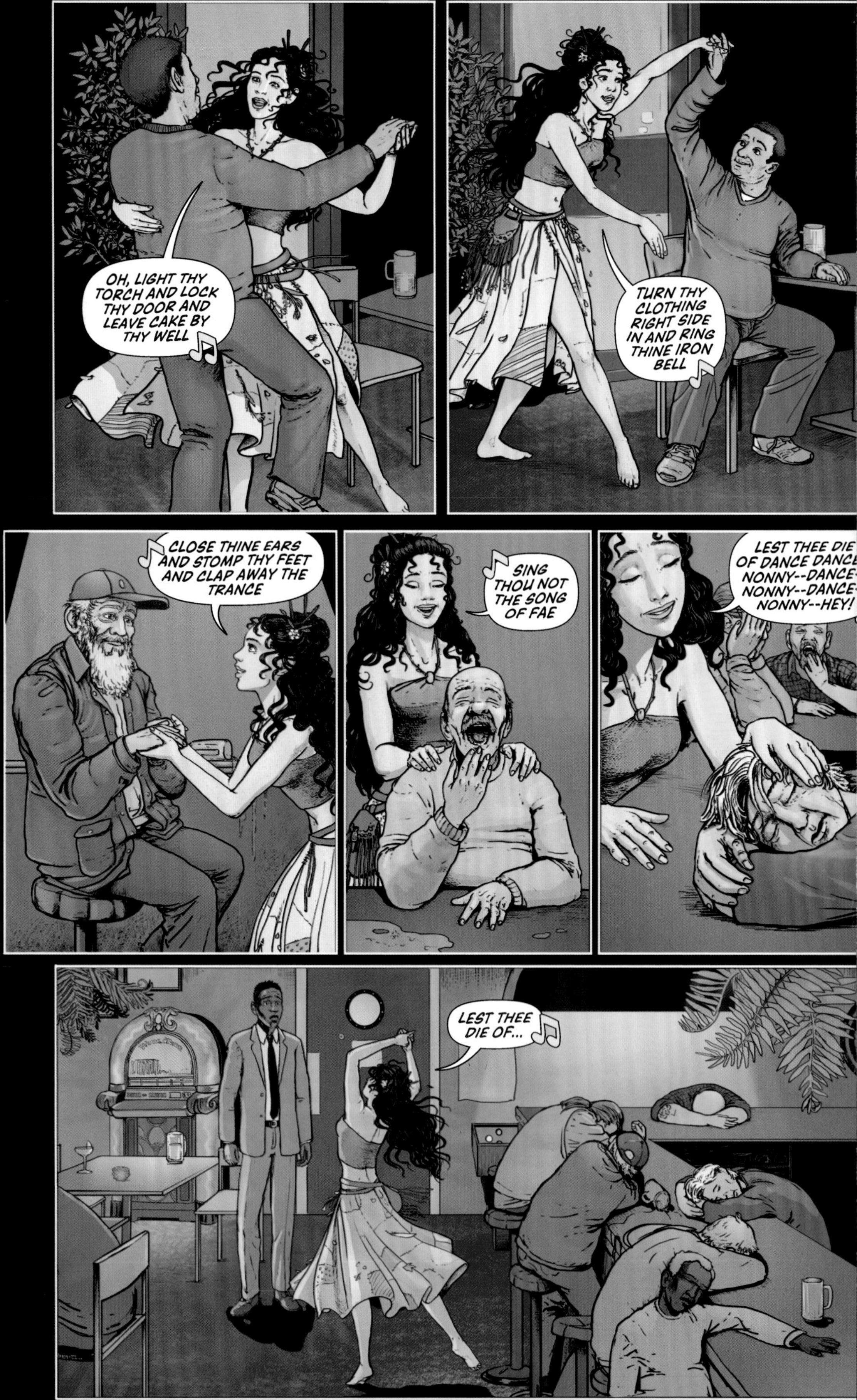
OH, LIGHT THY TORCH AND LOCK THY DOOR AND LEAVE CAKE BY THY WELL
TURN THY CLOTHING RIGHT SIDE IN AND RING THINE IRON BELL
CLOSE THINE EARS AND STOMP THY FEET AND CLAP AWAY THE TRANCE
SING THOU NOT THE SONG OF FAE
LEST THEE DIE OF DANCE DANCE NONNY--DANCE-- NONNY--DANCE-- NONNY--HEY!
LEST THEE DIE OF...

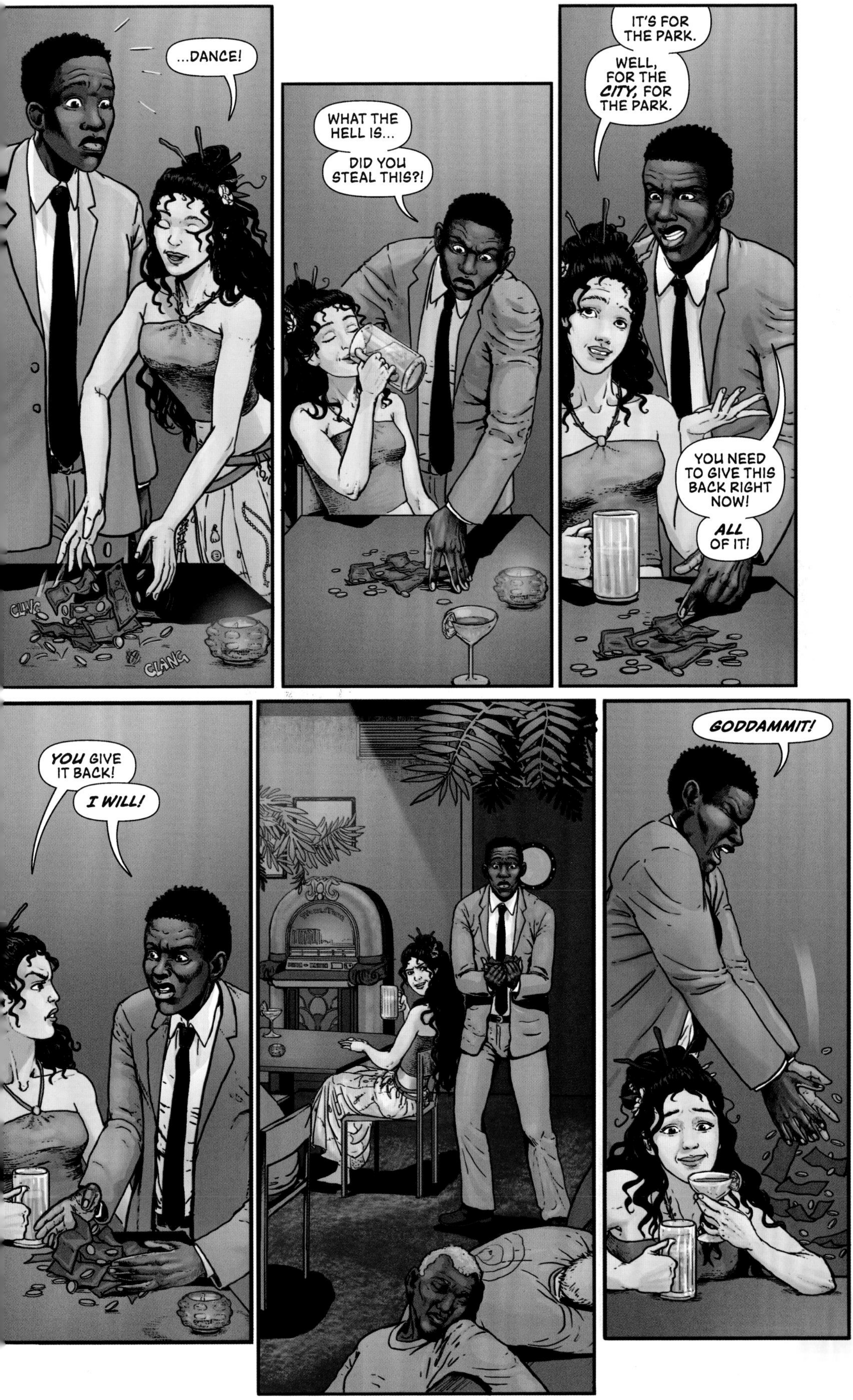
...DANCE!
CLANG
CLANG
WHAT THE HELL IS...
DID YOU STEAL THIS?!
IT'S FOR THE PARK.
WELL, FOR THE *CITY,* FOR THE PARK.
YOU NEED TO GIVE THIS BACK RIGHT NOW!
ALL OF IT!
YOU GIVE IT BACK!
I WILL!
GODDAMMIT!

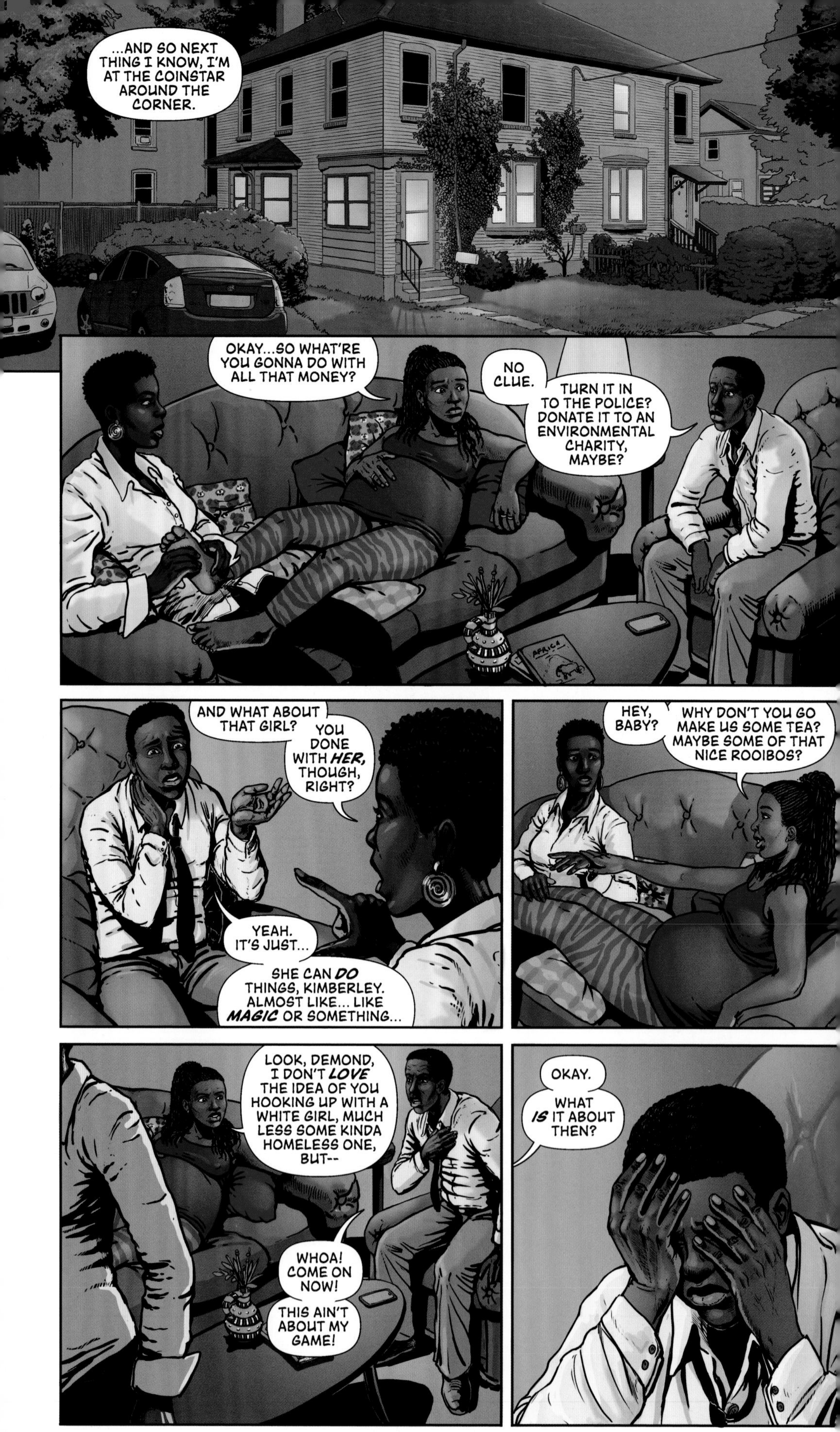

...AND SO NEXT THING I KNOW, I'M AT THE COINSTAR AROUND THE CORNER.
OKAY...SO WHAT'RE YOU GONNA DO WITH ALL THAT MONEY?
NO CLUE.
TURN IT IN TO THE POLICE? DONATE IT TO AN ENVIRONMENTAL CHARITY, MAYBE?
AND WHAT ABOUT THAT GIRL?
YOU DONE WITH *HER,* THOUGH, RIGHT?
YEAH. IT'S JUST...
SHE CAN *DO* THINGS, KIMBERLEY. ALMOST LIKE... LIKE *MAGIC* OR SOMETHING...
HEY, BABY?
WHY DON'T YOU GO MAKE US SOME TEA? MAYBE SOME OF THAT NICE ROOIBOS?
LOOK, DEMOND, I DON'T *LOVE* THE IDEA OF YOU HOOKING UP WITH A WHITE GIRL, MUCH LESS SOME KINDA HOMELESS ONE, BUT--
WHOA! COME ON NOW!
THIS AIN'T ABOUT MY GAME!
OKAY.
WHAT *IS* IT ABOUT THEN?
AFRICA

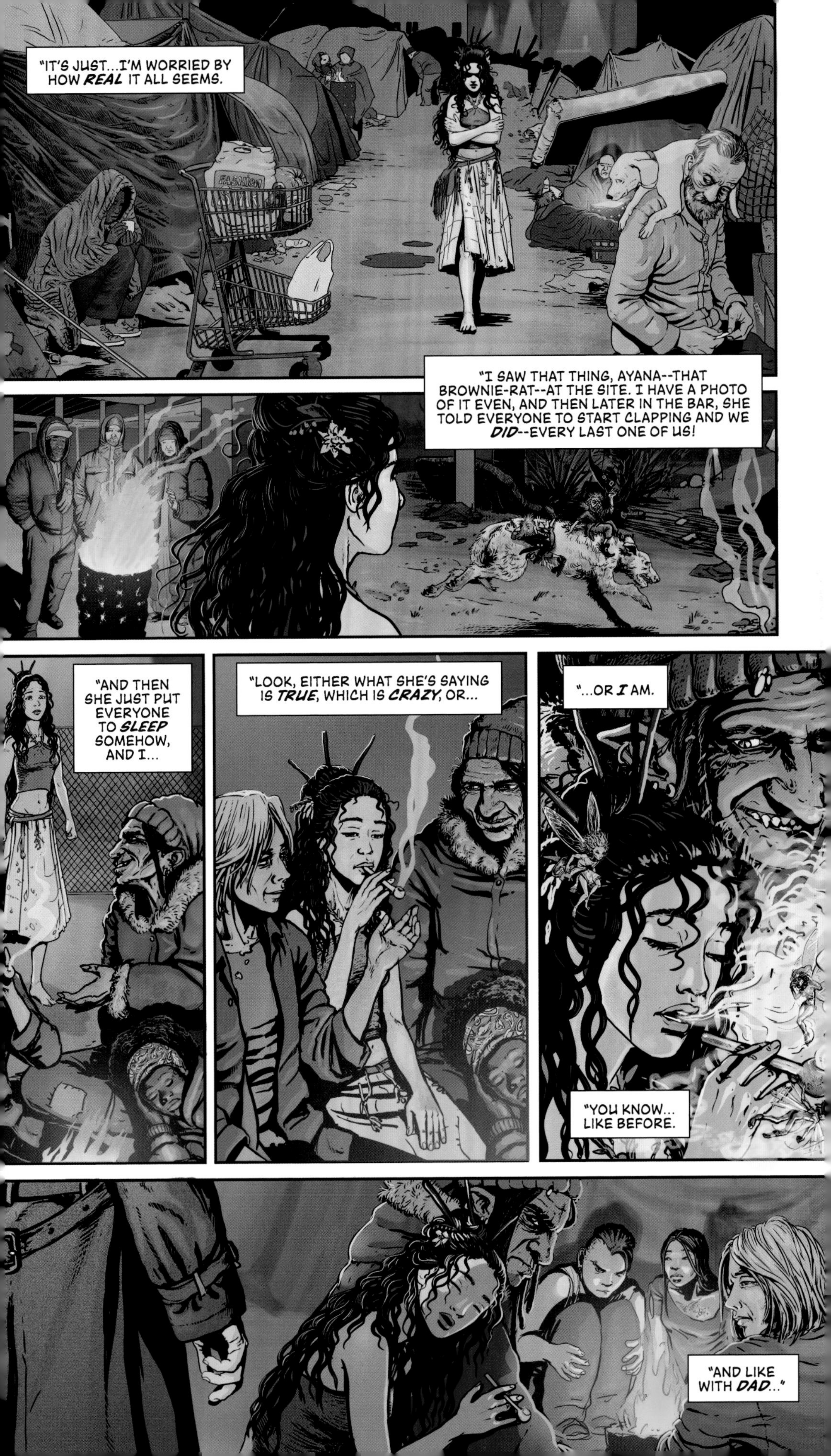
"IT'S JUST...I'M WORRIED BY HOW *REAL* IT ALL SEEMS.
"I SAW THAT THING, AYANA--THAT BROWNIE-RAT--AT THE SITE. I HAVE A PHOTO OF IT EVEN, AND THEN LATER IN THE BAR, SHE TOLD EVERYONE TO START CLAPPING AND WE *DID*--EVERY LAST ONE OF US!
"AND THEN SHE JUST PUT EVERYONE TO *SLEEP* SOMEHOW, AND I...
"LOOK, EITHER WHAT SHE'S SAYING IS *TRUE*, WHICH IS *CRAZY*, OR...
"...OR *I* AM.
"YOU KNOW... LIKE BEFORE.
"AND LIKE WITH *DAD*..."

Chapter II

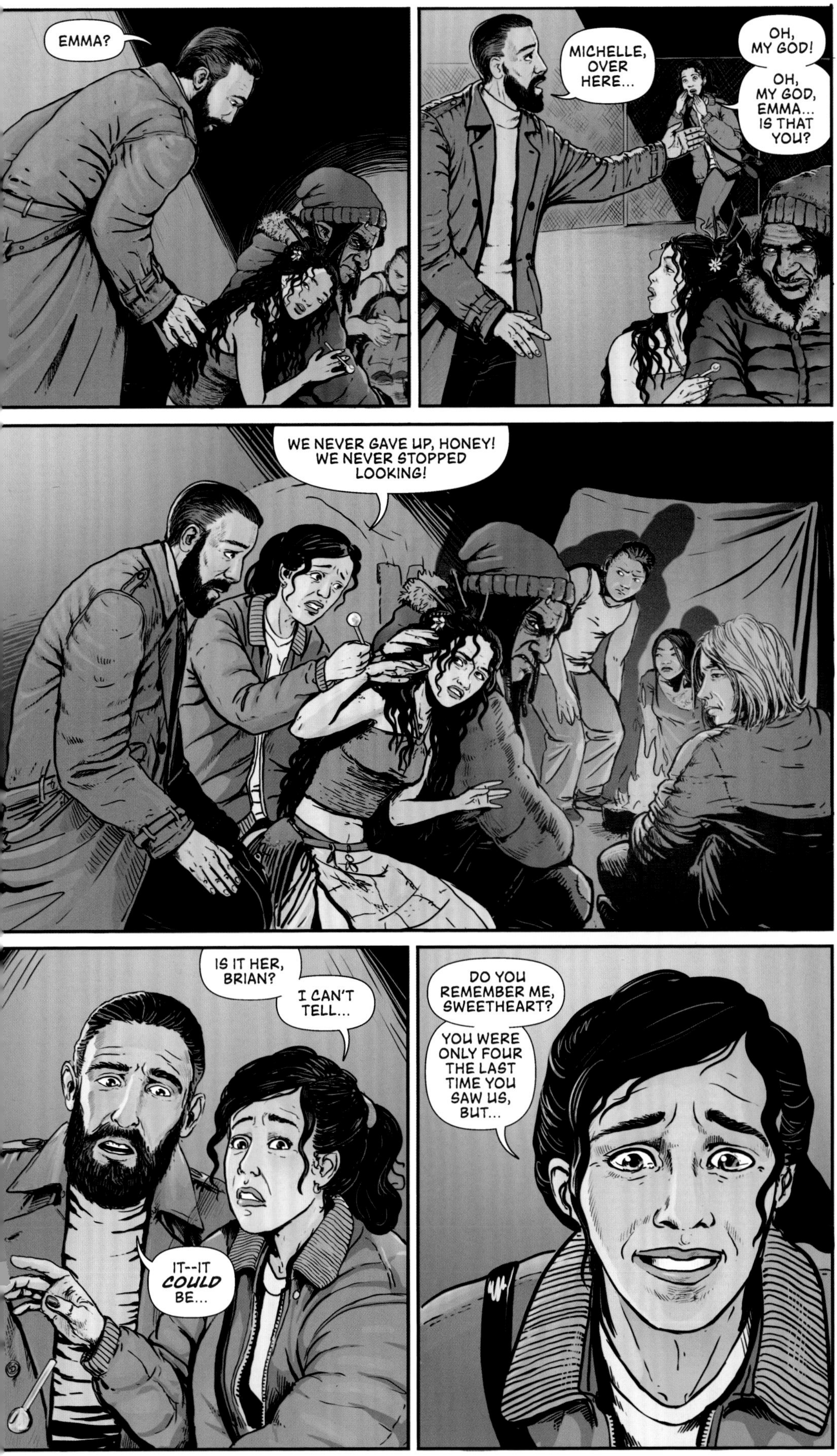
EMMA?
MICHELLE, OVER HERE...
OH, MY GOD!
OH, MY GOD, EMMA... IS THAT YOU?
WE NEVER GAVE UP, HONEY! WE NEVER STOPPED LOOKING!
IS IT HER, BRIAN?
I CAN'T TELL...
IT--IT *COULD* BE...
DO YOU REMEMBER ME, SWEETHEART?
YOU WERE ONLY FOUR THE LAST TIME YOU SAW US, BUT...

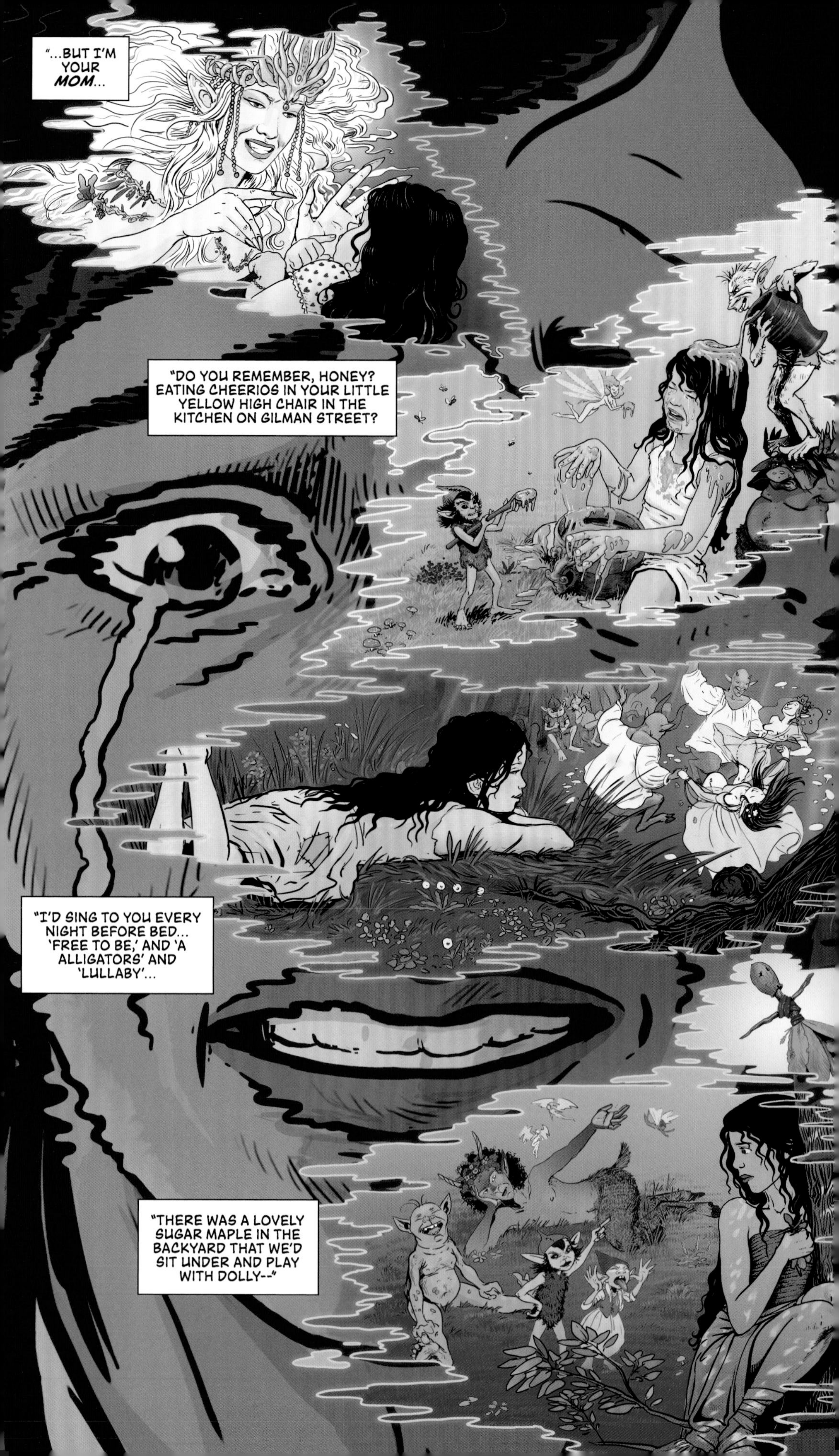
"...BUT I'M YOUR *MOM*...
"DO YOU REMEMBER, HONEY? EATING CHEERIOS IN YOUR LITTLE YELLOW HIGH CHAIR IN THE KITCHEN ON GILMAN STREET?
"I'D SING TO YOU EVERY NIGHT BEFORE BED... 'FREE TO BE,' AND 'A ALLIGATORS' AND 'LULLABY'...
"THERE WAS A LOVELY SUGAR MAPLE IN THE BACKYARD THAT WE'D SIT UNDER AND PLAY WITH DOLLY--"

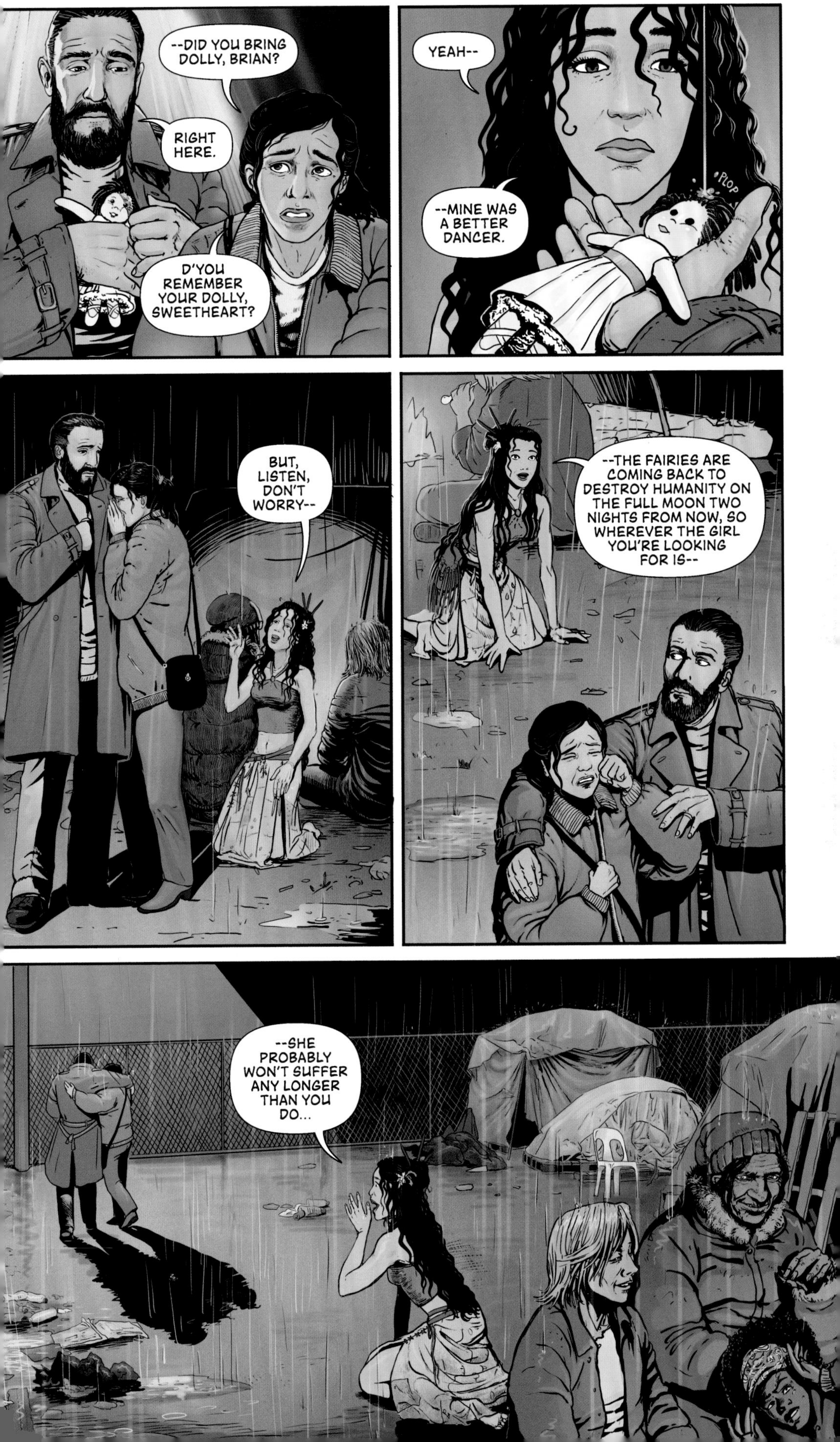
--DID YOU BRING DOLLY, BRIAN?
RIGHT HERE.
D'YOU REMEMBER YOUR DOLLY, SWEETHEART?
YEAH--
--MINE WAS A BETTER DANCER.
PLOP
BUT, LISTEN, DON'T WORRY--
--THE FAIRIES ARE COMING BACK TO DESTROY HUMANITY ON THE FULL MOON TWO NIGHTS FROM NOW, SO WHEREVER THE GIRL YOU'RE LOOKING FOR IS--
--SHE PROBABLY WON'T SUFFER ANY LONGER THAN YOU DO...

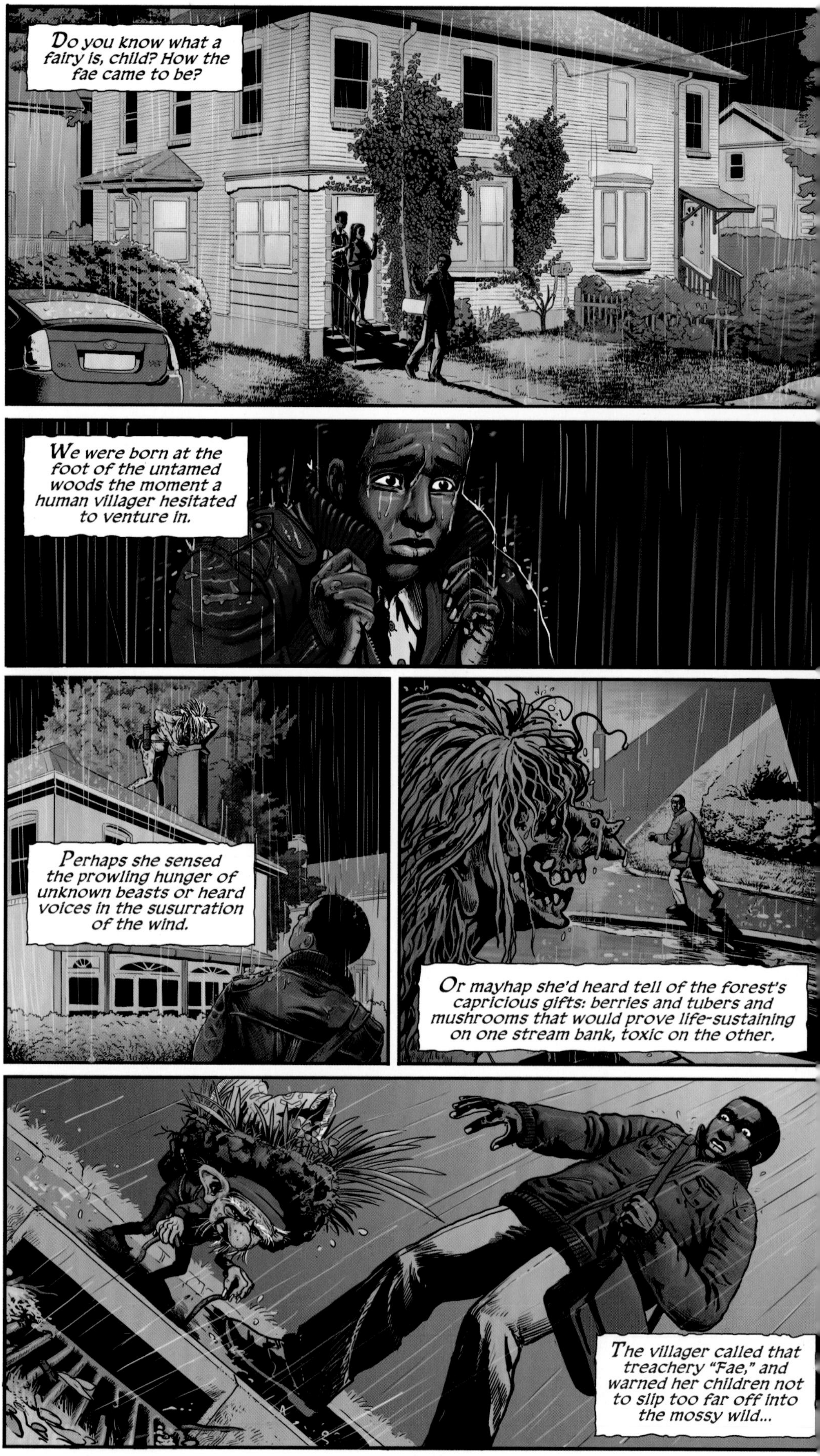
Do you know what a fairy is, child? How the fae came to be?
We were born at the foot of the untamed woods the moment a human villager hesitated to venture in.
Perhaps she sensed the prowling hunger of unknown beasts or heard voices in the susurration of the wind.
Or mayhap she'd heard tell of the forest's capricious gifts: berries and tubers and mushrooms that would prove life-sustaining on one stream bank, toxic on the other.
The villager called that treachery "Fae," and warned her children not to slip too far off into the mossy wild...

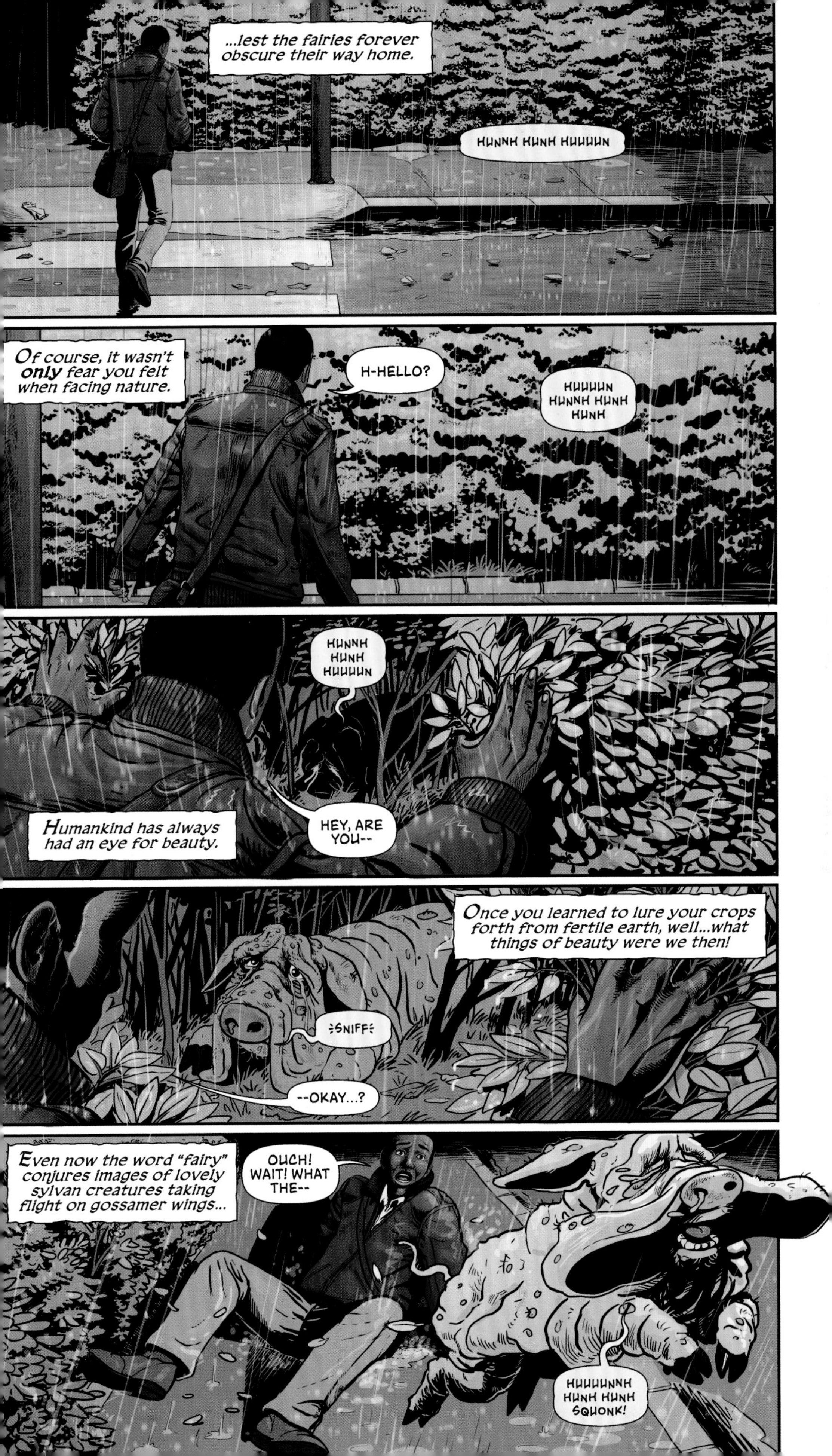
...lest the fairies forever obscure their way home.
HUNNH HUNH HUUUUN
Of course, it wasn't **only** fear you felt when facing nature.
H-HELLO?
HUUUUN HUNNH HUNH HUNH
HUNNH HUNH HUUUUN
Humankind has always had an eye for beauty.
HEY, ARE YOU--
Once you learned to lure your crops forth from fertile earth, well...what things of beauty were we then!
SNIFF
--OKAY...?
Even now the word "fairy" conjures images of lovely sylvan creatures taking flight on gossamer wings...
OUCH! WAIT! WHAT THE--
HUUUUNNH HUNH HUNH SQUONK!

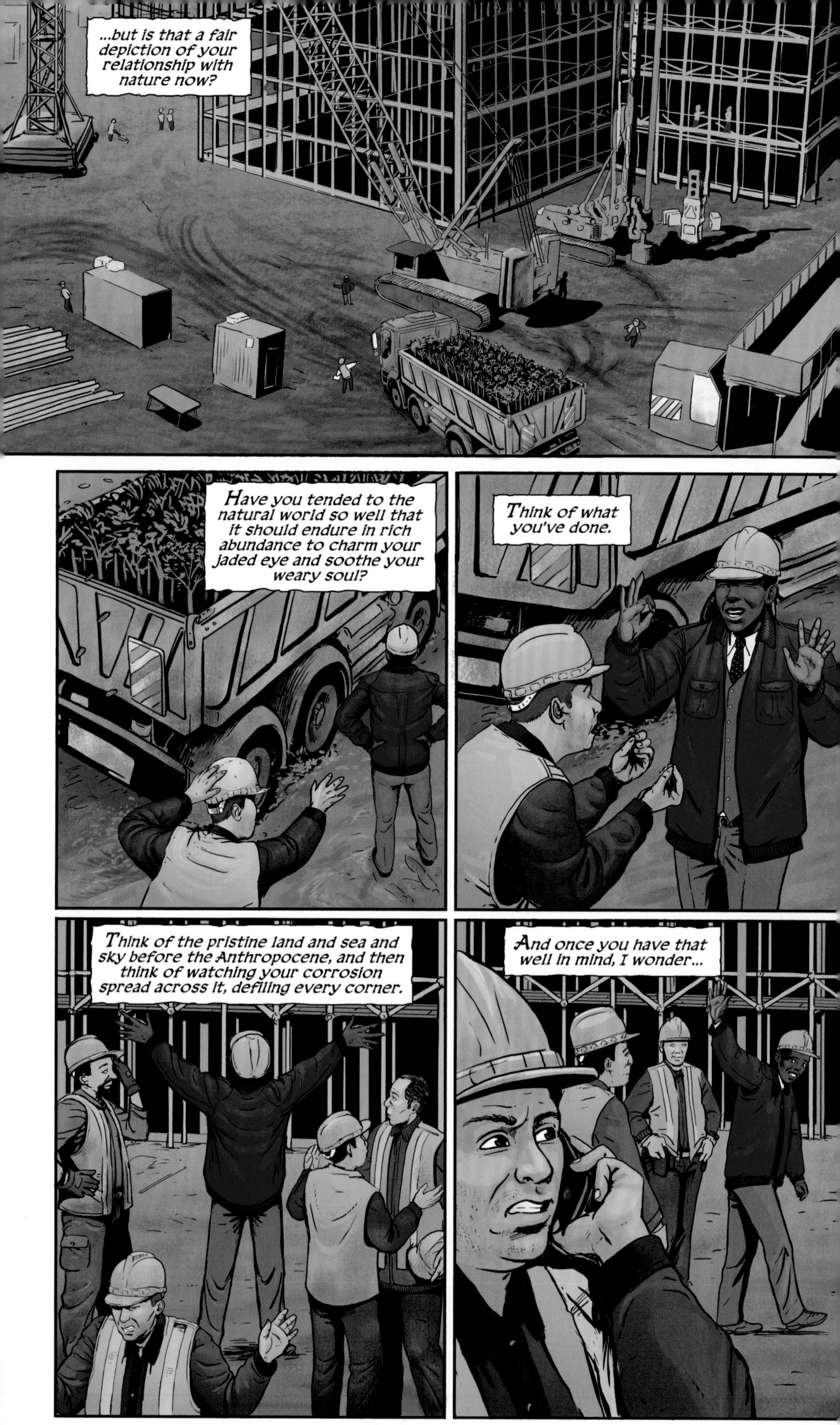
...but is that a fair depiction of your relationship with nature now?
Have you tended to the natural world so well that it should endure in rich abundance to charm your jaded eye and soothe your weary soul?
Think of what you've done.
Think of the pristine land and sea and sky before the Anthropocene, and then think of watching your corrosion spread across it, defiling every corner.
And once you have that well in mind, I wonder...

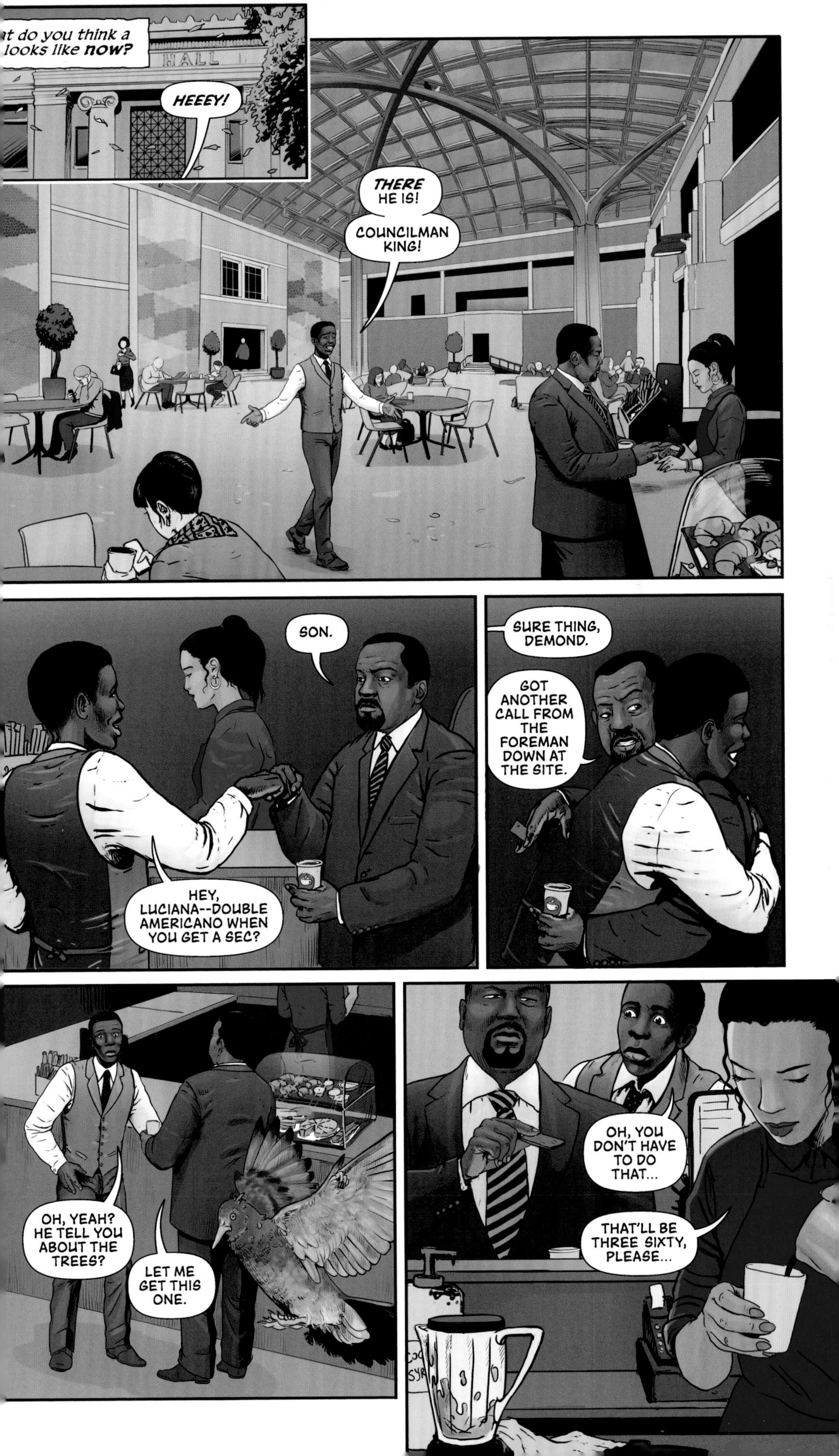

...at do you think a ... looks like ***now?***
HALL
HEEEY!
THERE HE IS!
COUNCILMAN KING!
SON.
HEY, LUCIANA--DOUBLE AMERICANO WHEN YOU GET A SEC?
SURE THING, DEMOND.
GOT ANOTHER CALL FROM THE FOREMAN DOWN AT THE SITE.
OH, YEAH? HE TELL YOU ABOUT THE TREES?
LET ME GET THIS ONE.
OH, YOU DON'T HAVE TO DO THAT...
THAT'LL BE THREE SIXTY, PLEASE...

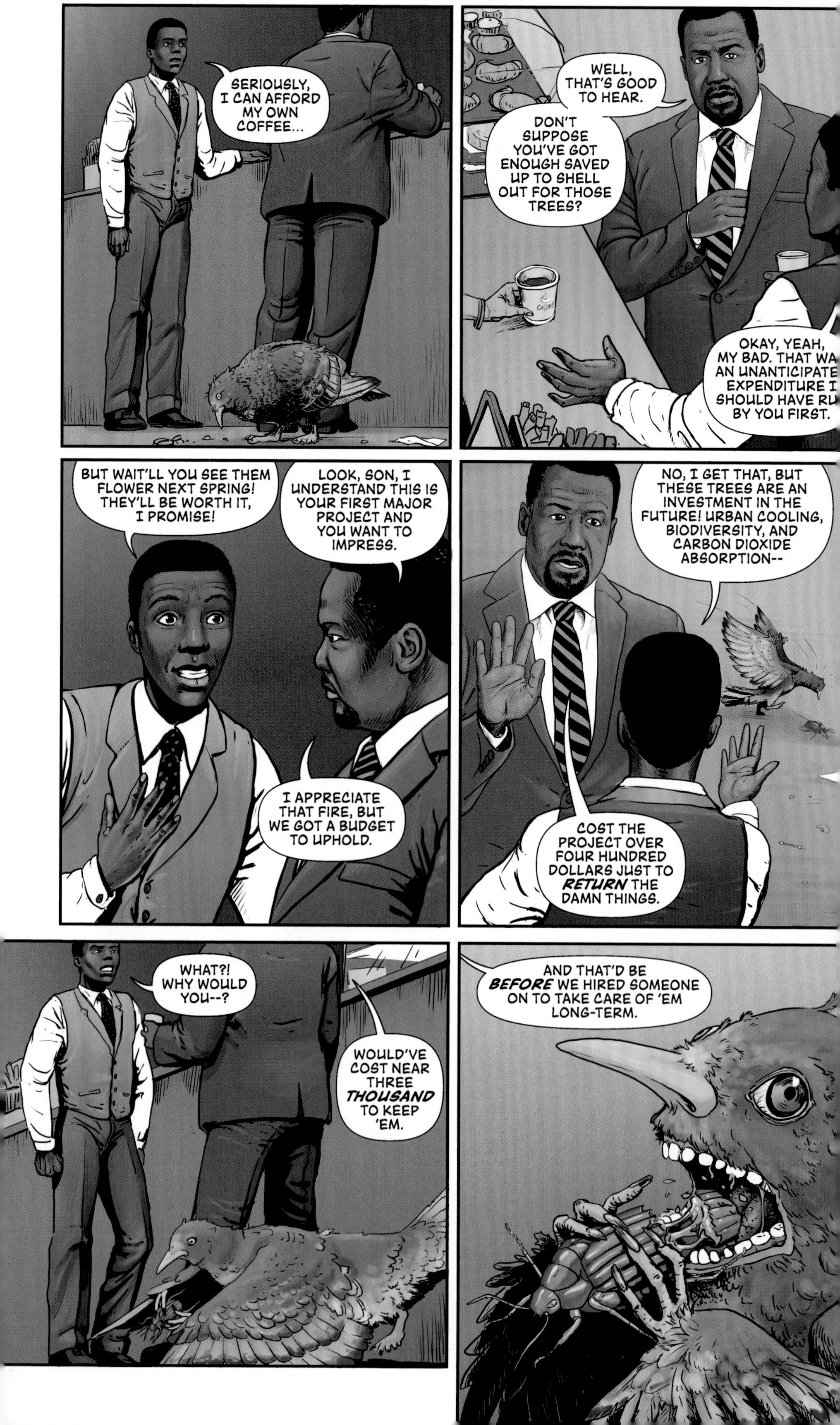
SERIOUSLY, I CAN AFFORD MY OWN COFFEE...
WELL, THAT'S GOOD TO HEAR.
DON'T SUPPOSE YOU'VE GOT ENOUGH SAVED UP TO SHELL OUT FOR THOSE TREES?
OKAY, YEAH, MY BAD. THAT WA AN UNANTICIPATE EXPENDITURE I SHOULD HAVE RU BY YOU FIRST.
BUT WAIT'LL YOU SEE THEM FLOWER NEXT SPRING! THEY'LL BE WORTH IT, I PROMISE!
LOOK, SON, I UNDERSTAND THIS IS YOUR FIRST MAJOR PROJECT AND YOU WANT TO IMPRESS.
I APPRECIATE THAT FIRE, BUT WE GOT A BUDGET TO UPHOLD.
NO, I GET THAT, BUT THESE TREES ARE AN INVESTMENT IN THE FUTURE! URBAN COOLING, BIODIVERSITY, AND CARBON DIOXIDE ABSORPTION--
COST THE PROJECT OVER FOUR HUNDRED DOLLARS JUST TO *RETURN* THE DAMN THINGS.
WHAT?! WHY WOULD YOU--?
WOULD'VE COST NEAR THREE *THOUSAND* TO KEEP 'EM.
AND THAT'D BE *BEFORE* WE HIRED SOMEONE ON TO TAKE CARE OF 'EM LONG-TERM.

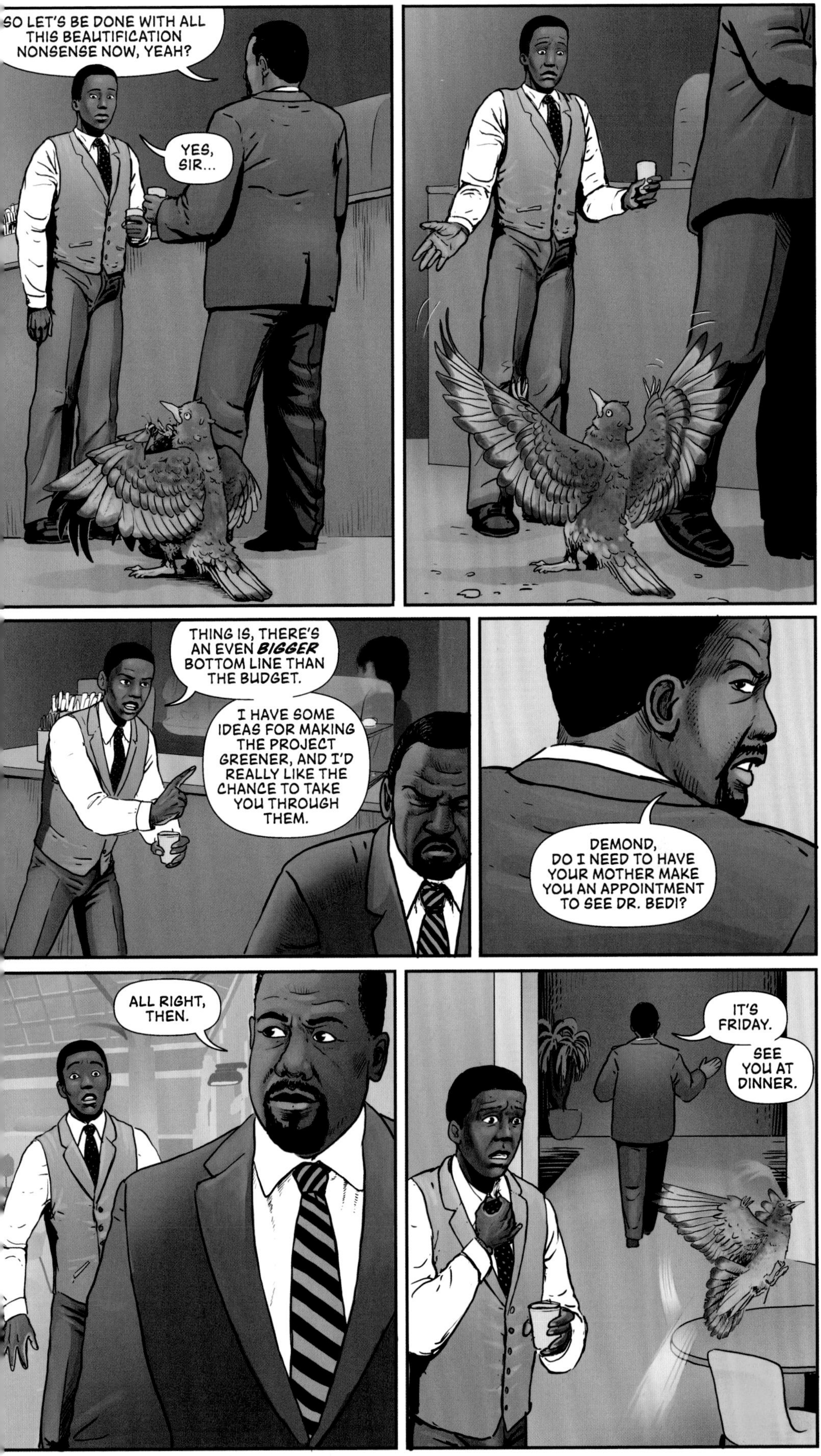
SO LET'S BE DONE WITH ALL THIS BEAUTIFICATION NONSENSE NOW, YEAH?
YES, SIR...
THING IS, THERE'S AN EVEN *BIGGER* BOTTOM LINE THAN THE BUDGET.
I HAVE SOME IDEAS FOR MAKING THE PROJECT GREENER, AND I'D REALLY LIKE THE CHANCE TO TAKE YOU THROUGH THEM.
DEMOND, DO I NEED TO HAVE YOUR MOTHER MAKE YOU AN APPOINTMENT TO SEE DR. BEDI?
ALL RIGHT, THEN.
IT'S FRIDAY.
SEE YOU AT DINNER.

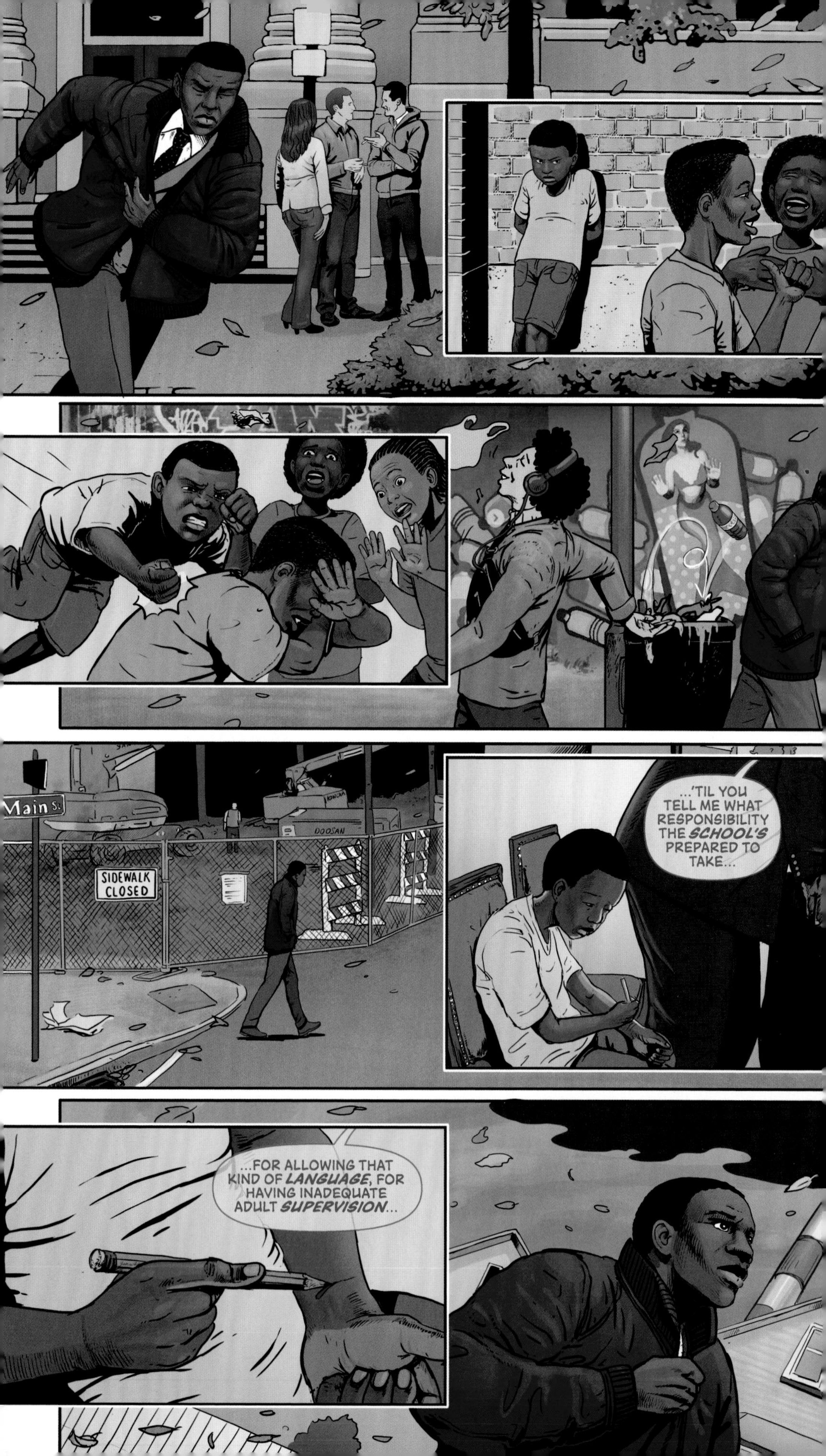
Main St
SIDEWALK CLOSED
DOOSAN
...'TIL YOU TELL ME WHAT RESPONSIBILITY THE SCHOOL'S PREPARED TO TAKE...
...FOR ALLOWING THAT KIND OF LANGUAGE, FOR HAVING INADEQUATE ADULT SUPERVISION...

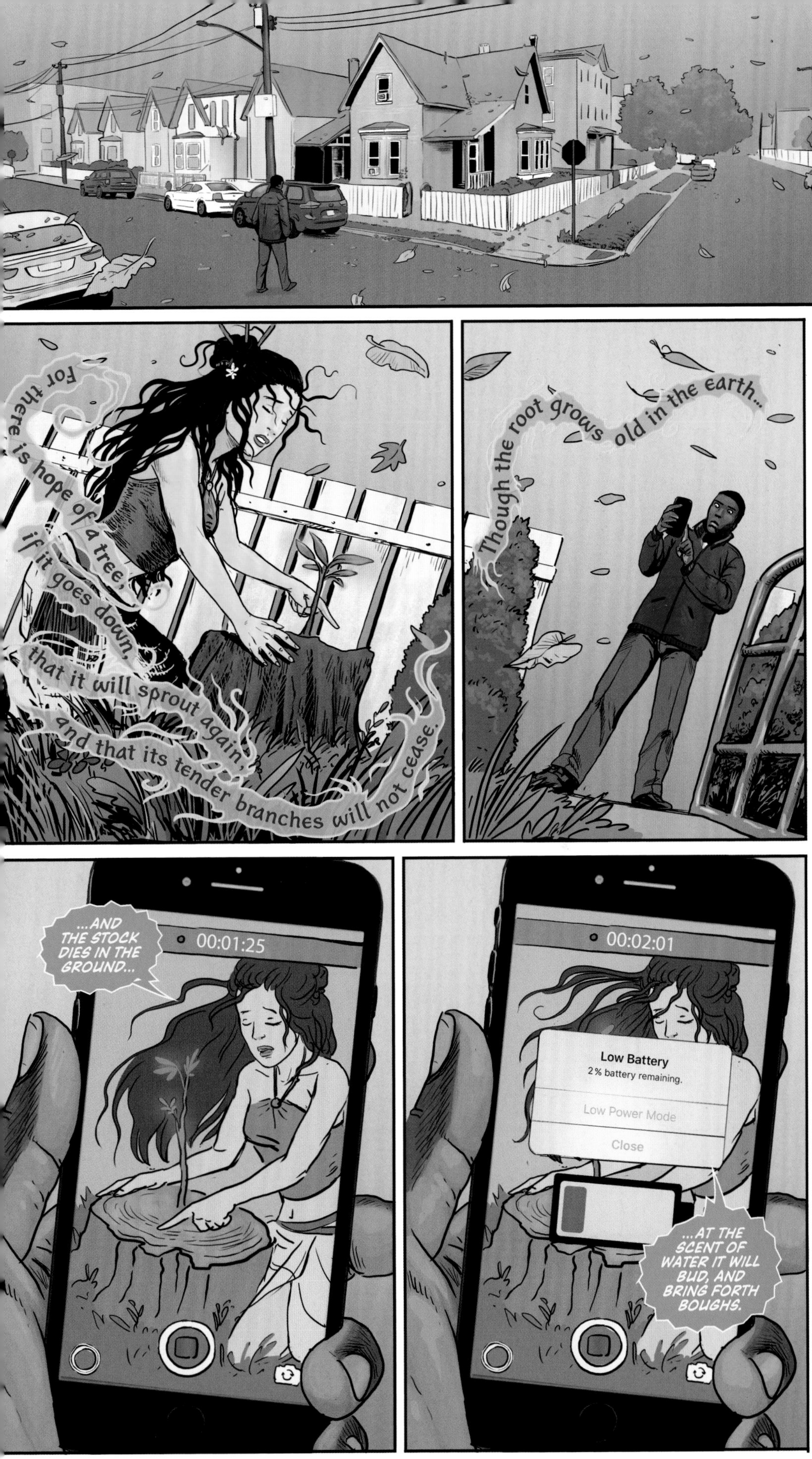
For there is hope of a tree, if it goes down, that it will sprout again, and that its tender branches will not cease.
Though the root grows old in the earth...
...AND THE STOCK DIES IN THE GROUND...
00:01:25
00:02:01
Low Battery
2% battery remaining.
Low Power Mode
Close
...AT THE SCENT OF WATER IT WILL BUD, AND BRING FORTH BOUGHS.

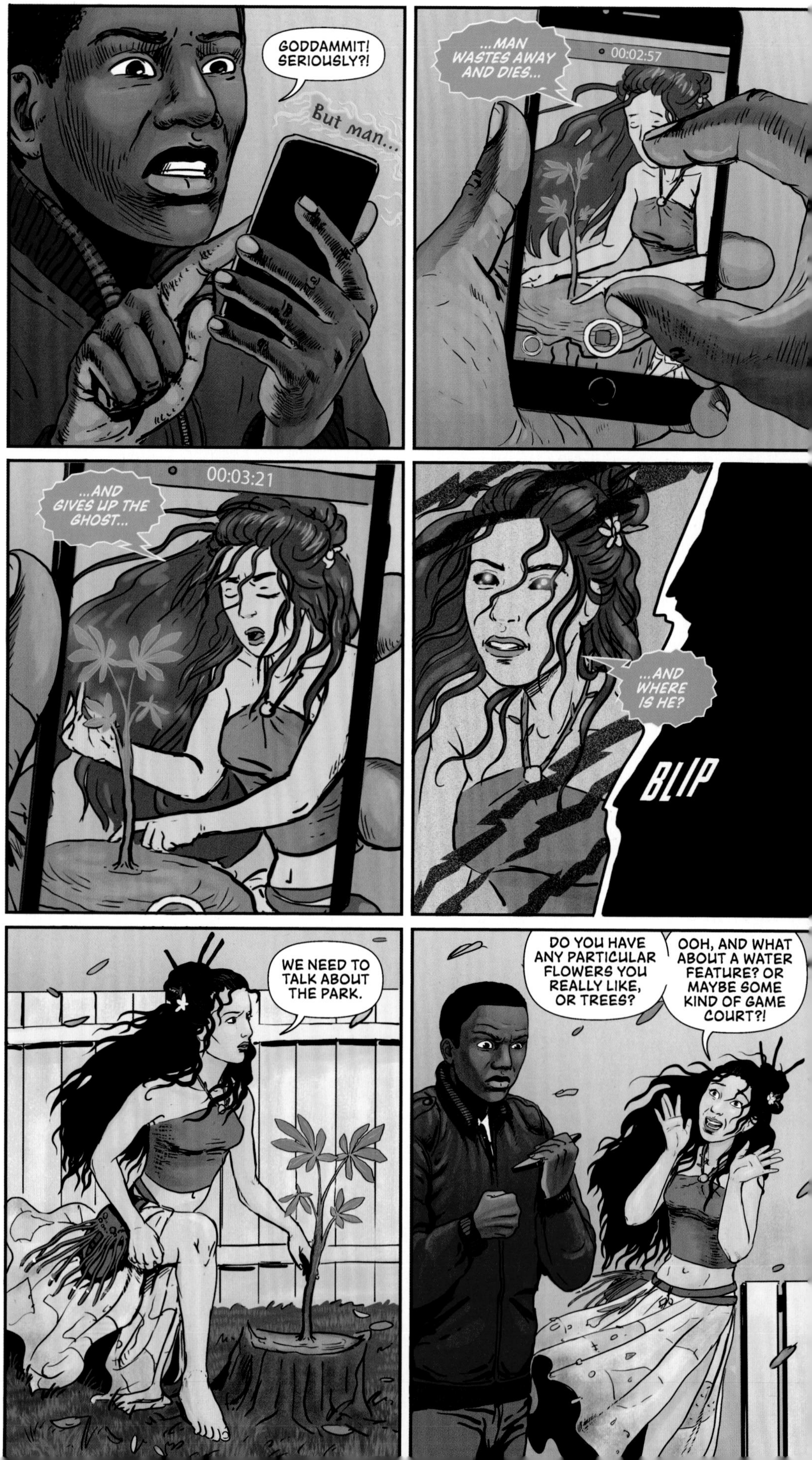
GODDAMMIT! SERIOUSLY?!
But man...
...MAN WASTES AWAY AND DIES...
00:02:57
00:03:21
...AND GIVES UP THE GHOST...
...AND WHERE IS HE?
BLIP
WE NEED TO TALK ABOUT THE PARK.
DO YOU HAVE ANY PARTICULAR FLOWERS YOU REALLY LIKE, OR TREES?
OOH, AND WHAT ABOUT A WATER FEATURE? OR MAYBE SOME KIND OF GAME COURT?!

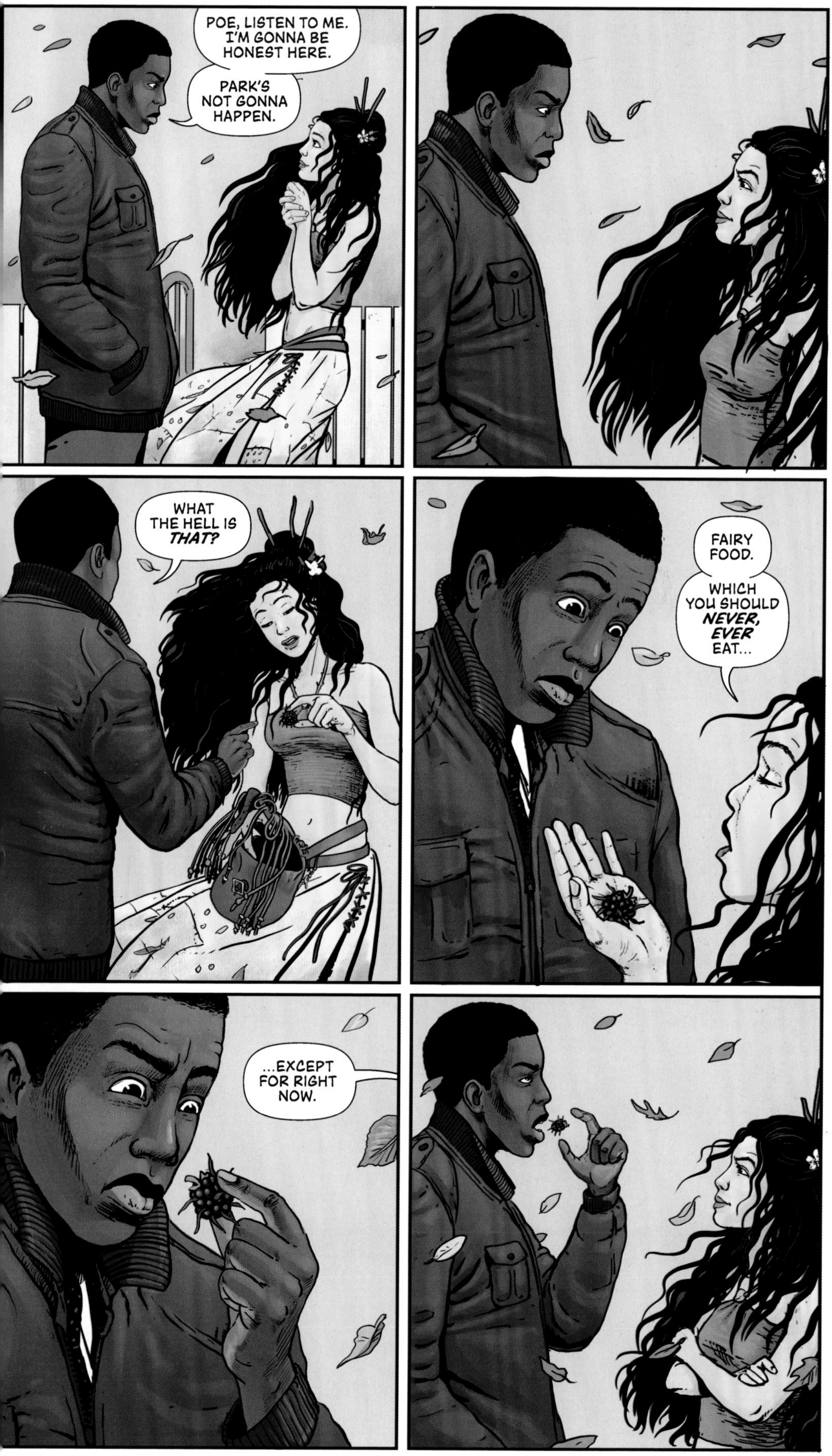

POE, LISTEN TO ME. I'M GONNA BE HONEST HERE.
PARK'S NOT GONNA HAPPEN.
WHAT THE HELL IS *THAT?*
FAIRY FOOD.
WHICH YOU SHOULD ***NEVER, EVER*** EAT...
...EXCEPT FOR RIGHT NOW.

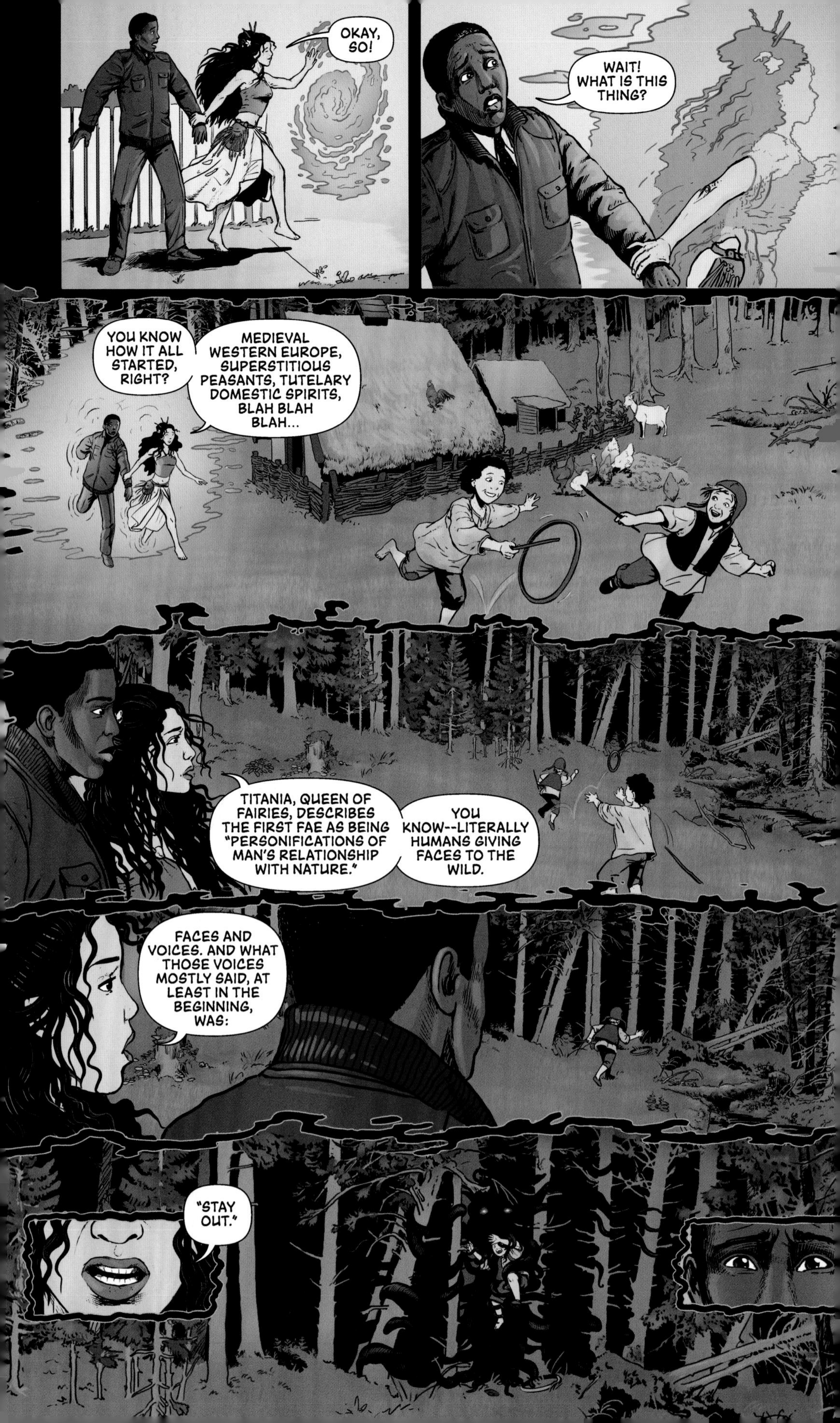
OKAY, SO!
WAIT! WHAT IS THIS THING?
YOU KNOW HOW IT ALL STARTED, RIGHT?
MEDIEVAL WESTERN EUROPE, SUPERSTITIOUS PEASANTS, TUTELARY DOMESTIC SPIRITS, BLAH BLAH BLAH...
TITANIA, QUEEN OF FAIRIES, DESCRIBES THE FIRST FAE AS BEING "PERSONIFICATIONS OF MAN'S RELATIONSHIP WITH NATURE."
YOU KNOW--LITERALLY HUMANS GIVING FACES TO THE WILD.
FACES AND VOICES. AND WHAT THOSE VOICES MOSTLY SAID, AT LEAST IN THE BEGINNING, WAS:
"STAY OUT."

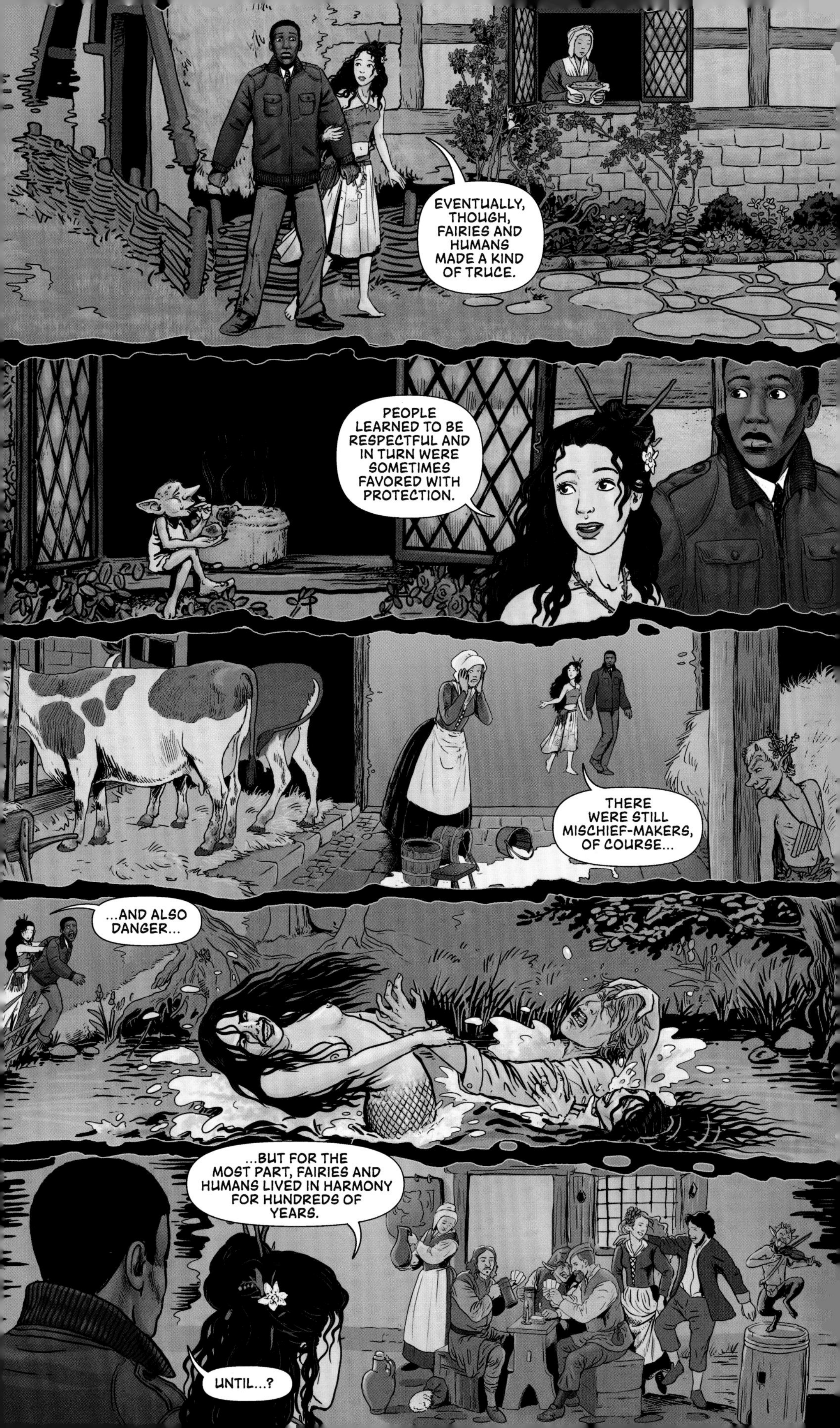

EVENTUALLY, THOUGH, FAIRIES AND HUMANS MADE A KIND OF TRUCE.
PEOPLE LEARNED TO BE RESPECTFUL AND IN TURN WERE SOMETIMES FAVORED WITH PROTECTION.
THERE WERE STILL MISCHIEF-MAKERS, OF COURSE...
...AND ALSO DANGER...
...BUT FOR THE MOST PART, FAIRIES AND HUMANS LIVED IN HARMONY FOR HUNDREDS OF YEARS.
UNTIL...?

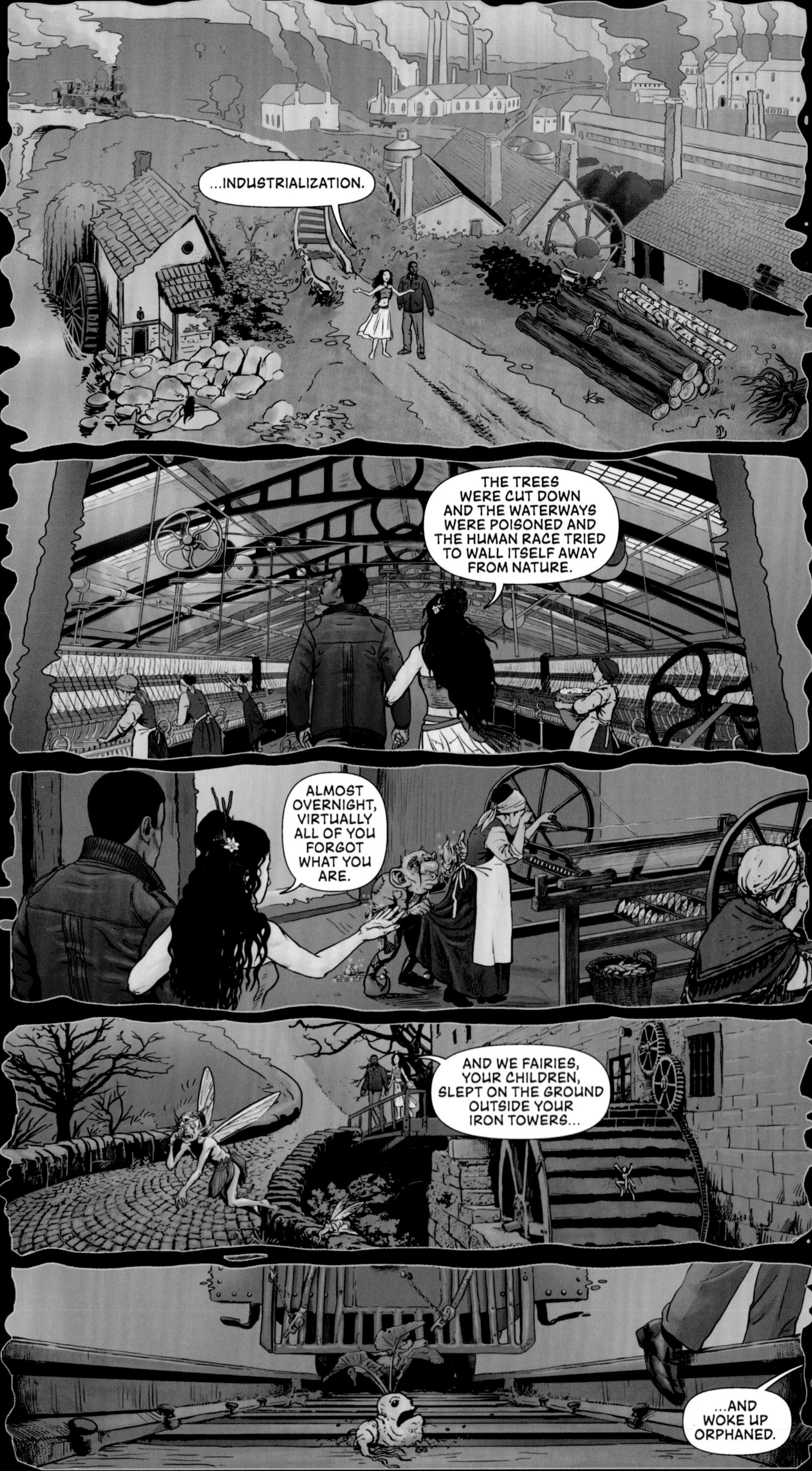
...INDUSTRIALIZATION.
THE TREES WERE CUT DOWN AND THE WATERWAYS WERE POISONED AND THE HUMAN RACE TRIED TO WALL ITSELF AWAY FROM NATURE.
ALMOST OVERNIGHT, VIRTUALLY ALL OF YOU FORGOT WHAT YOU ARE.
AND WE FAIRIES, YOUR CHILDREN, SLEPT ON THE GROUND OUTSIDE YOUR IRON TOWERS...
...AND WOKE UP ORPHANED.

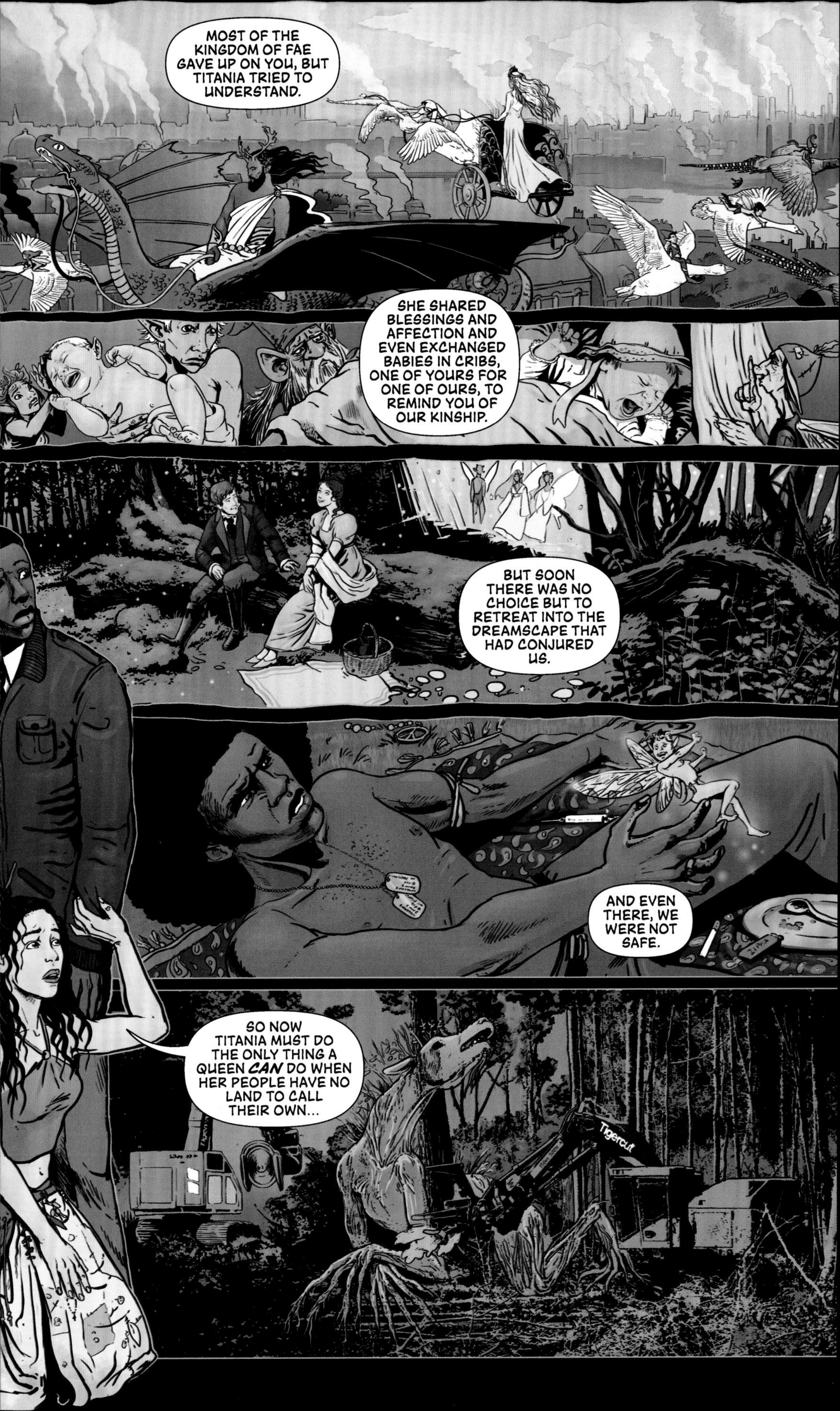
MOST OF THE KINGDOM OF FAE GAVE UP ON YOU, BUT TITANIA TRIED TO UNDERSTAND.
SHE SHARED BLESSINGS AND AFFECTION AND EVEN EXCHANGED BABIES IN CRIBS, ONE OF YOURS FOR ONE OF OURS, TO REMIND YOU OF OUR KINSHIP.
BUT SOON THERE WAS NO CHOICE BUT TO RETREAT INTO THE DREAMSCAPE THAT HAD CONJURED US.
AND EVEN THERE, WE WERE NOT SAFE.
SO NOW TITANIA MUST DO THE ONLY THING A QUEEN *CAN* DO WHEN HER PEOPLE HAVE NO LAND TO CALL THEIR OWN...
Tigercut

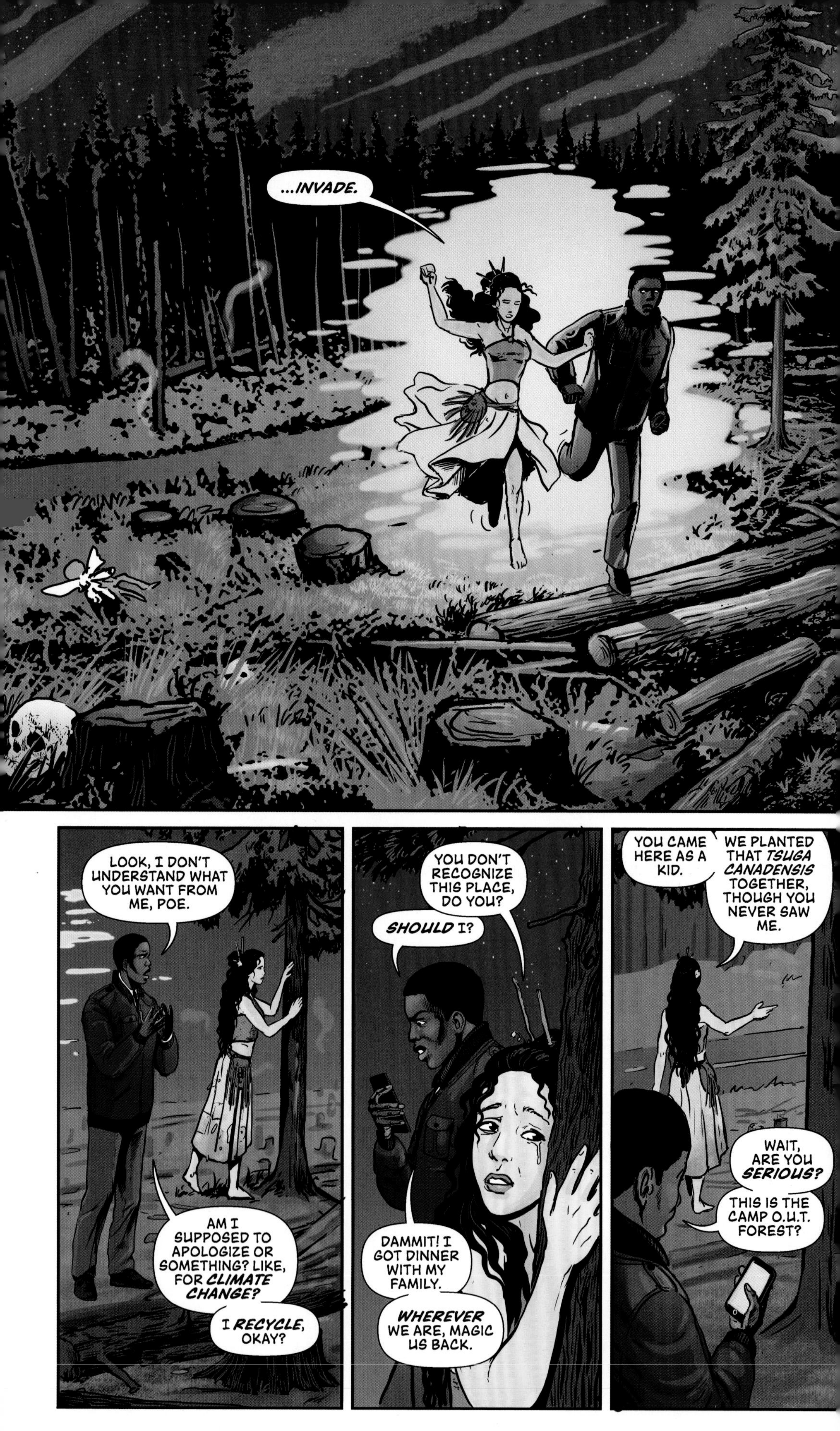
...INVADE.
LOOK, I DON'T UNDERSTAND WHAT YOU WANT FROM ME, POE.
AM I SUPPOSED TO APOLOGIZE OR SOMETHING? LIKE, FOR *CLIMATE CHANGE?*
I *RECYCLE*, OKAY?
YOU DON'T RECOGNIZE THIS PLACE, DO YOU?
SHOULD I?
DAMMIT! I GOT DINNER WITH MY FAMILY.
WHEREVER WE ARE, MAGIC US BACK.
YOU CAME HERE AS A KID.
WE PLANTED THAT *TSUGA CANADENSIS* TOGETHER, THOUGH YOU NEVER SAW ME.
WAIT, ARE YOU *SERIOUS?*
THIS IS THE CAMP O.U.T. FOREST?

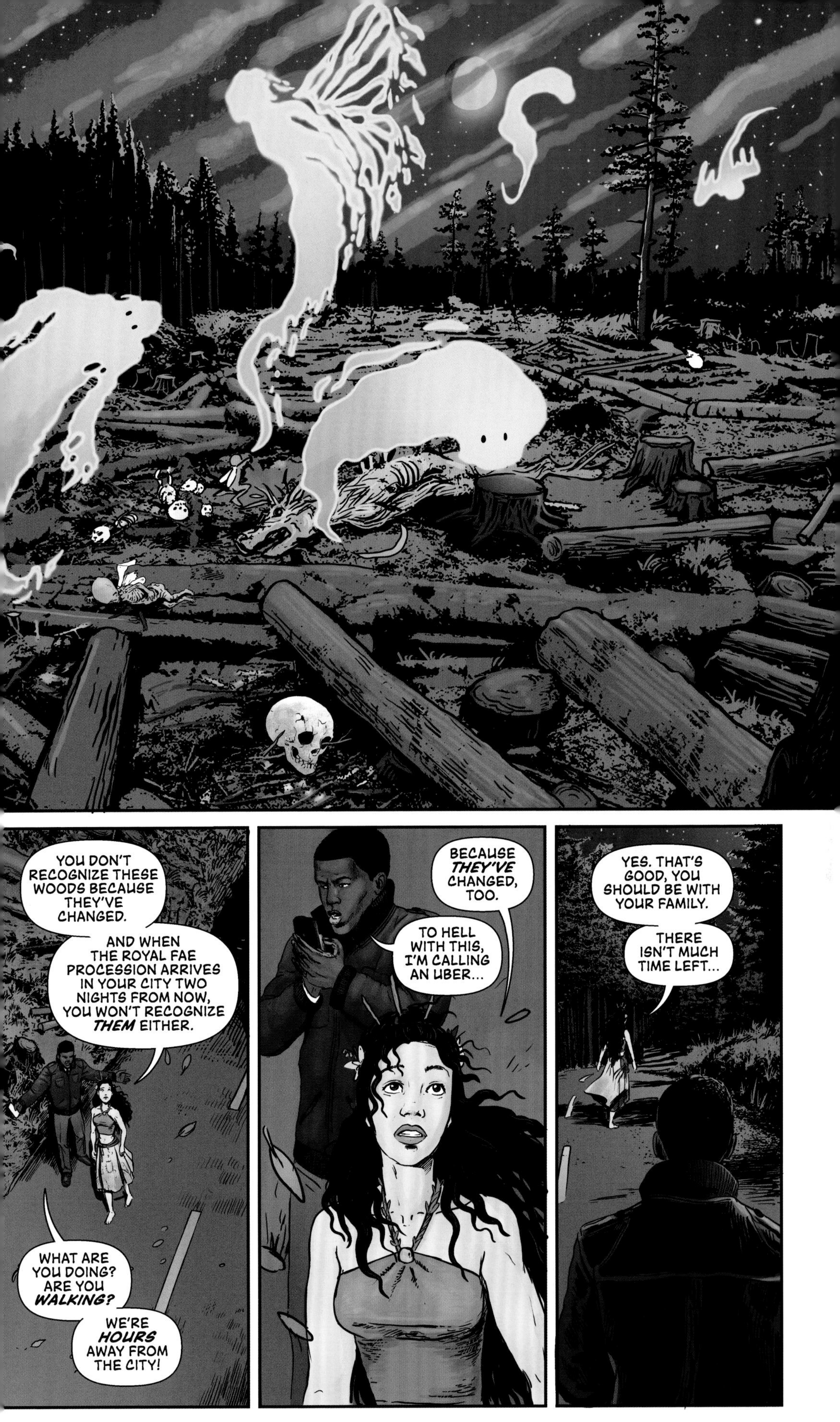
YOU DON'T RECOGNIZE THESE WOODS BECAUSE THEY'VE CHANGED.
AND WHEN THE ROYAL FAE PROCESSION ARRIVES IN YOUR CITY TWO NIGHTS FROM NOW, YOU WON'T RECOGNIZE *THEM* EITHER.
WHAT ARE YOU DOING? ARE YOU *WALKING?*
WE'RE *HOURS* AWAY FROM THE CITY!
BECAUSE *THEY'VE* CHANGED, TOO.
TO HELL WITH THIS, I'M CALLING AN UBER...
YES. THAT'S GOOD, YOU SHOULD BE WITH YOUR FAMILY.
THERE ISN'T MUCH TIME LEFT...

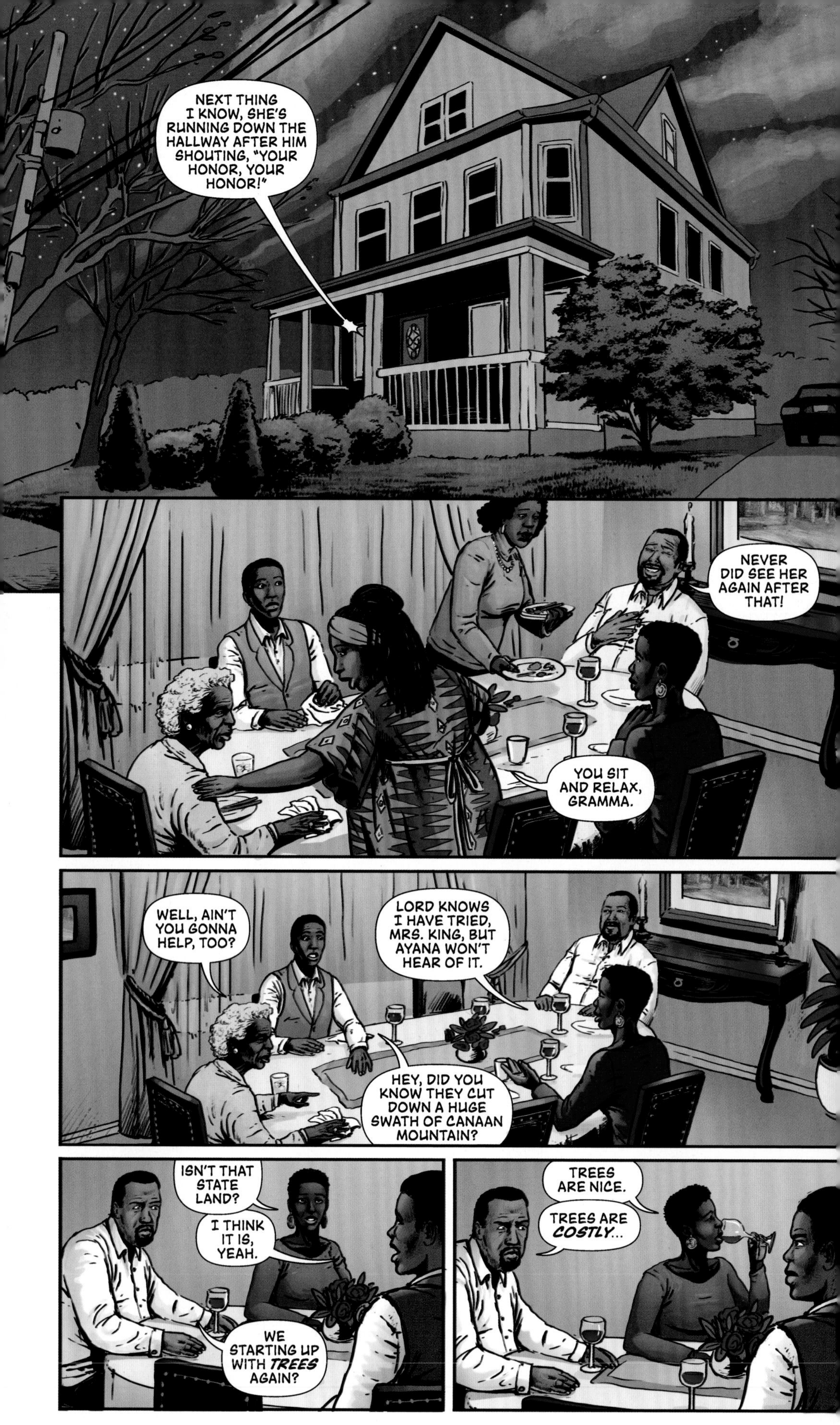
NEXT THING I KNOW, SHE'S RUNNING DOWN THE HALLWAY AFTER HIM SHOUTING, "YOUR HONOR, YOUR HONOR!"
NEVER DID SEE HER AGAIN AFTER THAT!
YOU SIT AND RELAX, GRAMMA.
WELL, AIN'T YOU GONNA HELP, TOO?
LORD KNOWS I HAVE TRIED, MRS. KING, BUT AYANA WON'T HEAR OF IT.
HEY, DID YOU KNOW THEY CUT DOWN A HUGE SWATH OF CANAAN MOUNTAIN?
ISN'T THAT STATE LAND?
I THINK IT IS, YEAH.
WE STARTING UP WITH *TREES* AGAIN?
TREES ARE NICE.
TREES ARE *COSTLY*...

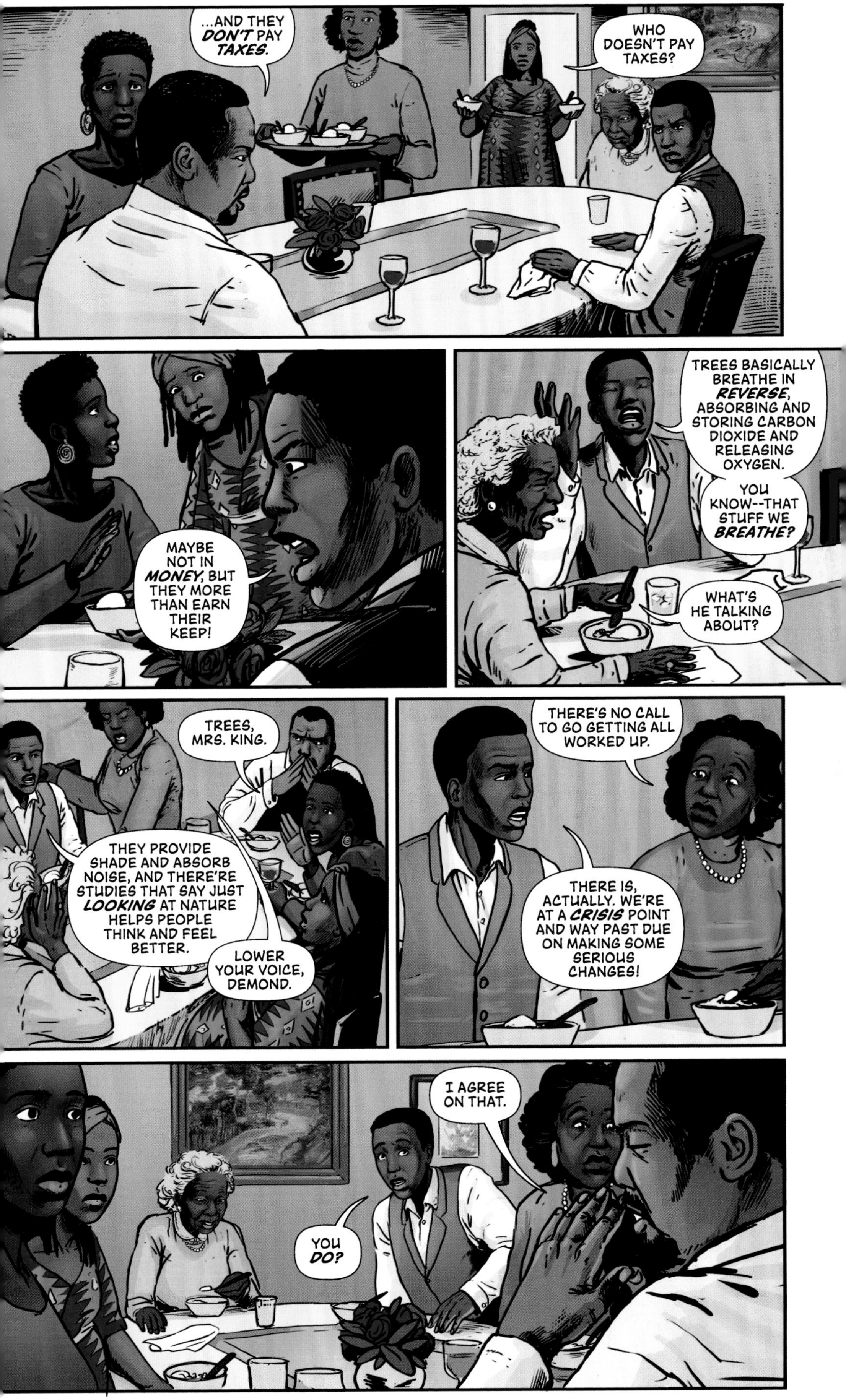
...AND THEY DON'T PAY TAXES.
WHO DOESN'T PAY TAXES?
MAYBE NOT IN MONEY, BUT THEY MORE THAN EARN THEIR KEEP!
TREES BASICALLY BREATHE IN REVERSE, ABSORBING AND STORING CARBON DIOXIDE AND RELEASING OXYGEN.
YOU KNOW--THAT STUFF WE BREATHE?
WHAT'S HE TALKING ABOUT?
TREES, MRS. KING.
THEY PROVIDE SHADE AND ABSORB NOISE, AND THERE'RE STUDIES THAT SAY JUST LOOKING AT NATURE HELPS PEOPLE THINK AND FEEL BETTER.
LOWER YOUR VOICE, DEMOND.
THERE'S NO CALL TO GO GETTING ALL WORKED UP.
THERE IS, ACTUALLY. WE'RE AT A CRISIS POINT AND WAY PAST DUE ON MAKING SOME SERIOUS CHANGES!
I AGREE ON THAT.
YOU DO?

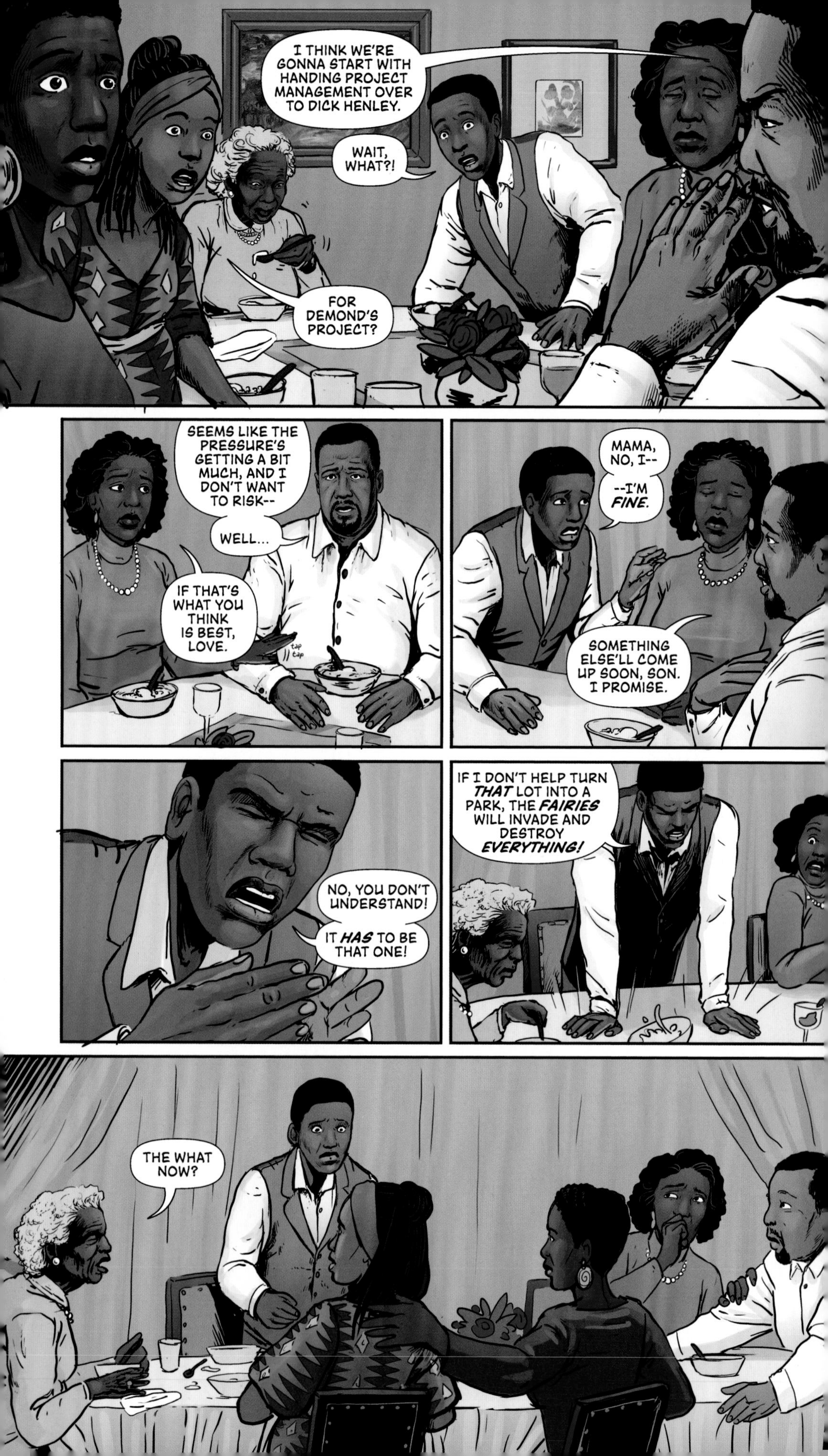
I THINK WE'RE GONNA START WITH HANDING PROJECT MANAGEMENT OVER TO DICK HENLEY.
WAIT, WHAT?!
FOR DEMOND'S PROJECT?
SEEMS LIKE THE PRESSURE'S GETTING A BIT MUCH, AND I DON'T WANT TO RISK--
WELL...
IF THAT'S WHAT YOU THINK IS BEST, LOVE.
tap tap
MAMA, NO, I--
--I'M *FINE*.
SOMETHING ELSE'LL COME UP SOON, SON. I PROMISE.
NO, YOU DON'T UNDERSTAND!
IT *HAS* TO BE THAT ONE!
IF I DON'T HELP TURN *THAT* LOT INTO A PARK, THE *FAIRIES* WILL INVADE AND DESTROY *EVERYTHING!*
THE WHAT NOW?

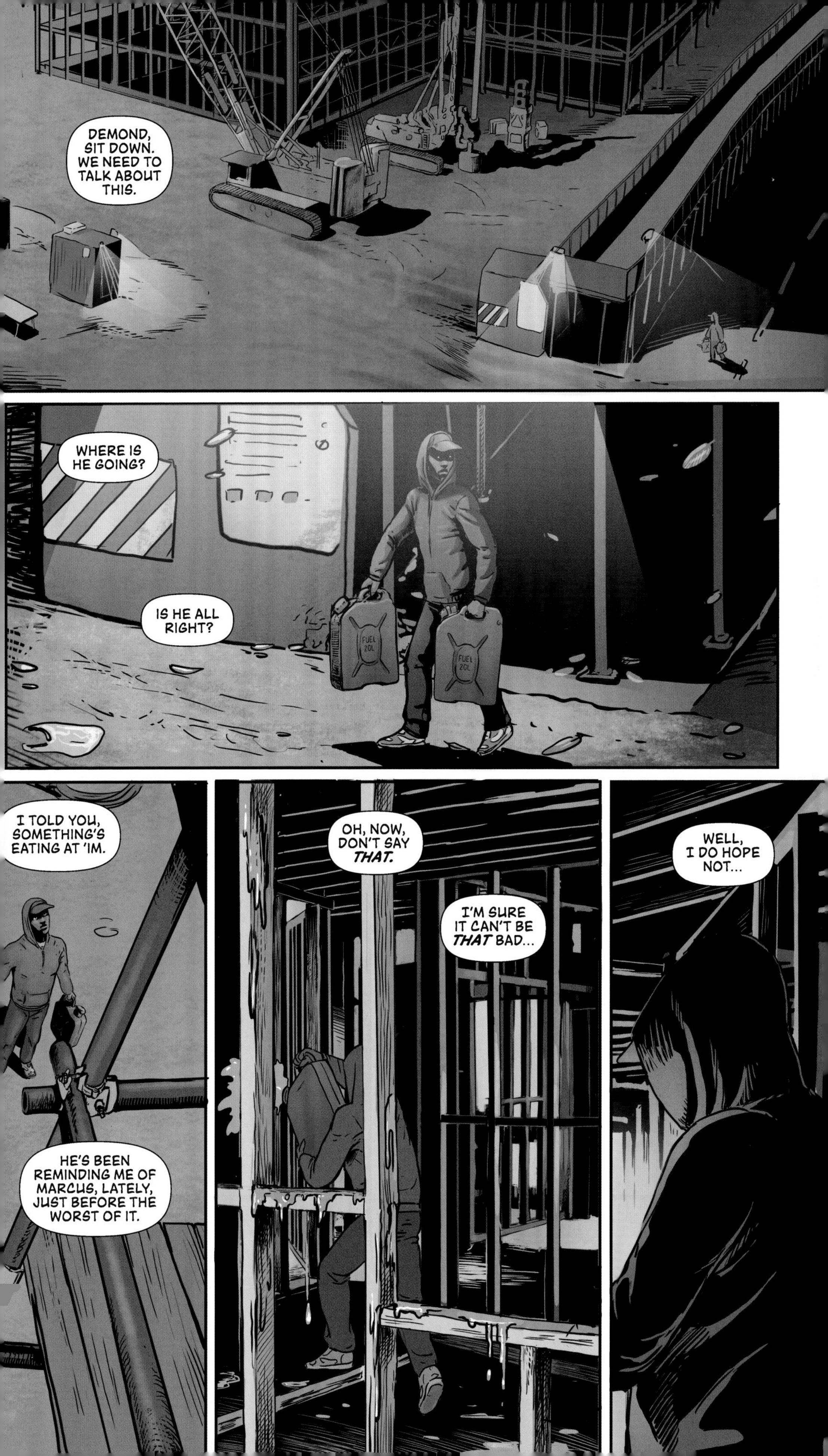
DEMOND, SIT DOWN. WE NEED TO TALK ABOUT THIS.
WHERE IS HE GOING?
IS HE ALL RIGHT?
FUEL 20L
FUEL 20L
I TOLD YOU, SOMETHING'S EATING AT 'IM.
HE'S BEEN REMINDING ME OF MARCUS, LATELY, JUST BEFORE THE WORST OF IT.
OH, NOW, DON'T SAY *THAT.*
I'M SURE IT CAN'T BE *THAT* BAD...
WELL, I DO HOPE NOT...

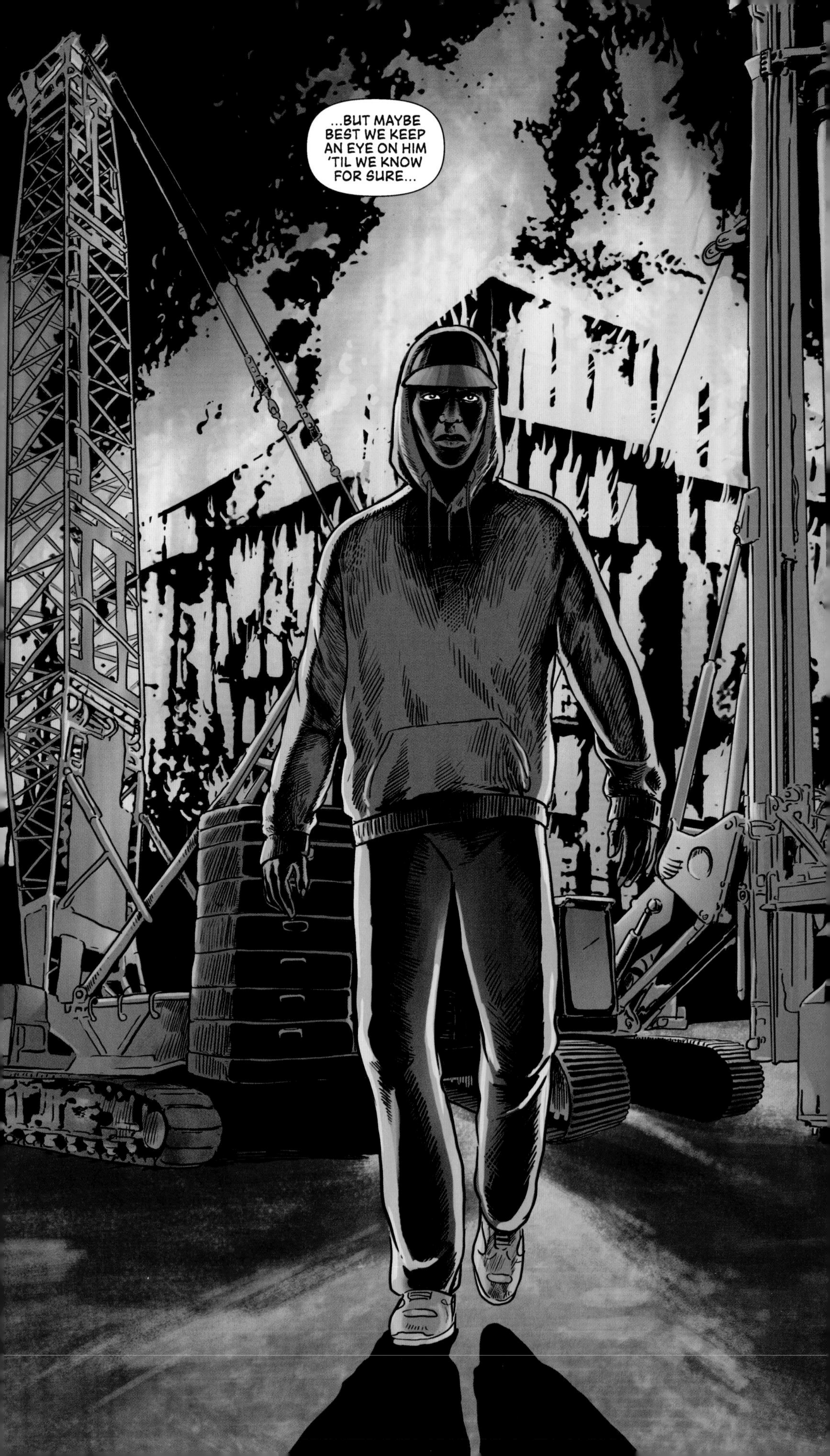
...BUT MAYBE BEST WE KEEP AN EYE ON HIM 'TIL WE KNOW FOR SURE...

Chapter III

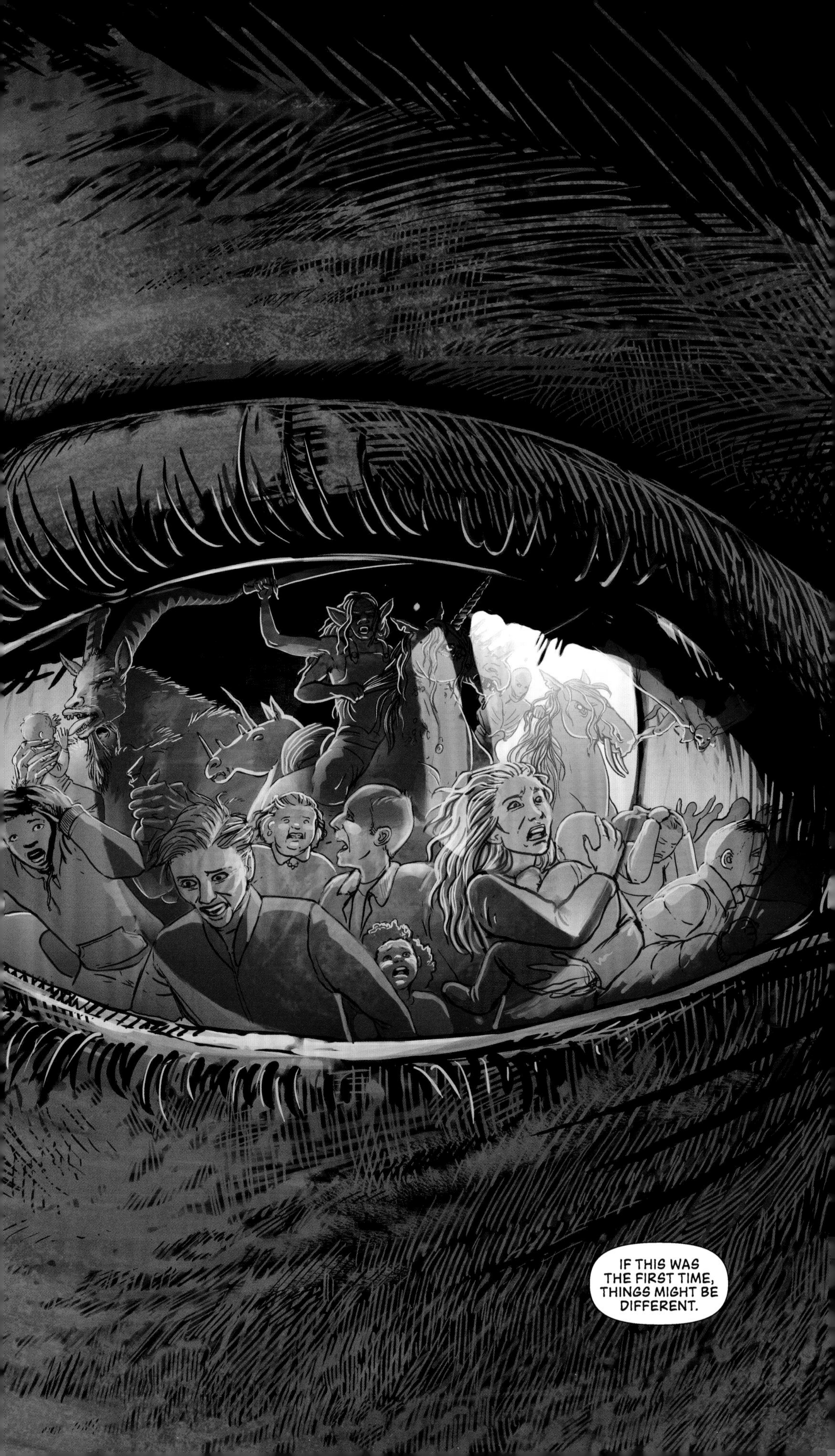
IF THIS WAS THE FIRST TIME, THINGS MIGHT BE DIFFERENT.

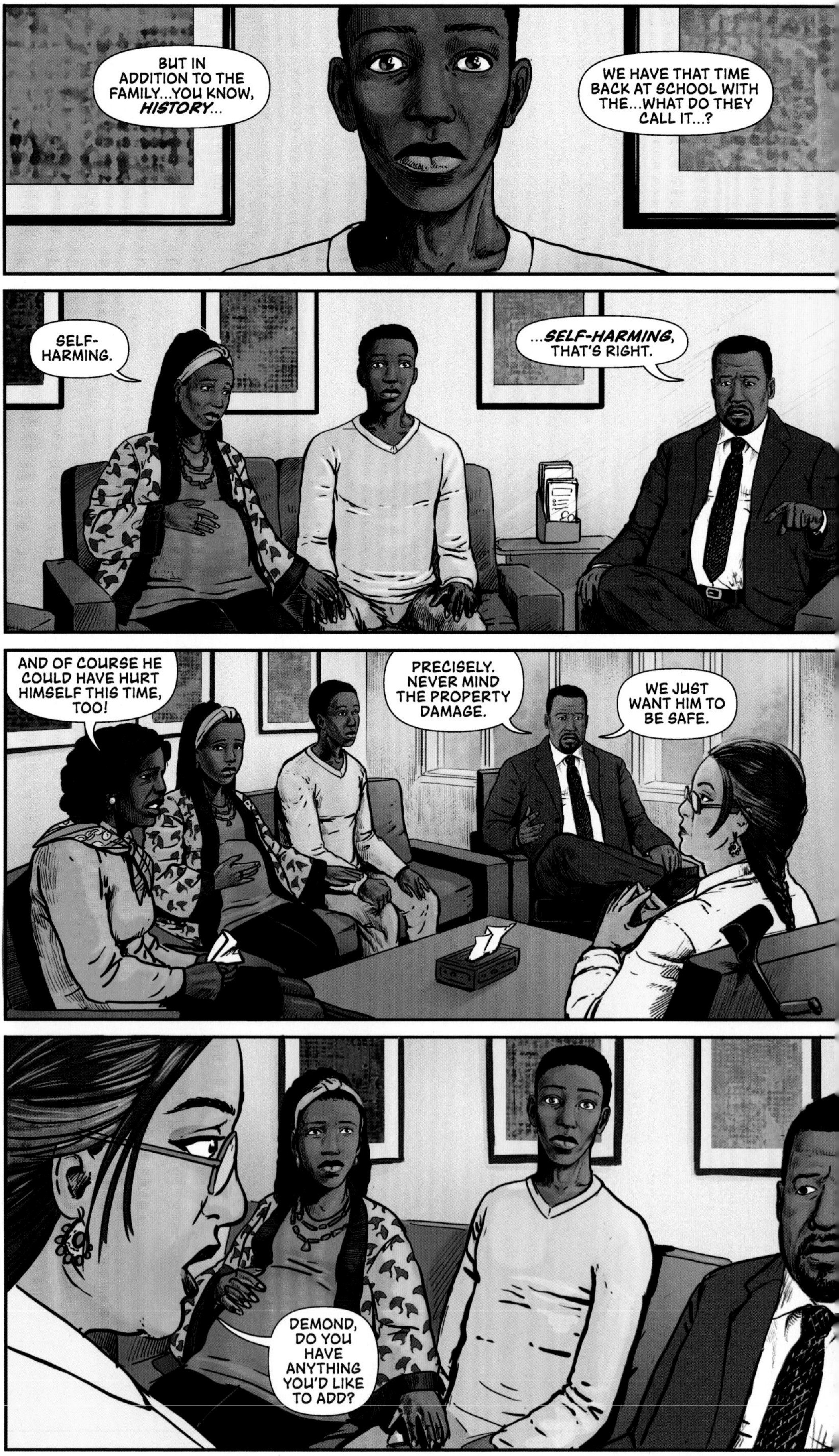
BUT IN ADDITION TO THE FAMILY...YOU KNOW, *HISTORY*...
WE HAVE THAT TIME BACK AT SCHOOL WITH THE...WHAT DO THEY CALL IT...?
SELF-HARMING.
...*SELF-HARMING*, THAT'S RIGHT.
AND OF COURSE HE COULD HAVE HURT HIMSELF THIS TIME, TOO!
PRECISELY. NEVER MIND THE PROPERTY DAMAGE.
WE JUST WANT HIM TO BE SAFE.
DEMOND, DO YOU HAVE ANYTHING YOU'D LIKE TO ADD?

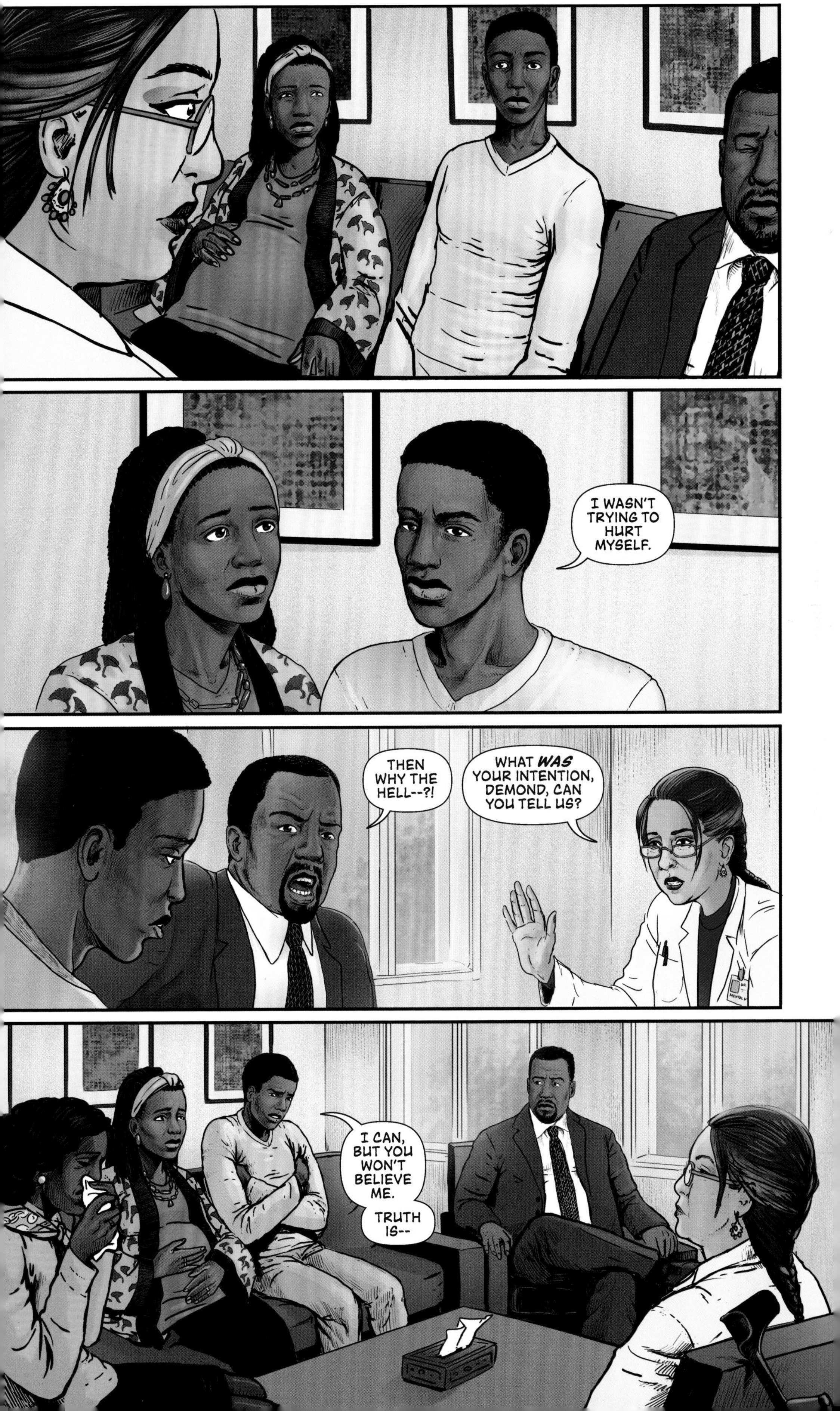
I WASN'T TRYING TO HURT MYSELF.
THEN WHY THE HELL--?!
WHAT *WAS* YOUR INTENTION, DEMOND, CAN YOU TELL US?
I CAN, BUT YOU WON'T BELIEVE ME.
TRUTH IS--

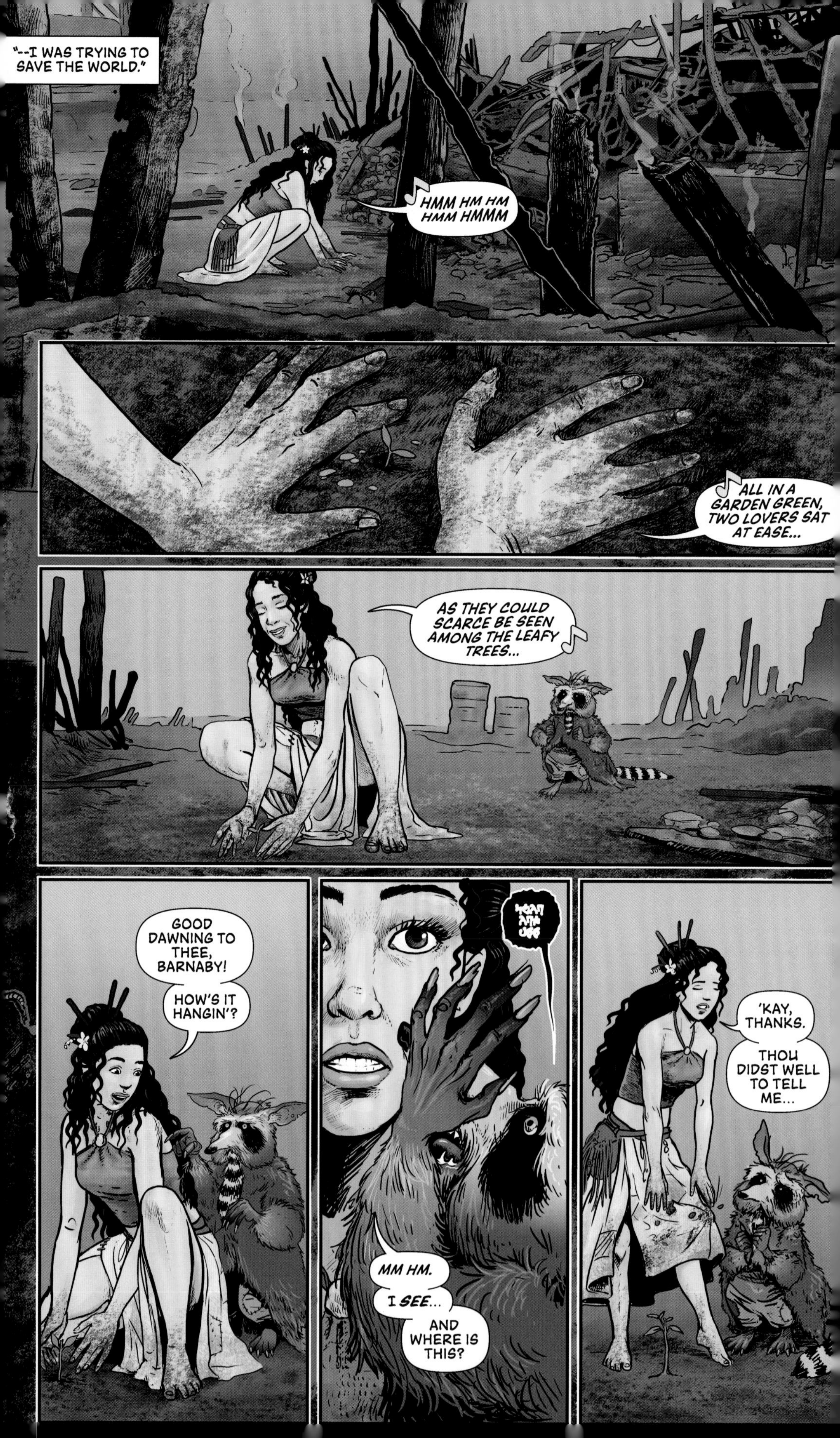
"--I WAS TRYING TO SAVE THE WORLD."
HMM HM HM HMM HMMM
ALL IN A GARDEN GREEN, TWO LOVERS SAT AT EASE...
AS THEY COULD SCARCE BE SEEN AMONG THE LEAFY TREES...
GOOD DAWNING TO THEE, BARNABY!
HOW'S IT HANGIN'?
MM HM.
I SEE...
AND WHERE IS THIS?
'KAY, THANKS.
THOU DIDST WELL TO TELL ME...

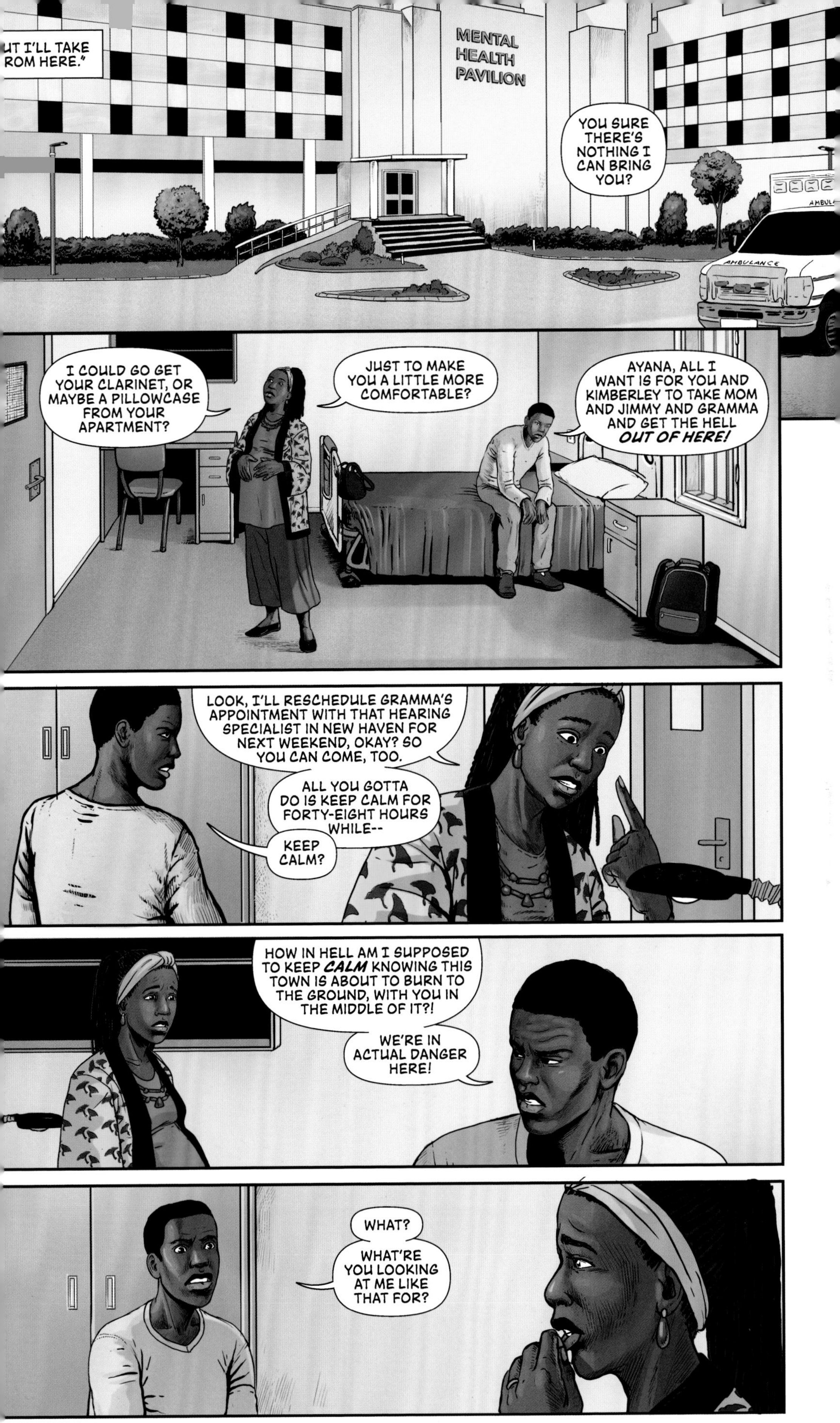
UT I'LL TAKE
ROM HERE."
MENTAL HEALTH PAVILION
YOU SURE THERE'S NOTHING I CAN BRING YOU?
AMBULANCE
I COULD GO GET YOUR CLARINET, OR MAYBE A PILLOWCASE FROM YOUR APARTMENT?
JUST TO MAKE YOU A LITTLE MORE COMFORTABLE?
AYANA, ALL I WANT IS FOR YOU AND KIMBERLEY TO TAKE MOM AND JIMMY AND GRAMMA AND GET THE HELL *OUT OF HERE!*
LOOK, I'LL RESCHEDULE GRAMMA'S APPOINTMENT WITH THAT HEARING SPECIALIST IN NEW HAVEN FOR NEXT WEEKEND, OKAY? SO YOU CAN COME, TOO.
ALL YOU GOTTA DO IS KEEP CALM FOR FORTY-EIGHT HOURS WHILE--
KEEP CALM?
HOW IN HELL AM I SUPPOSED TO KEEP *CALM* KNOWING THIS TOWN IS ABOUT TO BURN TO THE GROUND, WITH YOU IN THE MIDDLE OF IT?!
WE'RE IN ACTUAL DANGER HERE!
WHAT?
WHAT'RE YOU LOOKING AT ME LIKE THAT FOR?

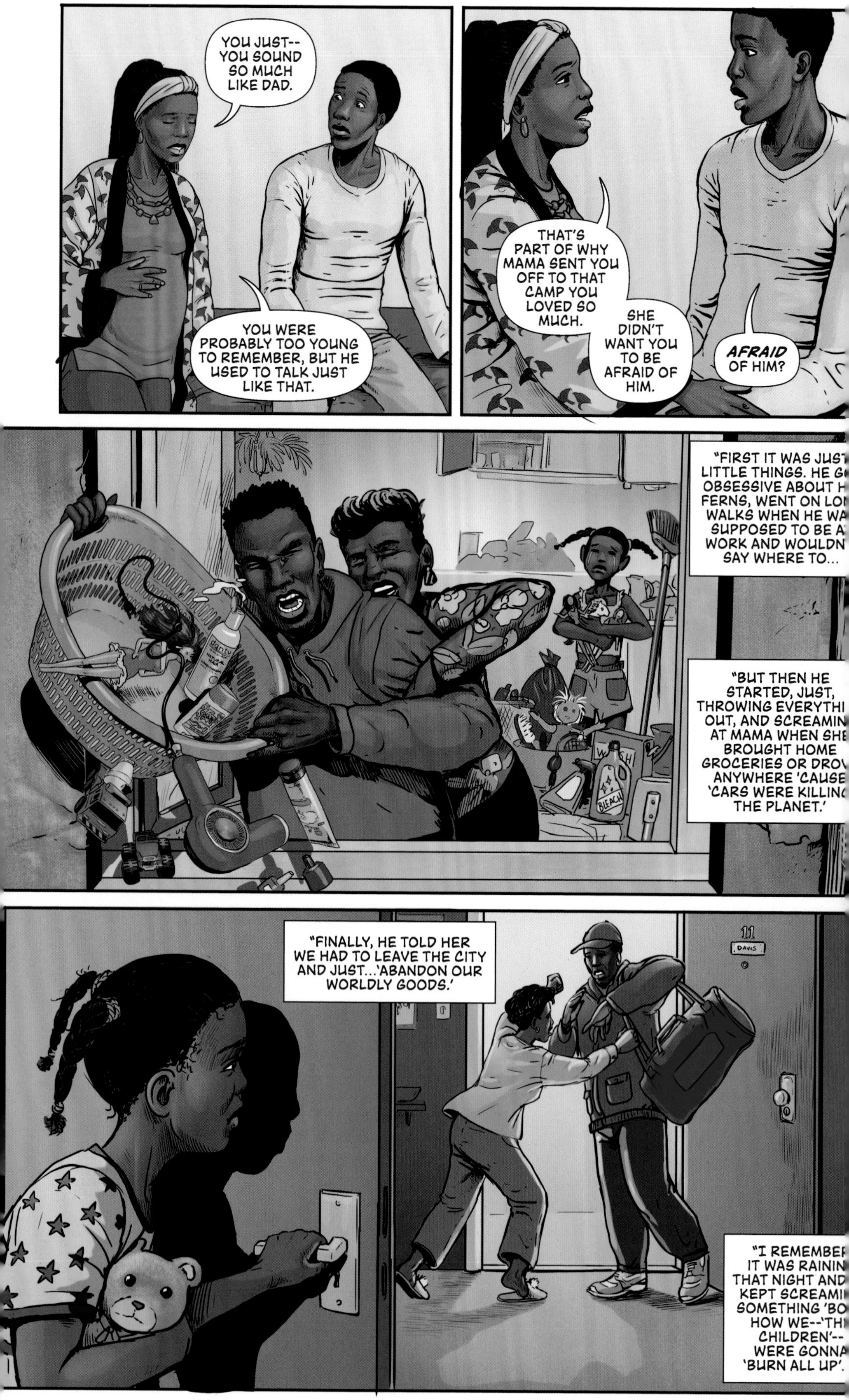
YOU JUST-- YOU SOUND SO MUCH LIKE DAD.
YOU WERE PROBABLY TOO YOUNG TO REMEMBER, BUT HE USED TO TALK JUST LIKE THAT.
THAT'S PART OF WHY MAMA SENT YOU OFF TO THAT CAMP YOU LOVED SO MUCH.
SHE DIDN'T WANT YOU TO BE AFRAID OF HIM.
AFRAID OF HIM?
"FIRST IT WAS JUS LITTLE THINGS. HE G OBSESSIVE ABOUT H FERNS, WENT ON LO WALKS WHEN HE WA SUPPOSED TO BE A WORK AND WOULDN SAY WHERE TO...
"BUT THEN HE STARTED, JUST, THROWING EVERYTHI OUT, AND SCREAMIN AT MAMA WHEN SHE BROUGHT HOME GROCERIES OR DRO ANYWHERE 'CAUSE 'CARS WERE KILLIN THE PLANET.'
"FINALLY, HE TOLD HER WE HAD TO LEAVE THE CITY AND JUST...'ABANDON OUR WORLDLY GOODS.'
11
DAVIS
"I REMEMBE IT WAS RAININ THAT NIGHT AND KEPT SCREAMI SOMETHING 'BO HOW WE--'TH CHILDREN'-- WERE GONNA 'BURN ALL UP'.

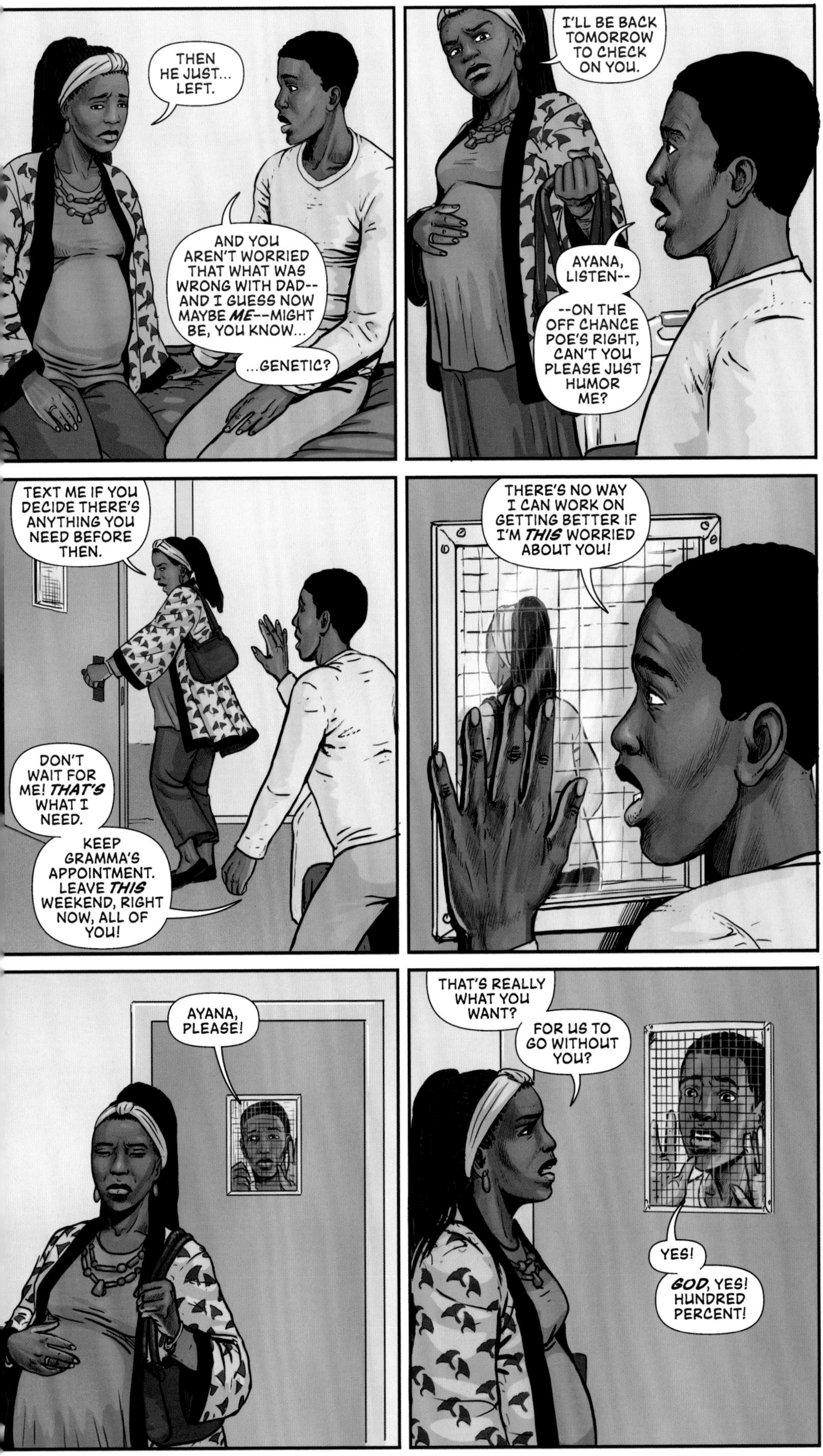
THEN HE JUST... LEFT.
AND YOU AREN'T WORRIED THAT WHAT WAS WRONG WITH DAD--AND I GUESS NOW MAYBE *ME*--MIGHT BE, YOU KNOW...
...GENETIC?
I'LL BE BACK TOMORROW TO CHECK ON YOU.
AYANA, LISTEN--
--ON THE OFF CHANCE POE'S RIGHT, CAN'T YOU PLEASE JUST HUMOR ME?
TEXT ME IF YOU DECIDE THERE'S ANYTHING YOU NEED BEFORE THEN.
DON'T WAIT FOR ME! *THAT'S* WHAT I NEED.
KEEP GRAMMA'S APPOINTMENT. LEAVE *THIS* WEEKEND, RIGHT NOW, ALL OF YOU!
THERE'S NO WAY I CAN WORK ON GETTING BETTER IF I'M *THIS* WORRIED ABOUT YOU!
AYANA, PLEASE!
THAT'S REALLY WHAT YOU WANT?
FOR US TO GO WITHOUT YOU?
YES!
GOD, YES! HUNDRED PERCENT!

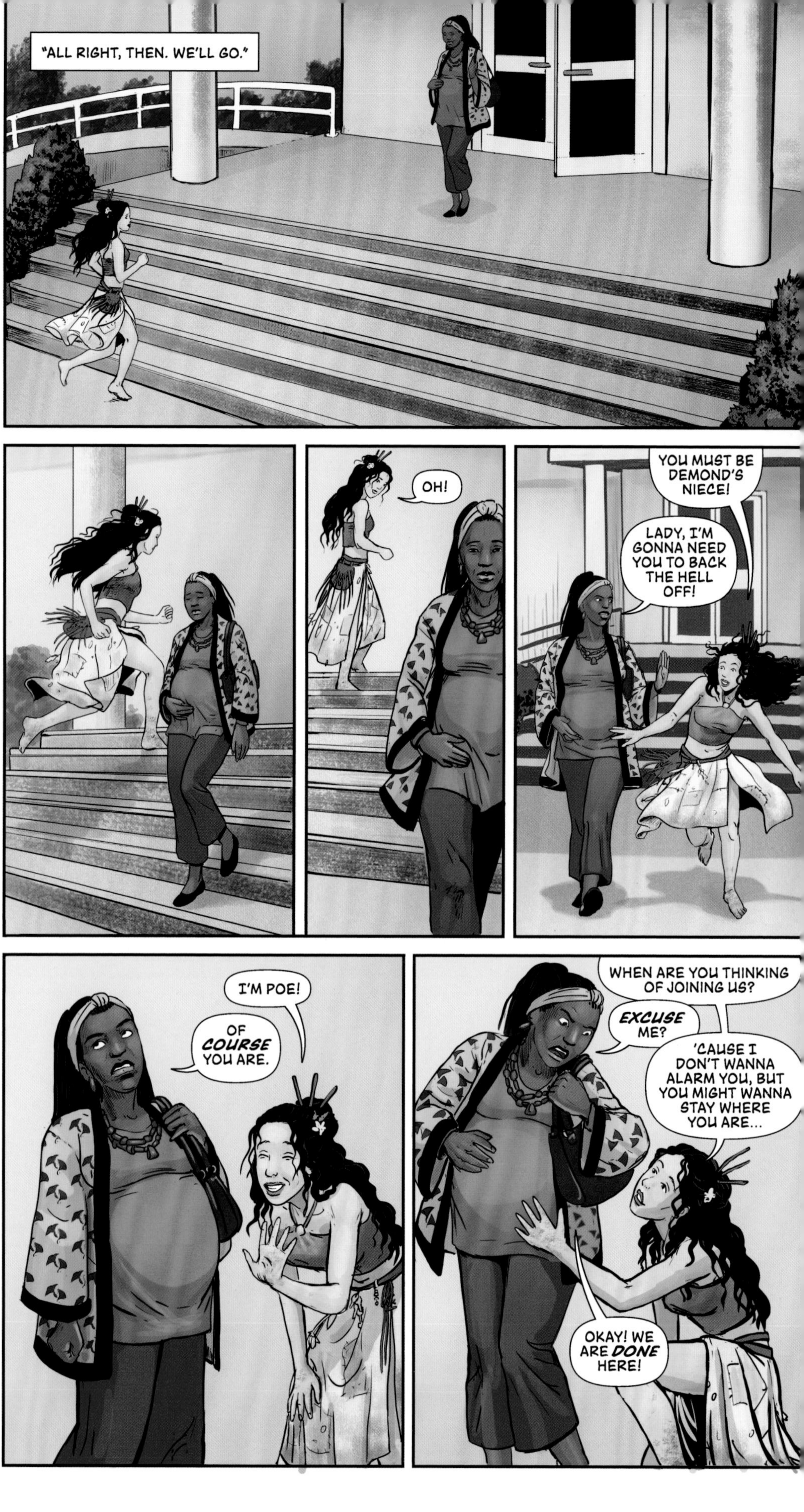
"ALL RIGHT, THEN. WE'LL GO."
OH!
YOU MUST BE DEMOND'S NIECE!
LADY, I'M GONNA NEED YOU TO BACK THE HELL OFF!
I'M POE!
OF *COURSE* YOU ARE.
WHEN ARE YOU THINKING OF JOINING US?
EXCUSE ME?
'CAUSE I DON'T WANNA ALARM YOU, BUT YOU MIGHT WANNA STAY WHERE YOU ARE...
OKAY! WE ARE *DONE* HERE!

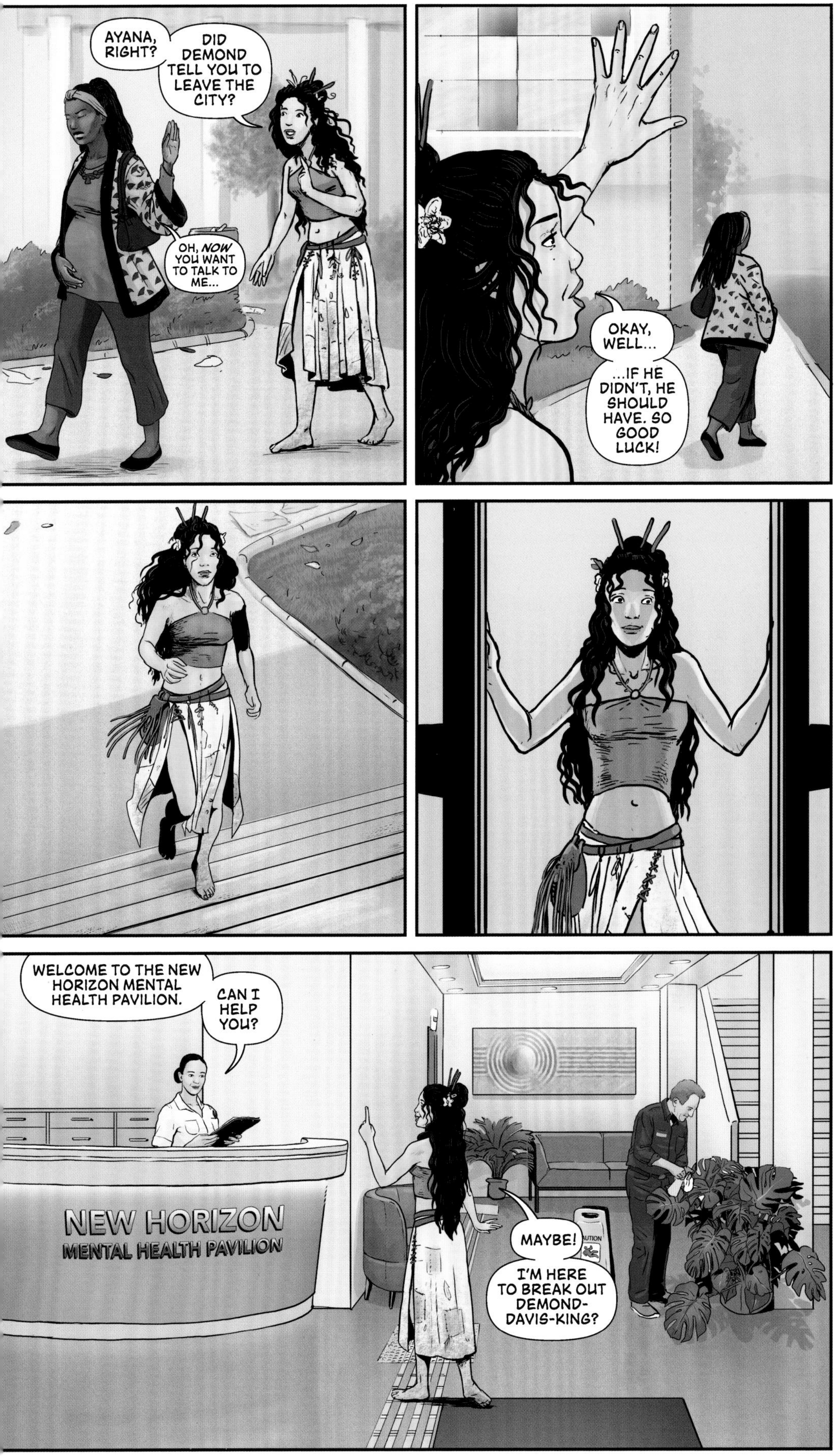
AYANA, RIGHT?
DID DEMOND TELL YOU TO LEAVE THE CITY?
OH, NOW YOU WANT TO TALK TO ME...
OKAY, WELL...
...IF HE DIDN'T, HE SHOULD HAVE. SO GOOD LUCK!
WELCOME TO THE NEW HORIZON MENTAL HEALTH PAVILION.
CAN I HELP YOU?
NEW HORIZON
MENTAL HEALTH PAVILION
MAYBE!
I'M HERE TO BREAK OUT DEMOND-DAVIS-KING?

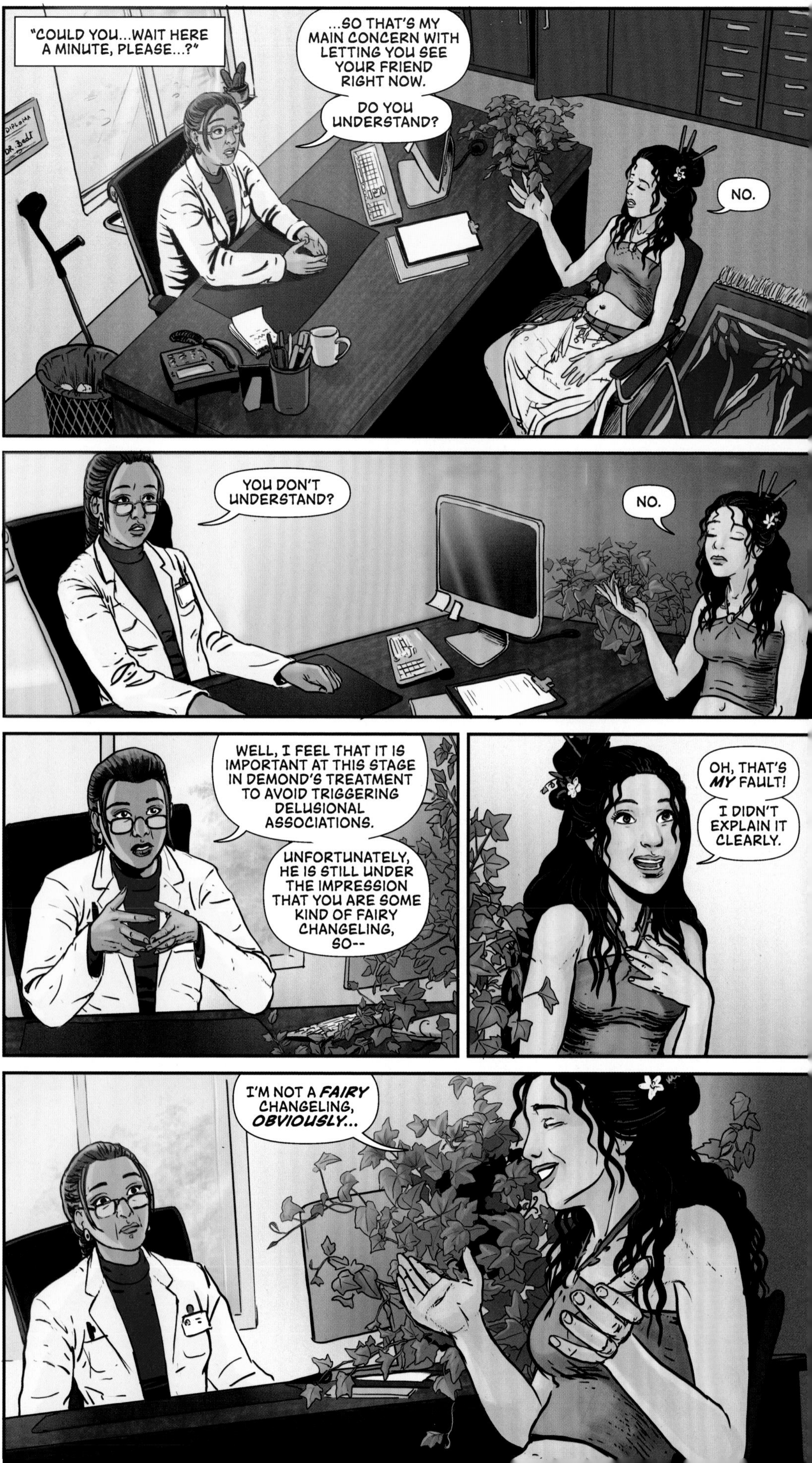
"COULD YOU...WAIT HERE A MINUTE, PLEASE...?"
...SO THAT'S MY MAIN CONCERN WITH LETTING YOU SEE YOUR FRIEND RIGHT NOW.
DO YOU UNDERSTAND?
NO.
YOU DON'T UNDERSTAND?
NO.
WELL, I FEEL THAT IT IS IMPORTANT AT THIS STAGE IN DEMOND'S TREATMENT TO AVOID TRIGGERING DELUSIONAL ASSOCIATIONS.
UNFORTUNATELY, HE IS STILL UNDER THE IMPRESSION THAT YOU ARE SOME KIND OF FAIRY CHANGELING, SO--
OH, THAT'S *MY* FAULT!
I DIDN'T EXPLAIN IT CLEARLY.
I'M NOT A *FAIRY* CHANGELING, *OBVIOUSLY*...

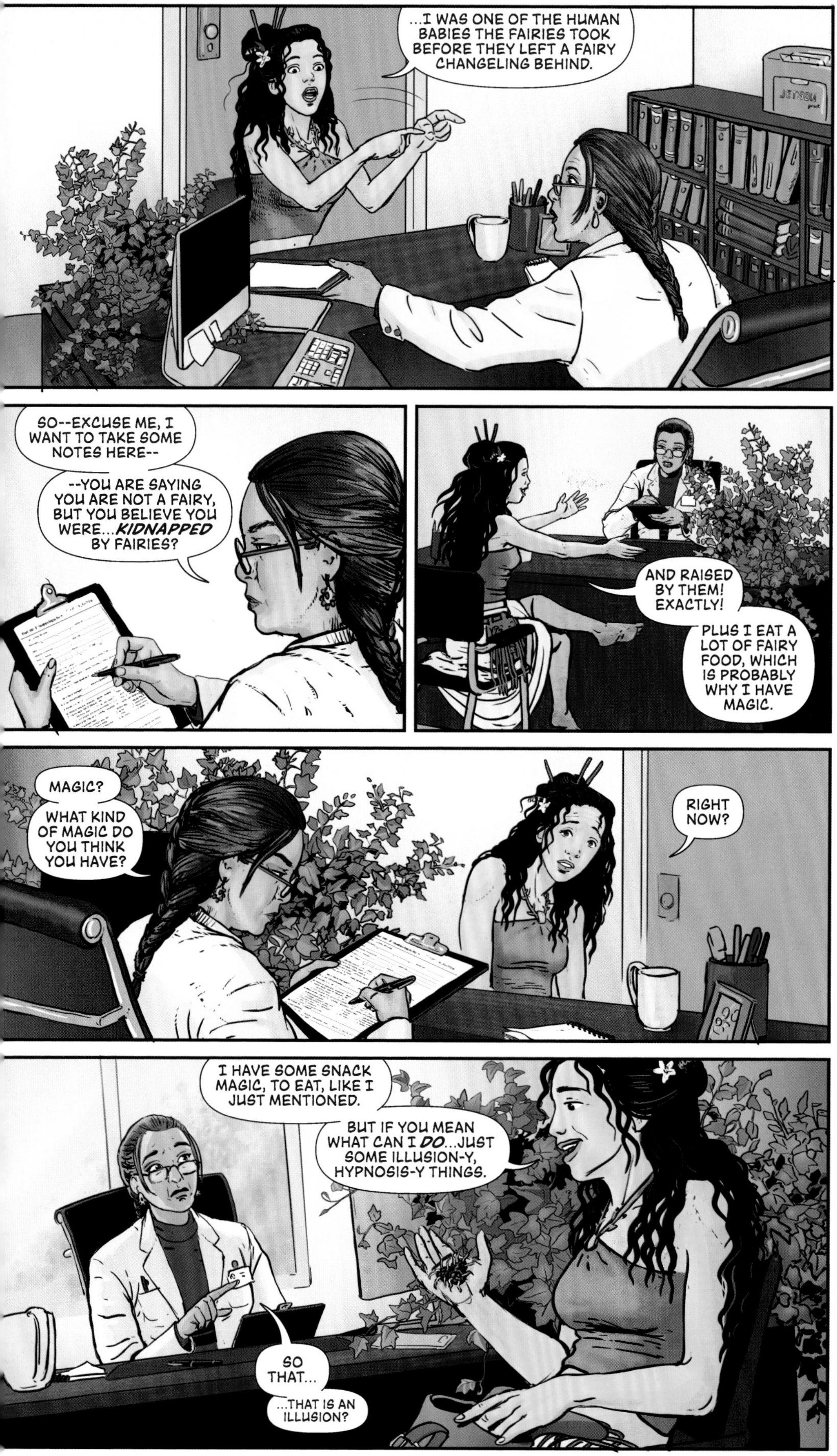

...I WAS ONE OF THE HUMAN BABIES THE FAIRIES TOOK BEFORE THEY LEFT A FAIRY CHANGELING BEHIND.
SO--EXCUSE ME, I WANT TO TAKE SOME NOTES HERE--
--YOU ARE SAYING YOU ARE NOT A FAIRY, BUT YOU BELIEVE YOU WERE...KIDNAPPED BY FAIRIES?
AND RAISED BY THEM! EXACTLY!
PLUS I EAT A LOT OF FAIRY FOOD, WHICH IS PROBABLY WHY I HAVE MAGIC.
MAGIC?
WHAT KIND OF MAGIC DO YOU THINK YOU HAVE?
RIGHT NOW?
I HAVE SOME SNACK MAGIC, TO EAT, LIKE I JUST MENTIONED.
BUT IF YOU MEAN WHAT CAN I DO...JUST SOME ILLUSION-Y, HYPNOSIS-Y THINGS.
SO THAT...
...THAT IS AN ILLUSION?

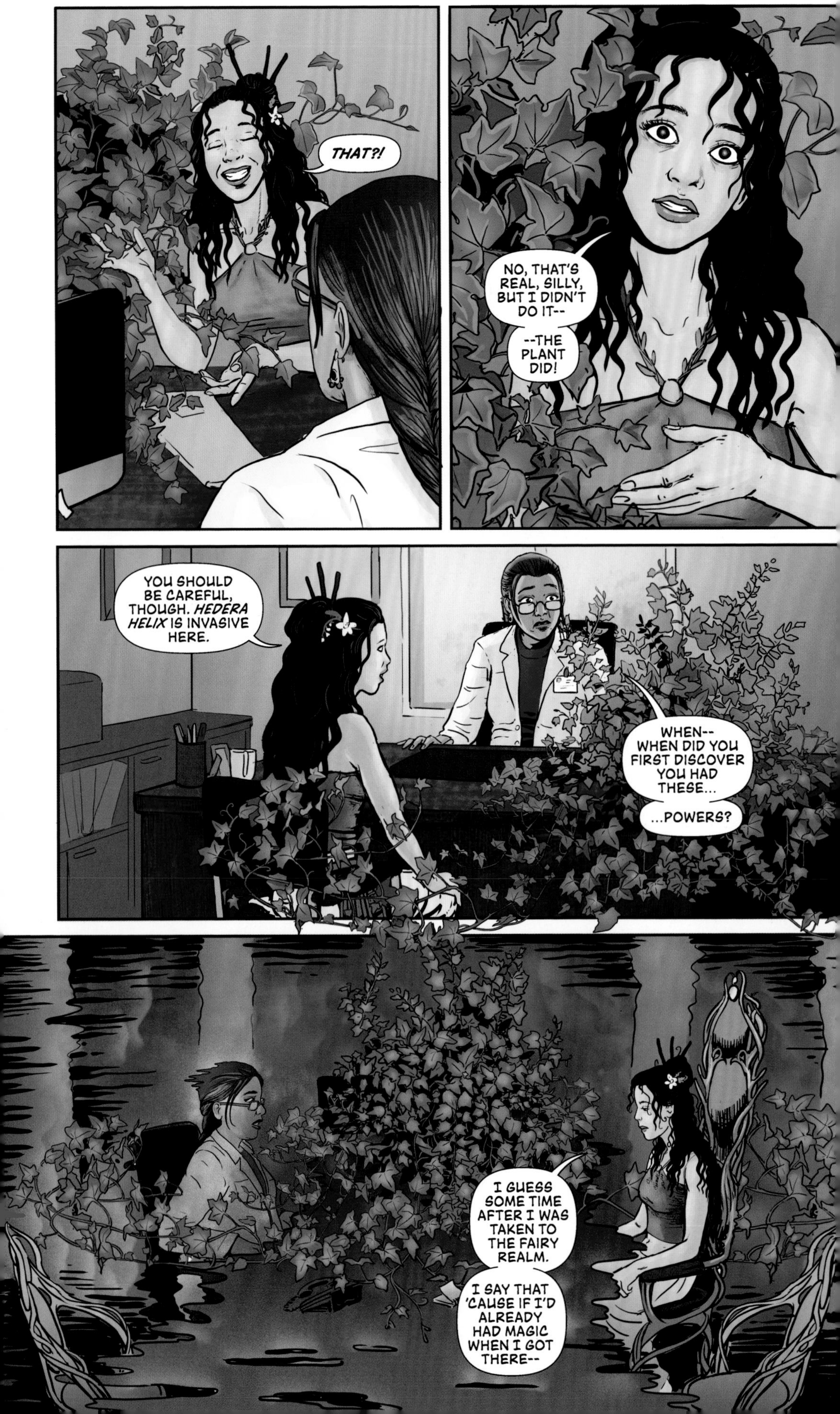
THAT?!
NO, THAT'S REAL, SILLY, BUT I DIDN'T DO IT--
--THE PLANT DID!
YOU SHOULD BE CAREFUL, THOUGH. HEDERA HELIX IS INVASIVE HERE.
WHEN-- WHEN DID YOU FIRST DISCOVER YOU HAD THESE...
...POWERS?
I GUESS SOME TIME AFTER I WAS TAKEN TO THE FAIRY REALM.
I SAY THAT 'CAUSE IF I'D ALREADY HAD MAGIC WHEN I GOT THERE--

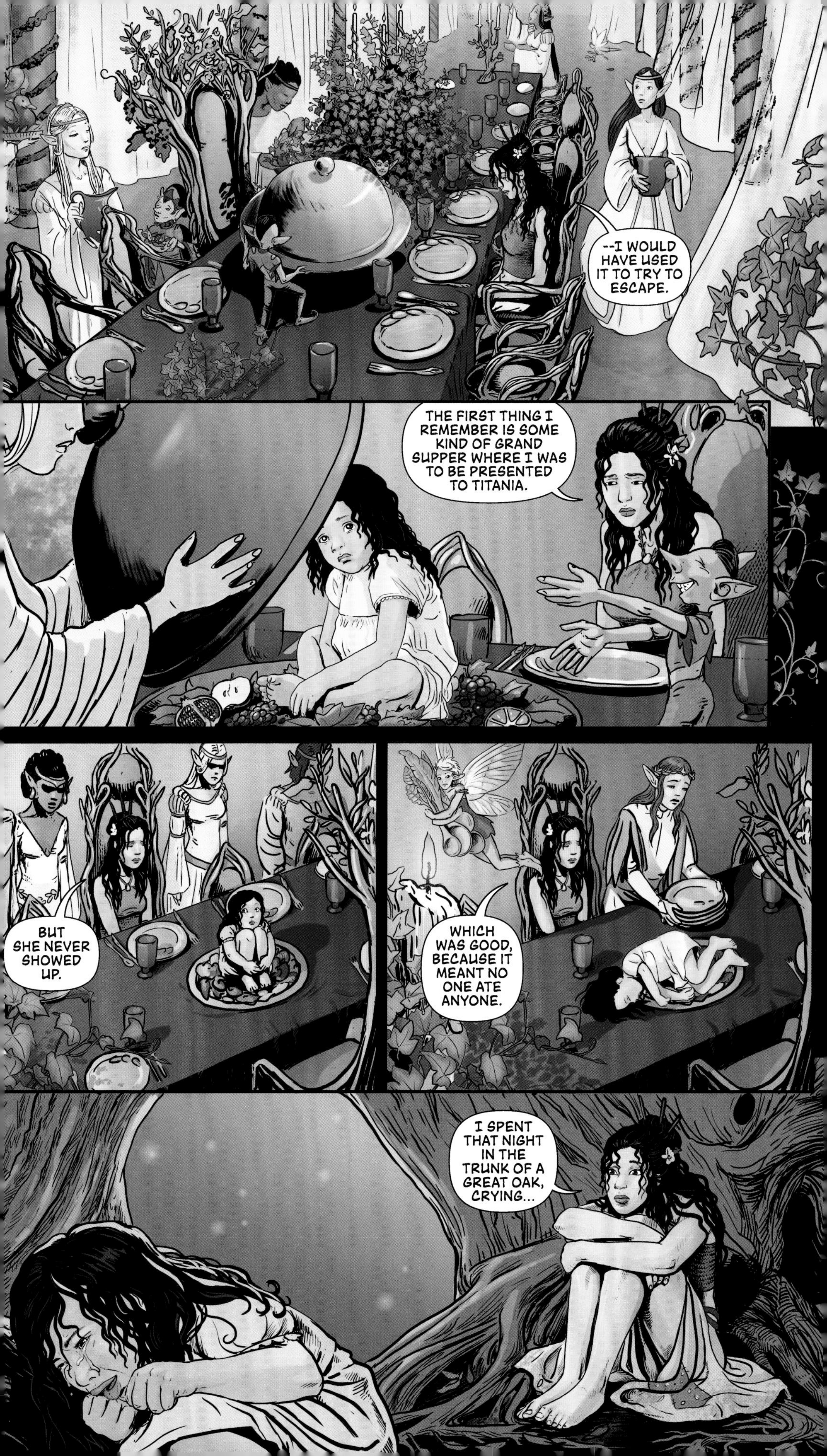
--I WOULD HAVE USED IT TO TRY TO ESCAPE.
THE FIRST THING I REMEMBER IS SOME KIND OF GRAND SUPPER WHERE I WAS TO BE PRESENTED TO TITANIA.
BUT SHE NEVER SHOWED UP.
WHICH WAS GOOD, BECAUSE IT MEANT NO ONE ATE ANYONE.
I SPENT THAT NIGHT IN THE TRUNK OF A GREAT OAK, CRYING...

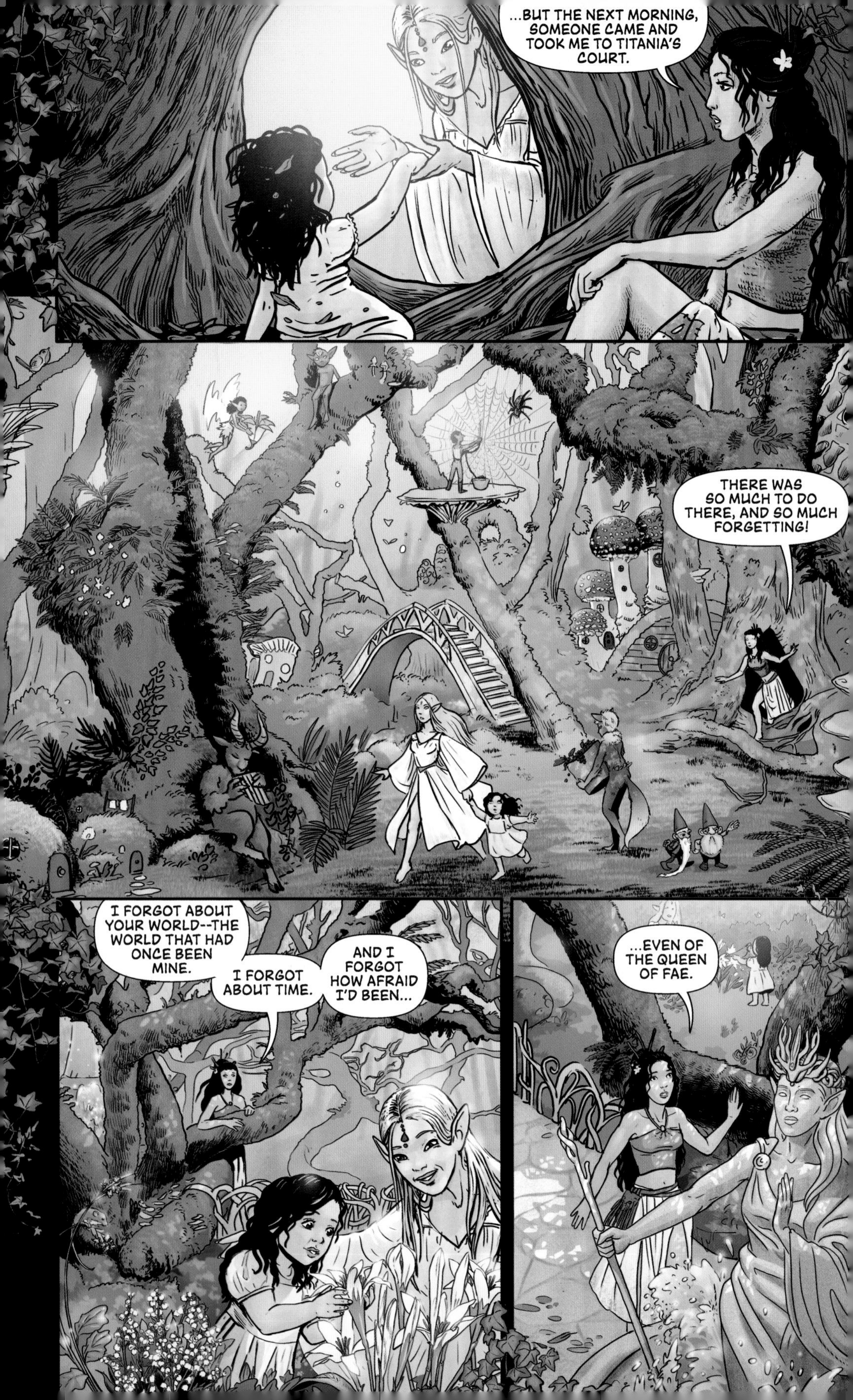
...BUT THE NEXT MORNING, SOMEONE CAME AND TOOK ME TO TITANIA'S COURT.
THERE WAS SO MUCH TO DO THERE, AND SO MUCH FORGETTING!
I FORGOT ABOUT YOUR WORLD--THE WORLD THAT HAD ONCE BEEN MINE.
I FORGOT ABOUT TIME.
AND I FORGOT HOW AFRAID I'D BEEN...
...EVEN OF THE QUEEN OF FAE.

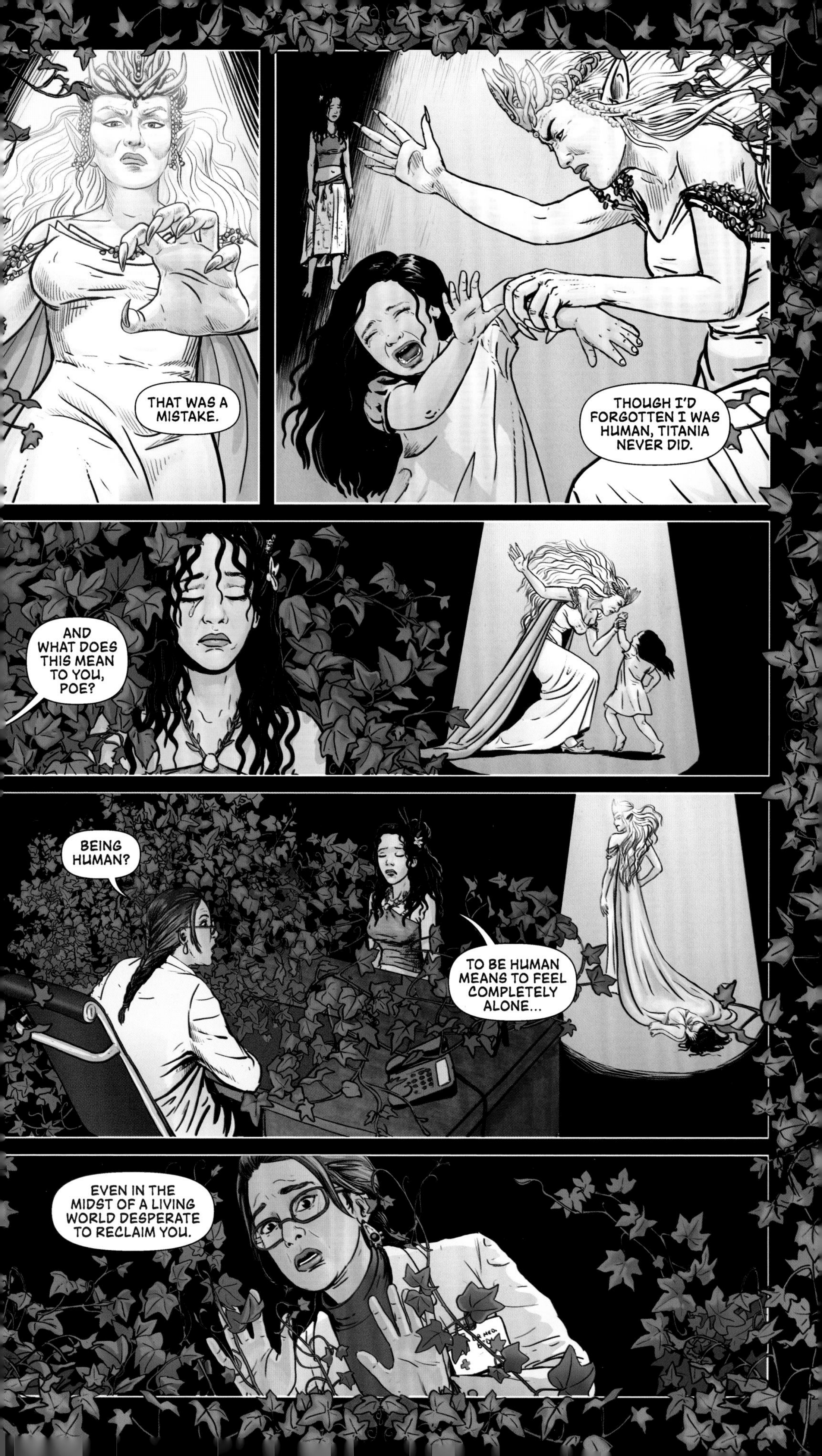
THAT WAS A MISTAKE.
THOUGH I'D FORGOTTEN I WAS HUMAN, TITANIA NEVER DID.
AND WHAT DOES THIS MEAN TO YOU, POE?
BEING HUMAN?
TO BE HUMAN MEANS TO FEEL COMPLETELY ALONE...
EVEN IN THE MIDST OF A LIVING WORLD DESPERATE TO RECLAIM YOU.

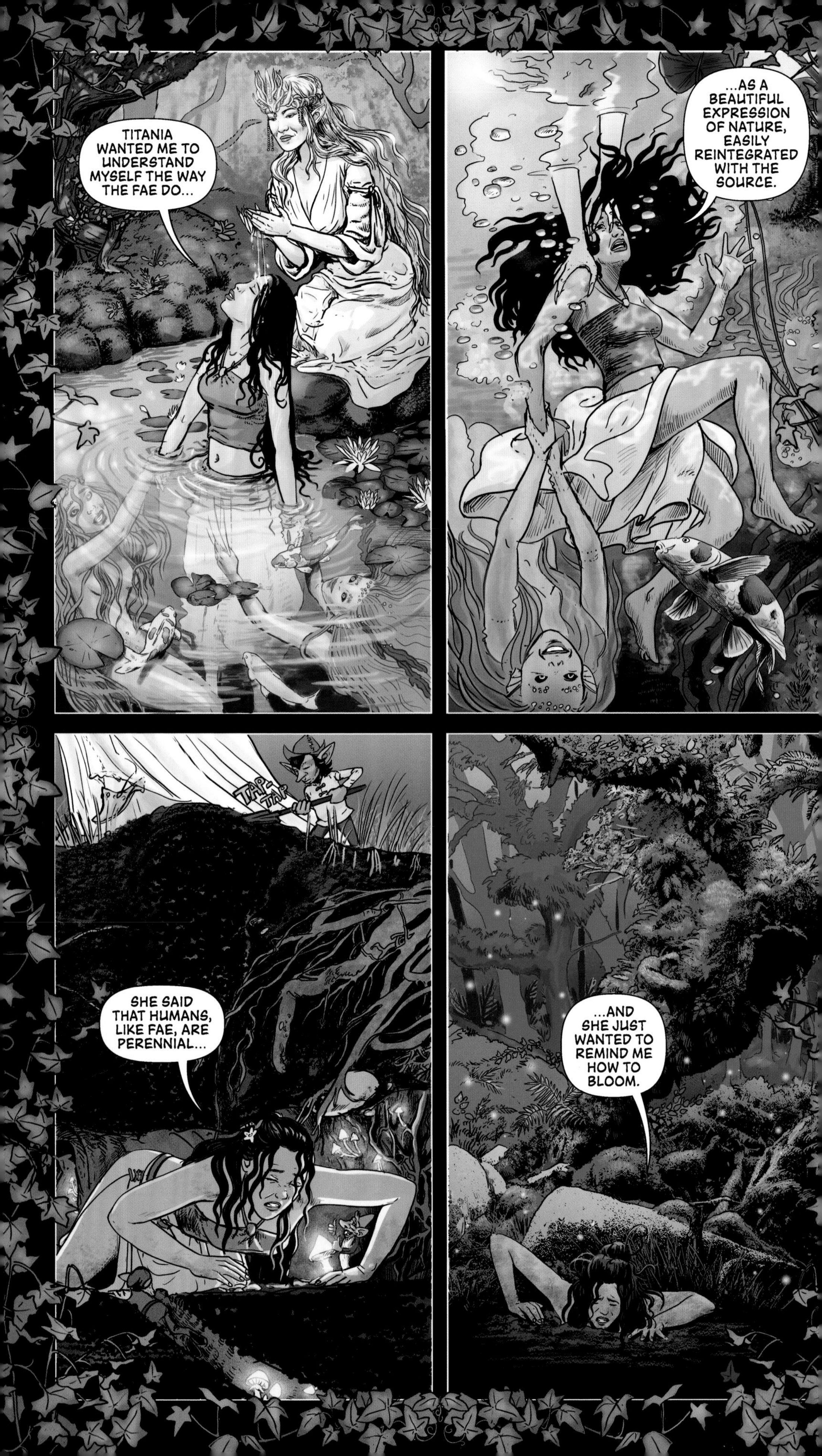
TITANIA WANTED ME TO UNDERSTAND MYSELF THE WAY THE FAE DO...
...AS A BEAUTIFUL EXPRESSION OF NATURE, EASILY REINTEGRATED WITH THE SOURCE.
TAP TAP
SHE SAID THAT HUMANS, LIKE FAE, ARE PERENNIAL...
...AND SHE JUST WANTED TO REMIND ME HOW TO BLOOM.

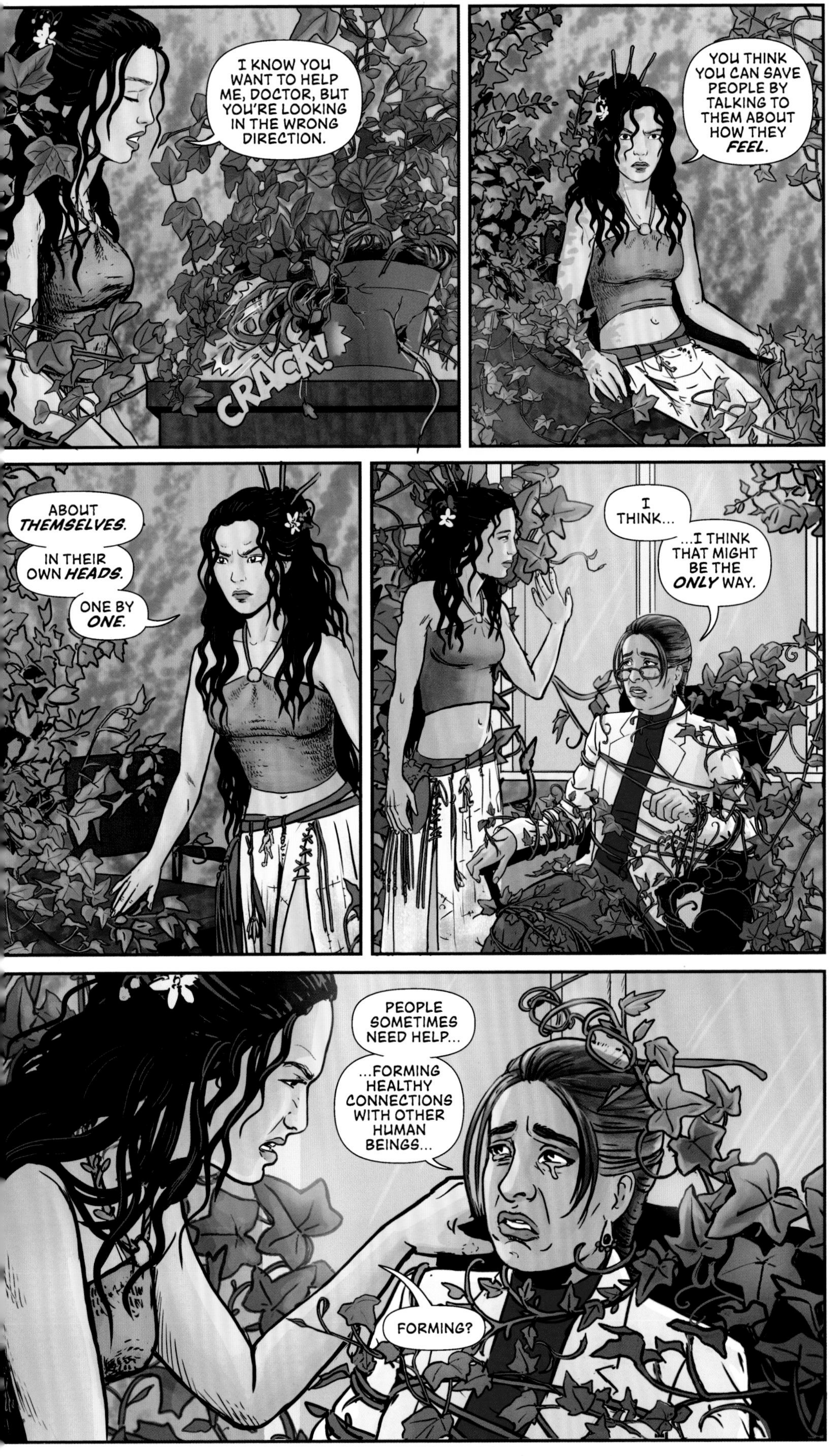
I KNOW YOU WANT TO HELP ME, DOCTOR, BUT YOU'RE LOOKING IN THE WRONG DIRECTION.
CRACK!
YOU THINK YOU CAN SAVE PEOPLE BY TALKING TO THEM ABOUT HOW THEY *FEEL*.
ABOUT *THEMSELVES*.
IN THEIR OWN *HEADS*.
ONE BY *ONE*.
I THINK...
...I THINK THAT MIGHT BE THE *ONLY* WAY.
PEOPLE SOMETIMES NEED HELP...
...FORMING HEALTHY CONNECTIONS WITH OTHER HUMAN BEINGS...
FORMING?

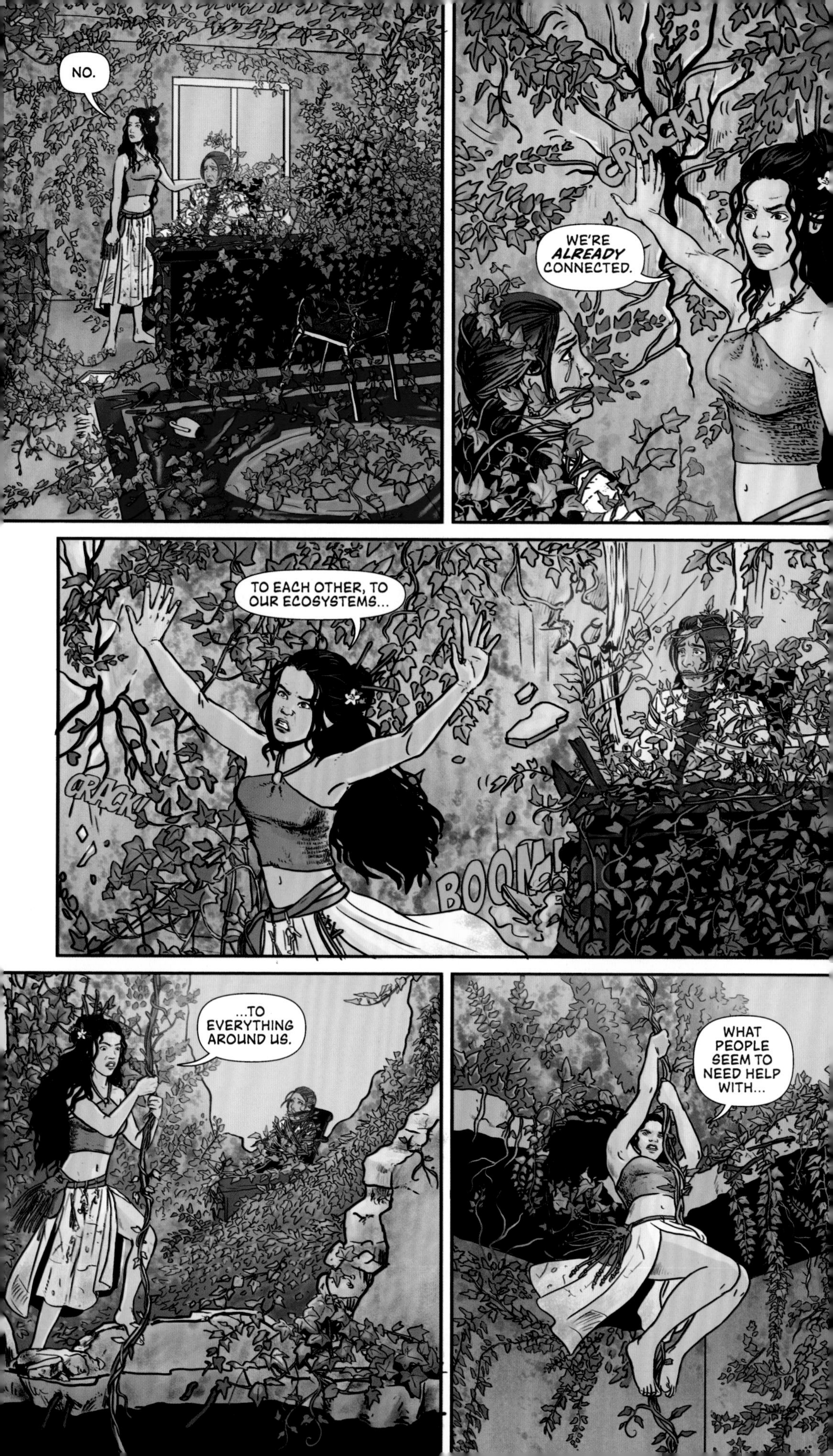
NO.
CRACK!
WE'RE *ALREADY* CONNECTED.
TO EACH OTHER, TO OUR ECOSYSTEMS...
CRACK!
BOOM!
...TO EVERYTHING AROUND US.
WHAT PEOPLE SEEM TO NEED HELP WITH...

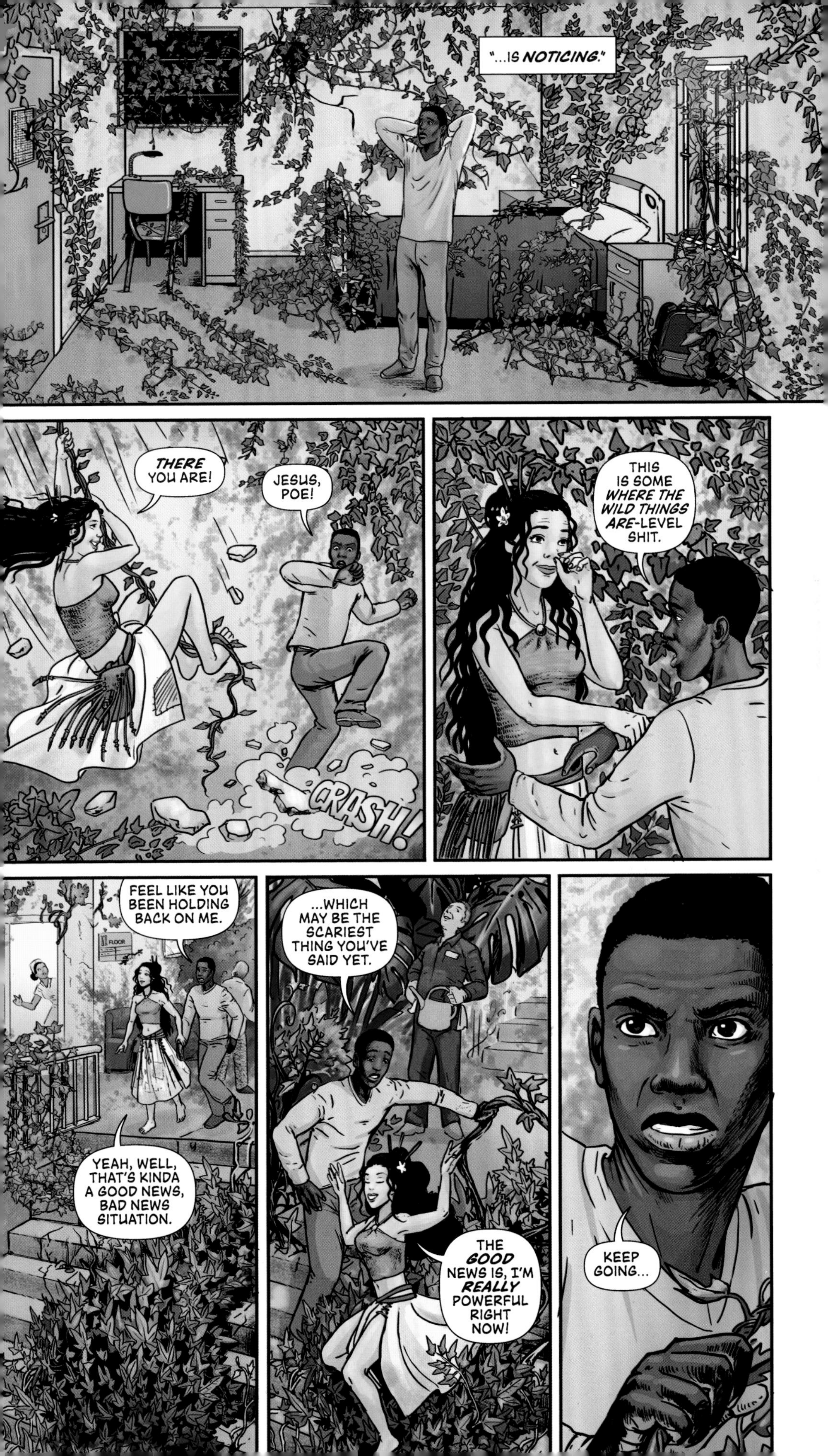
"...IS NOTICING."
THERE YOU ARE!
JESUS, POE!
CRASH!
THIS IS SOME WHERE THE WILD THINGS ARE-LEVEL SHIT.
FEEL LIKE YOU BEEN HOLDING BACK ON ME.
YEAH, WELL, THAT'S KINDA A GOOD NEWS, BAD NEWS SITUATION.
...WHICH MAY BE THE SCARIEST THING YOU'VE SAID YET.
THE GOOD NEWS IS, I'M REALLY POWERFUL RIGHT NOW!
KEEP GOING...

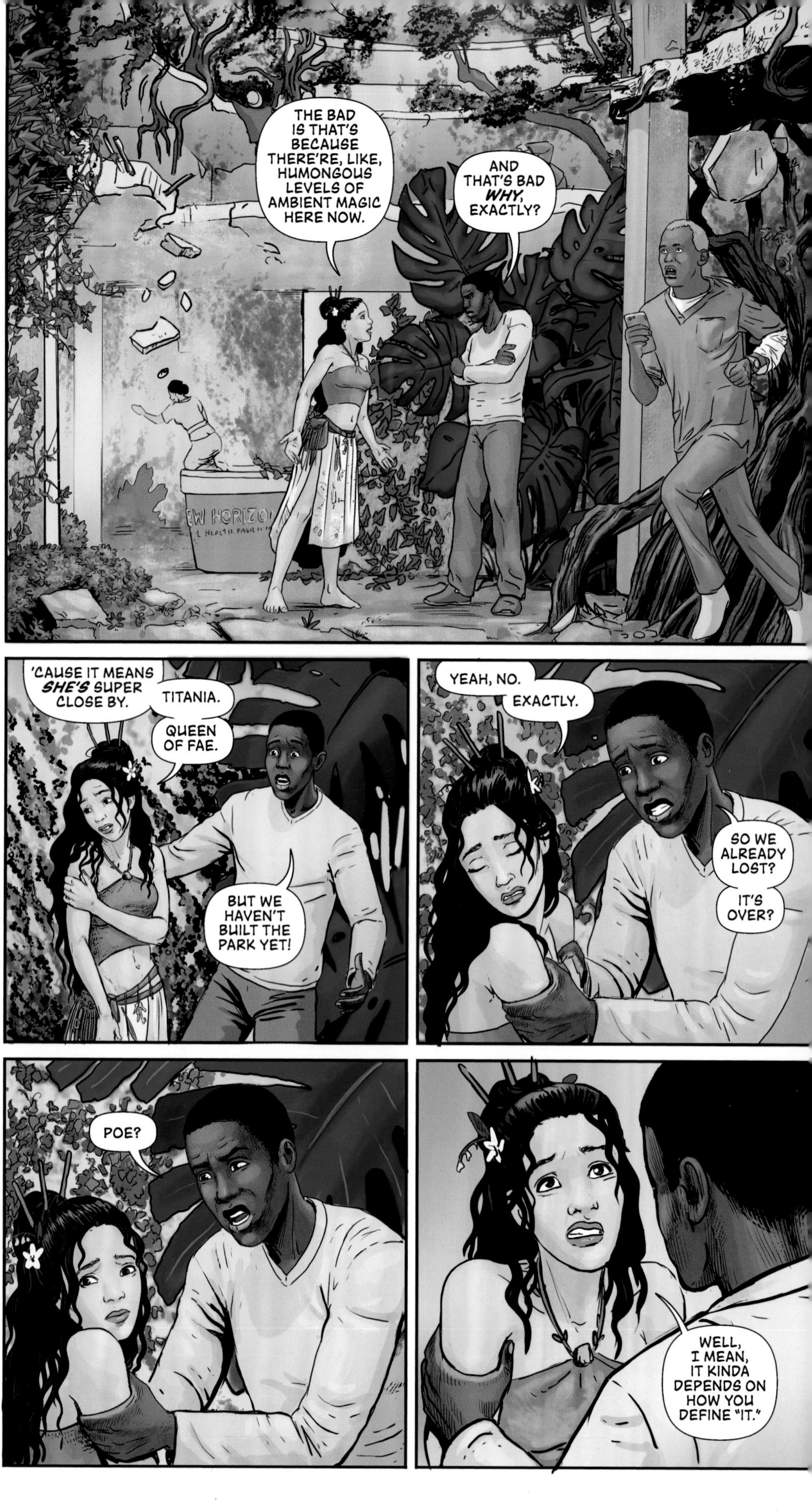
THE BAD IS THAT'S BECAUSE THERE'RE, LIKE, HUMONGOUS LEVELS OF AMBIENT MAGIC HERE NOW.
AND THAT'S BAD *WHY*, EXACTLY?
'CAUSE IT MEANS *SHE'S* SUPER CLOSE BY.
TITANIA.
QUEEN OF FAE.
BUT WE HAVEN'T BUILT THE PARK YET!
YEAH, NO.
EXACTLY.
SO WE ALREADY LOST?
IT'S OVER?
POE?
WELL, I MEAN, IT KINDA DEPENDS ON HOW YOU DEFINE "IT."

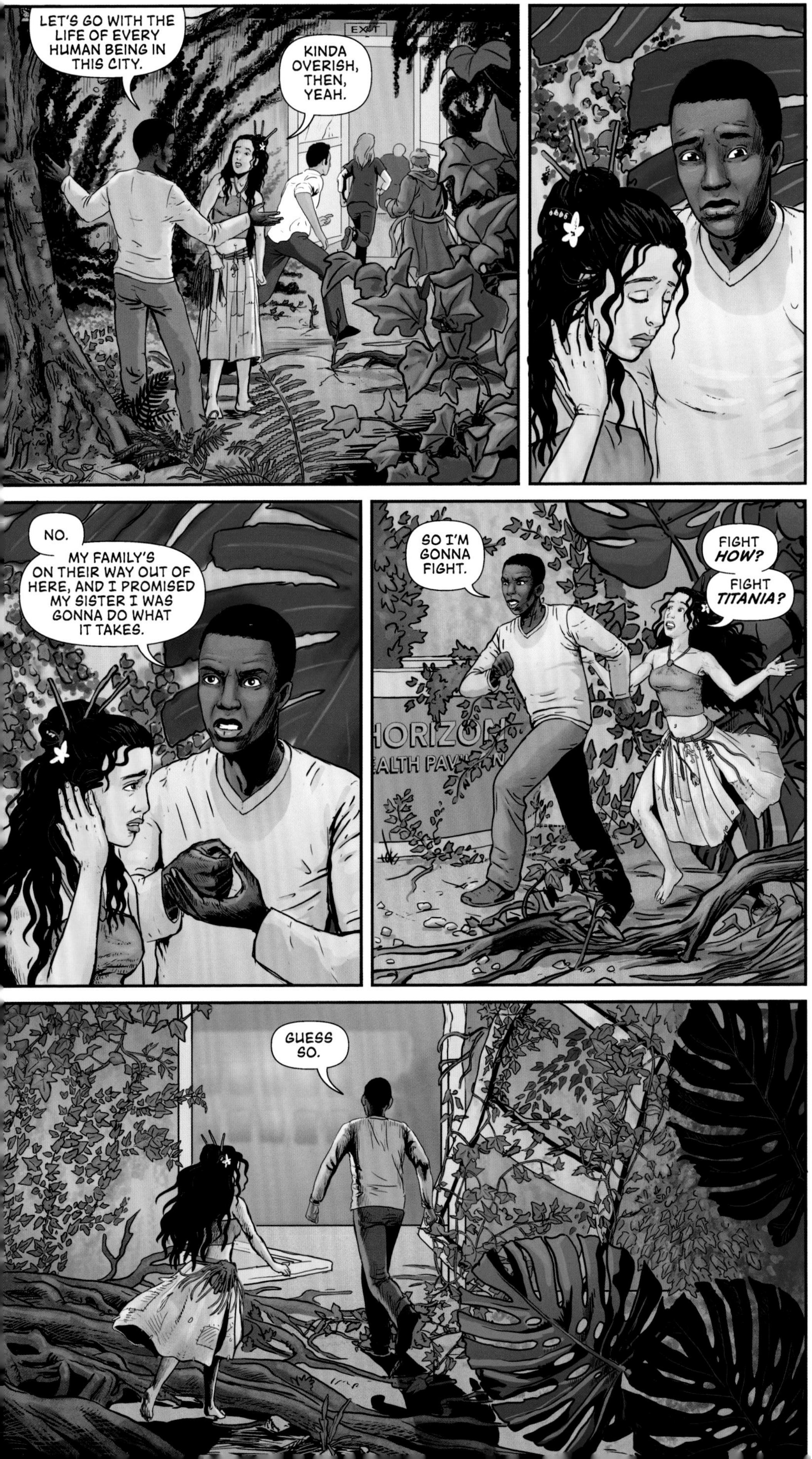
LET'S GO WITH THE LIFE OF EVERY HUMAN BEING IN THIS CITY.
KINDA OVERISH, THEN, YEAH.
NO.
MY FAMILY'S ON THEIR WAY OUT OF HERE, AND I PROMISED MY SISTER I WAS GONNA DO WHAT IT TAKES.
SO I'M GONNA FIGHT.
FIGHT *HOW?*
FIGHT *TITANIA?*
GUESS SO.

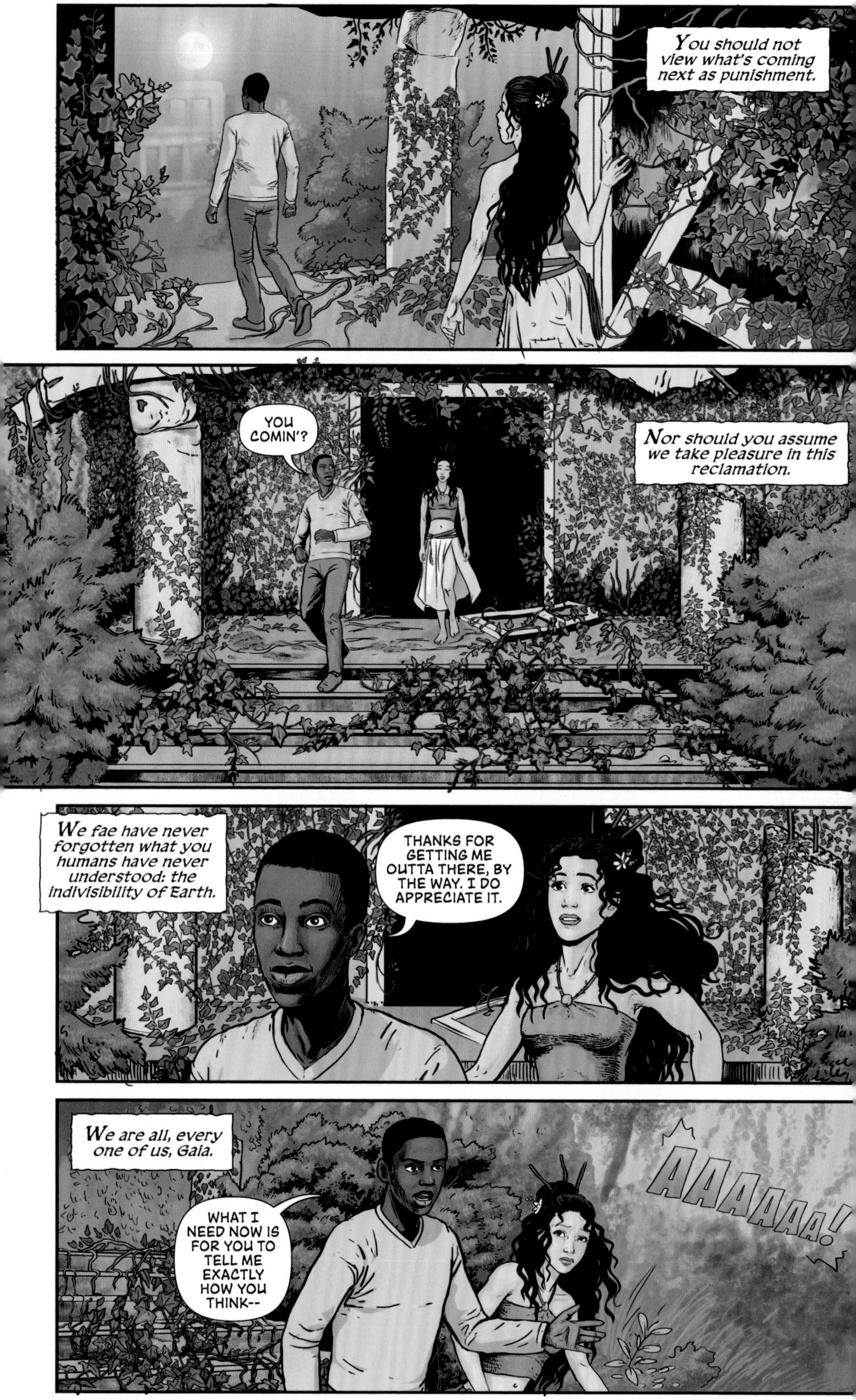
You should not view what's coming next as punishment.
YOU COMIN'?
Nor should you assume we take pleasure in this reclamation.
We fae have never forgotten what you humans have never understood: the indivisibility of Earth.
THANKS FOR GETTING ME OUTTA THERE, BY THE WAY. I DO APPRECIATE IT.
We are all, every one of us, Gaia.
WHAT I NEED NOW IS FOR YOU TO TELL ME EXACTLY HOW YOU THINK--
AAAAAA!

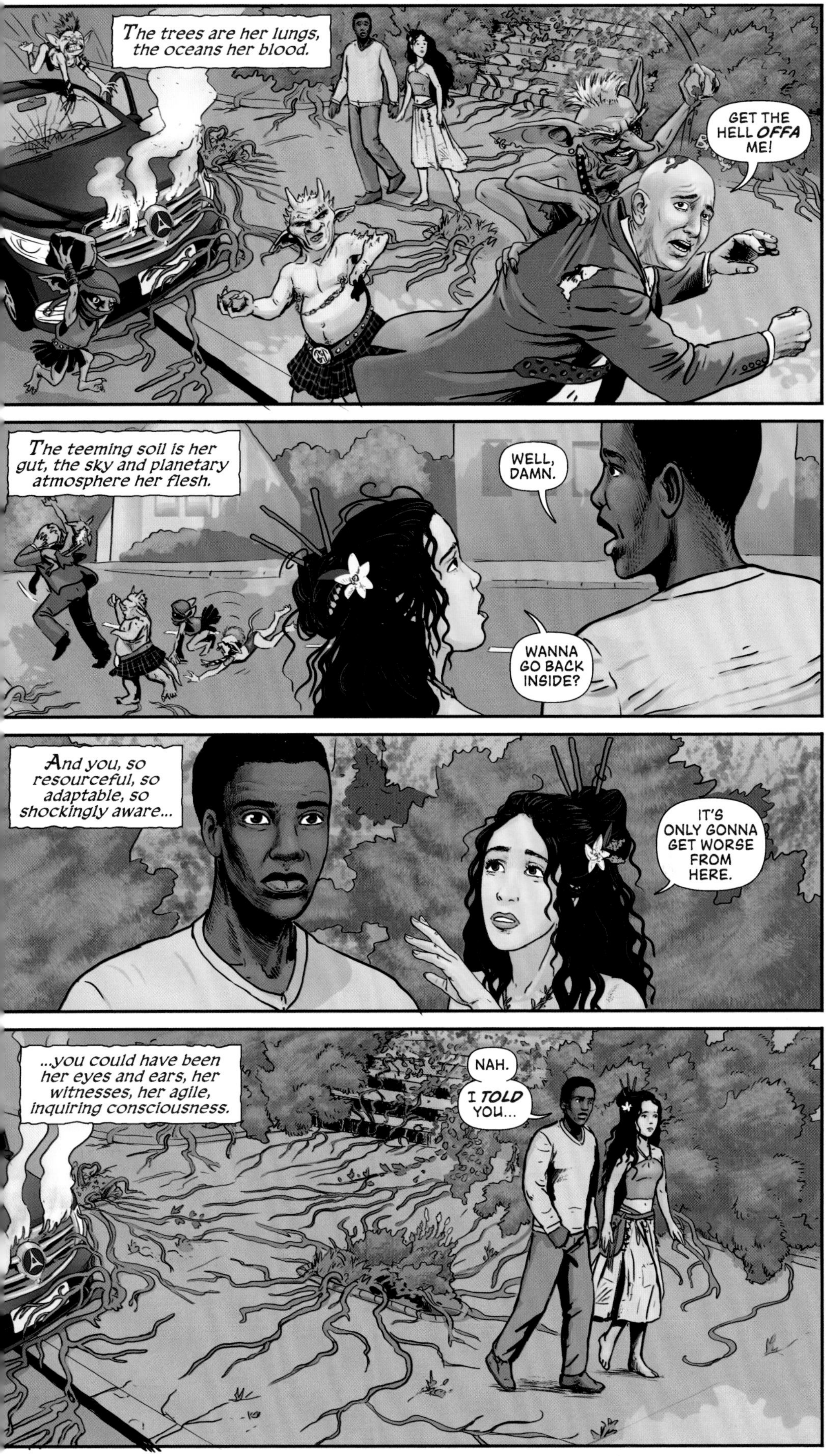

The trees are her lungs, the oceans her blood.
GET THE HELL OFFA ME!
The teeming soil is her gut, the sky and planetary atmosphere her flesh.
WELL, DAMN.
WANNA GO BACK INSIDE?
And you, so resourceful, so adaptable, so shockingly aware...
IT'S ONLY GONNA GET WORSE FROM HERE.
...you could have been her eyes and ears, her witnesses, her agile, inquiring consciousness.
NAH.
I TOLD YOU...

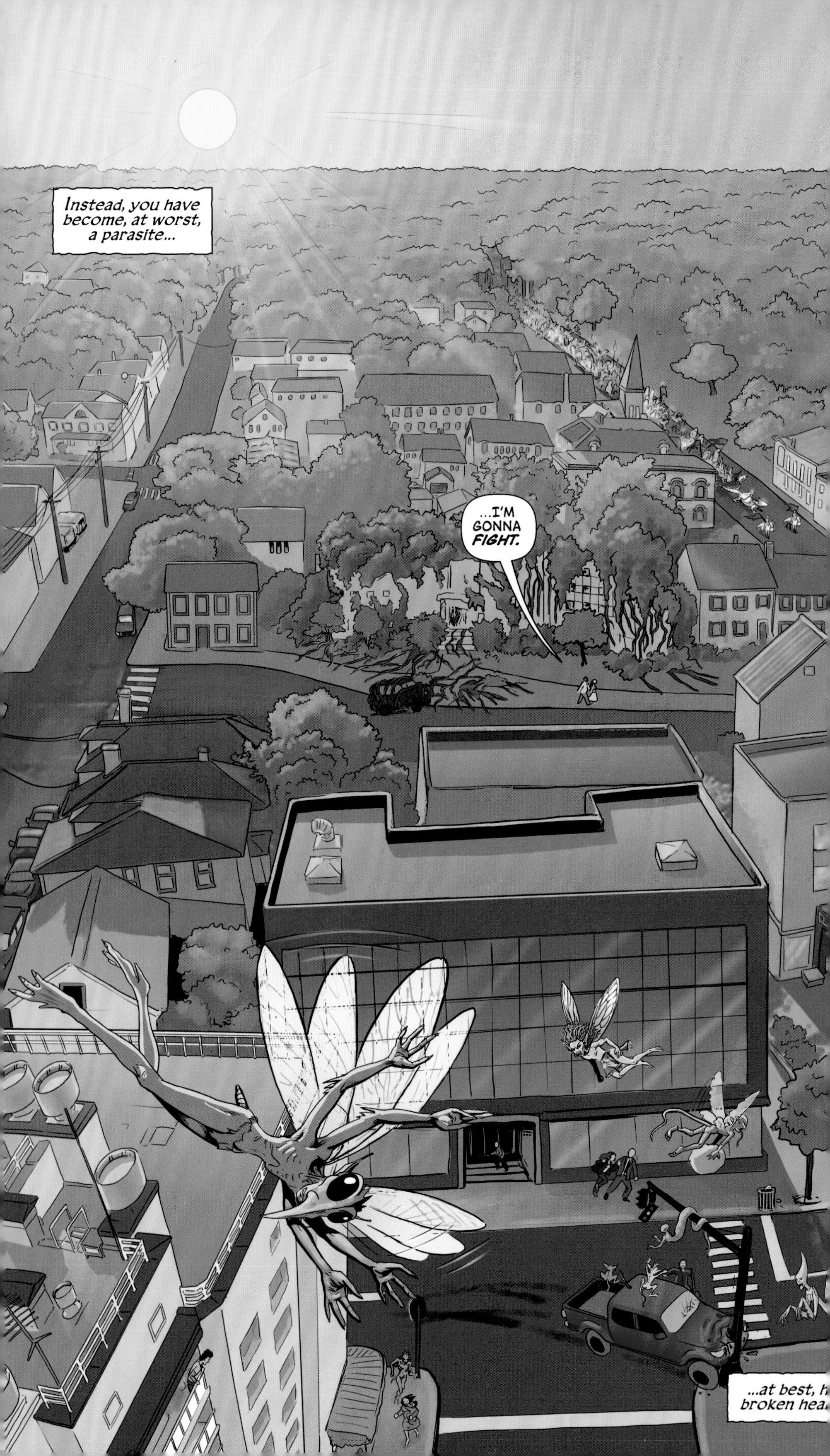
Instead, you have become, at worst, a parasite...
...I'M GONNA FIGHT.
...at best, h
broken hea

Chapter IV

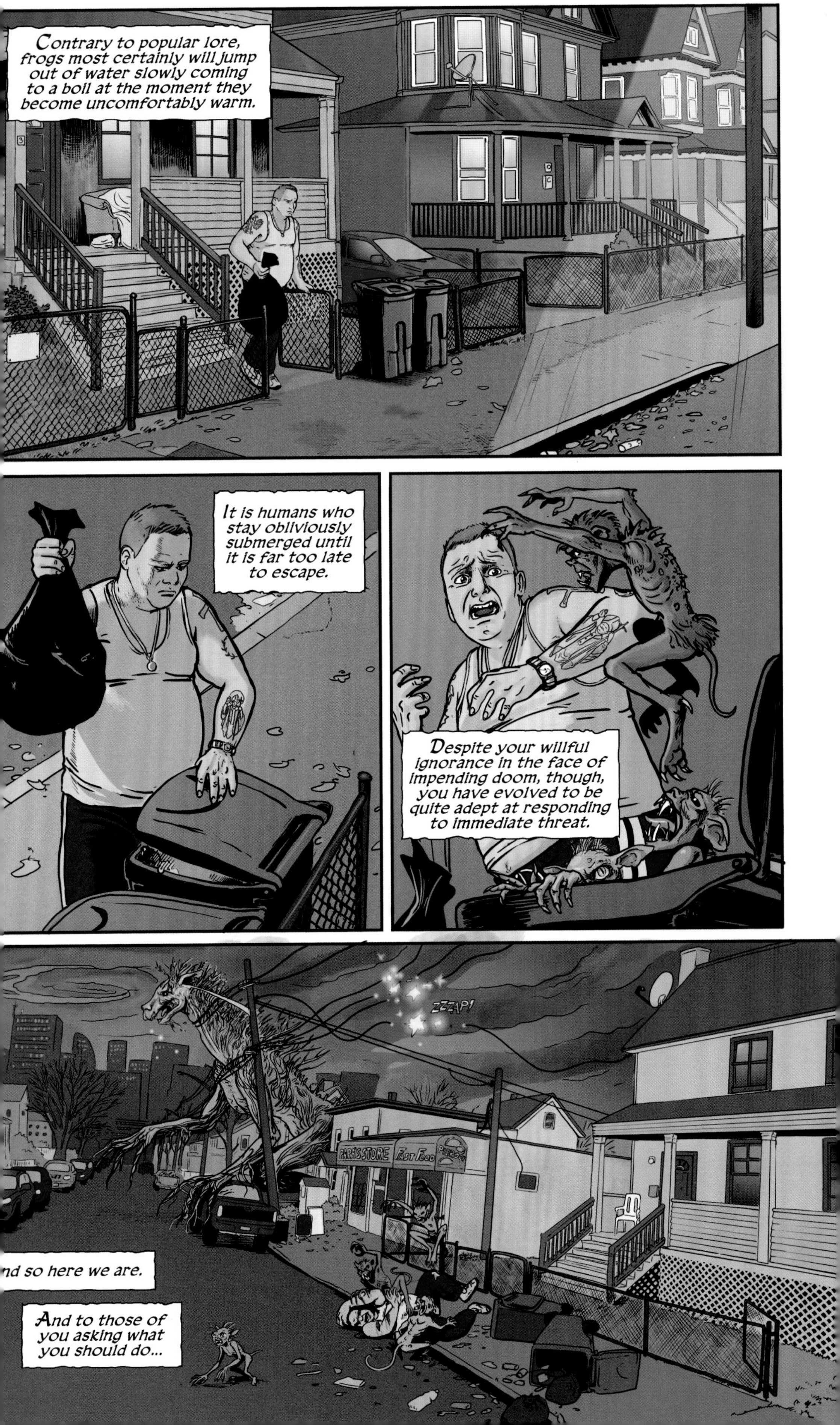

Contrary to popular lore, frogs most certainly will jump out of water slowly coming to a boil at the moment they become uncomfortably warm.
It is humans who stay obliviously submerged until it is far too late to escape.
Despite your willful ignorance in the face of impending doom, though, you have evolved to be quite adept at responding to immediate threat.
ZZZAP!
PAPA'S STORE
FAST FOOD
PIEROGI
nd so here we are.
And to those of you asking what you should do...

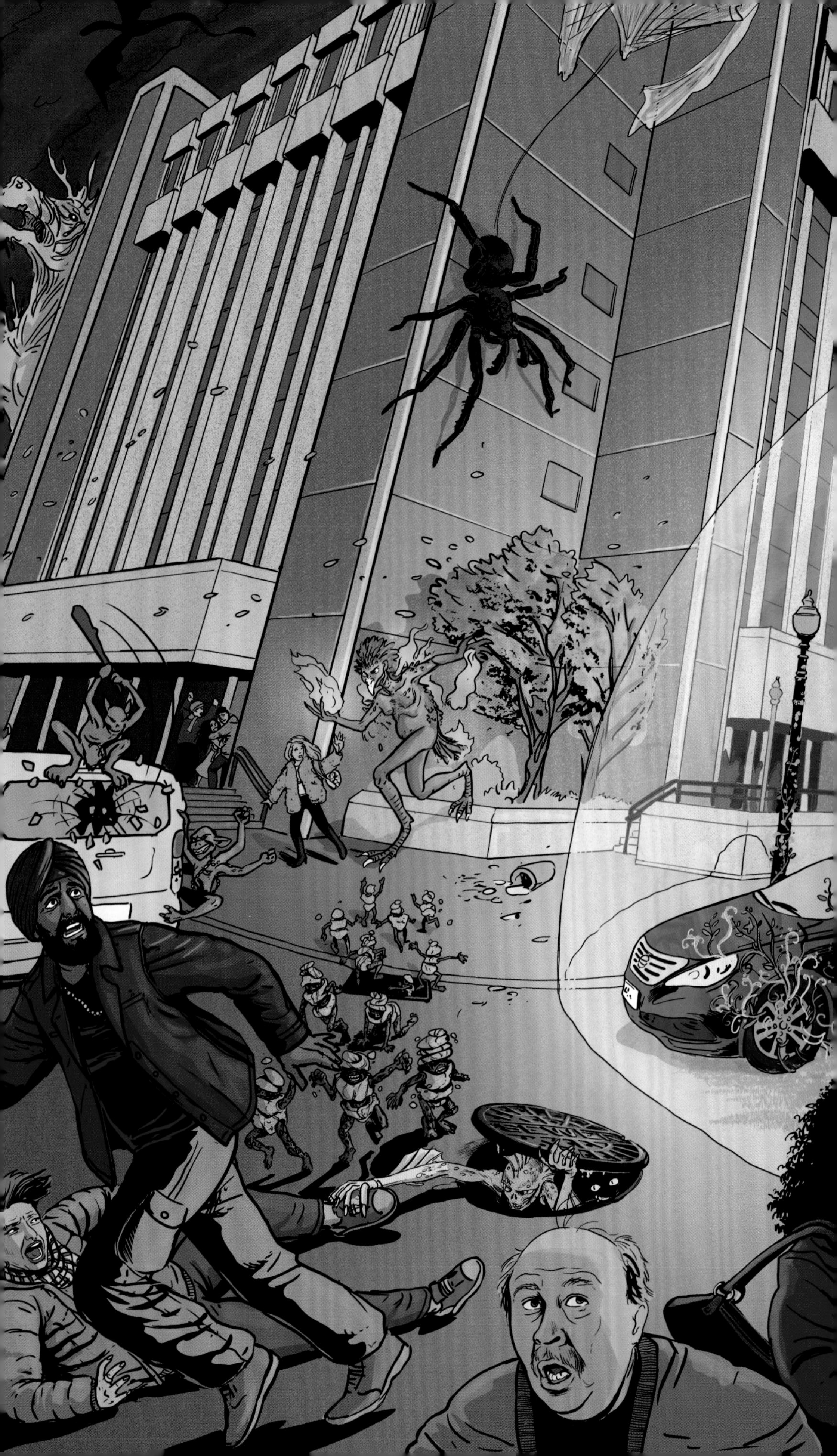

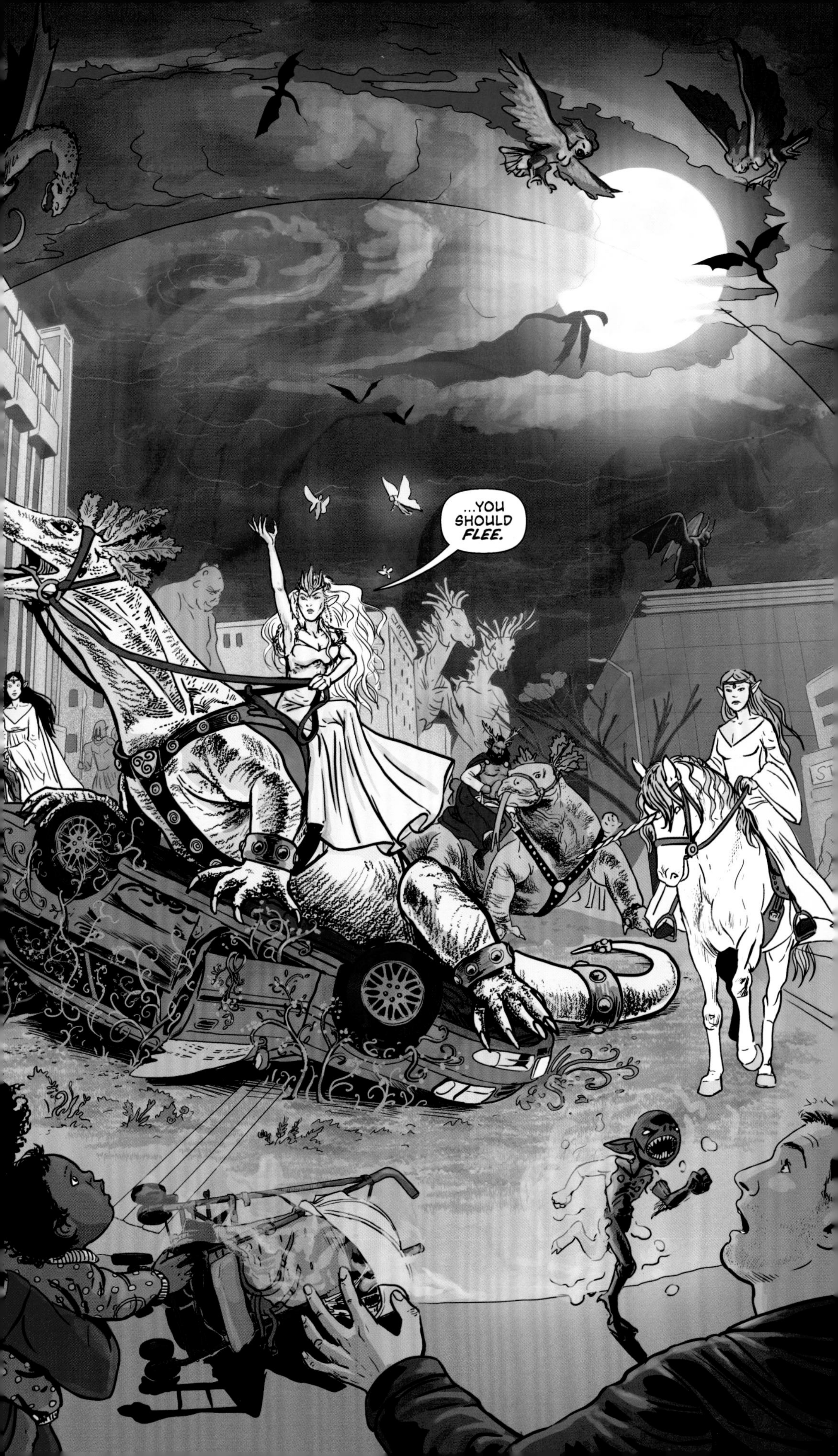
...YOU SHOULD *FLEE.*

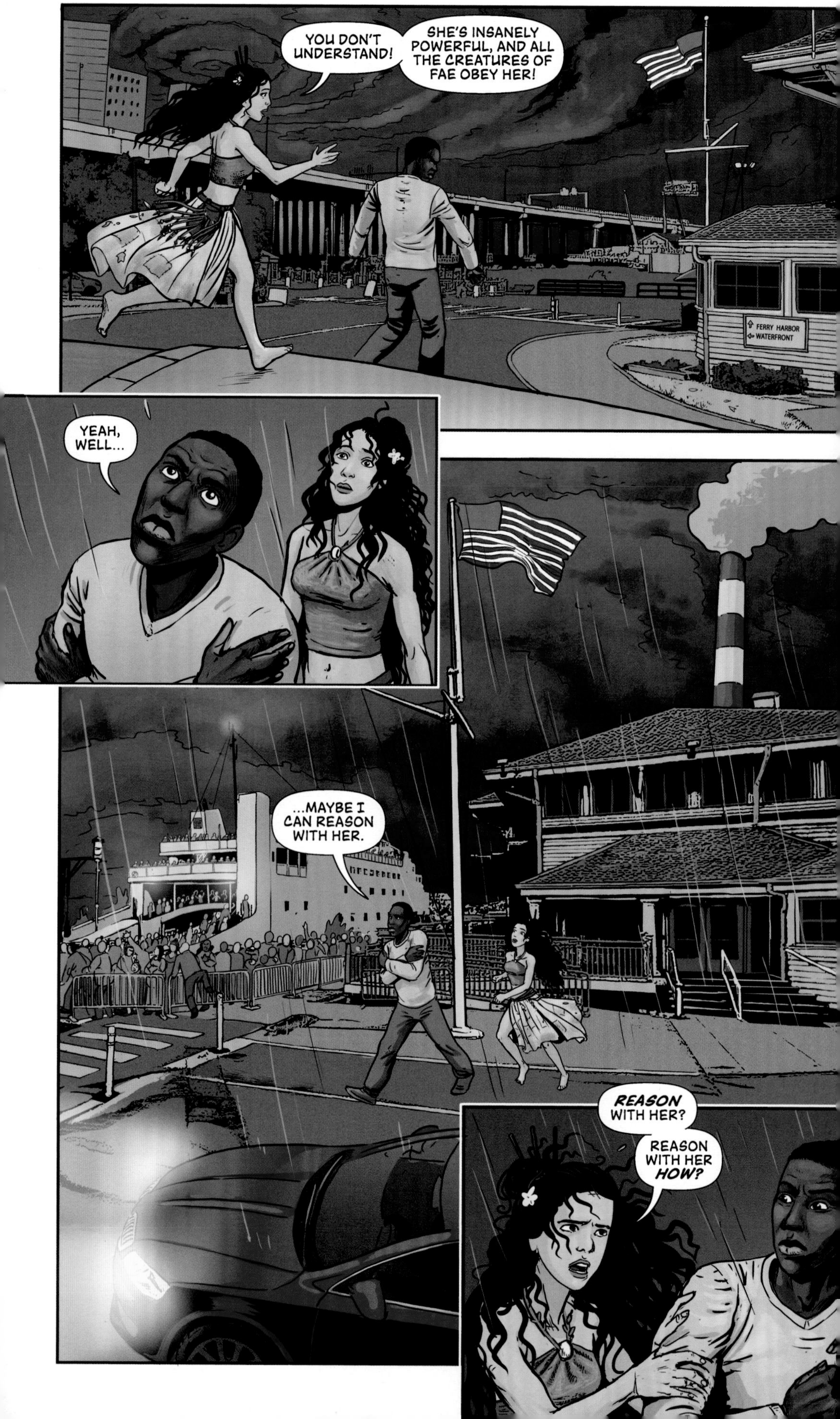
YOU DON'T UNDERSTAND!
SHE'S INSANELY POWERFUL, AND ALL THE CREATURES OF FAE OBEY HER!
FERRY HARBOR
WATERFRONT
YEAH, WELL...
...MAYBE I CAN REASON WITH HER.
REASON WITH HER?
REASON WITH HER *HOW?*

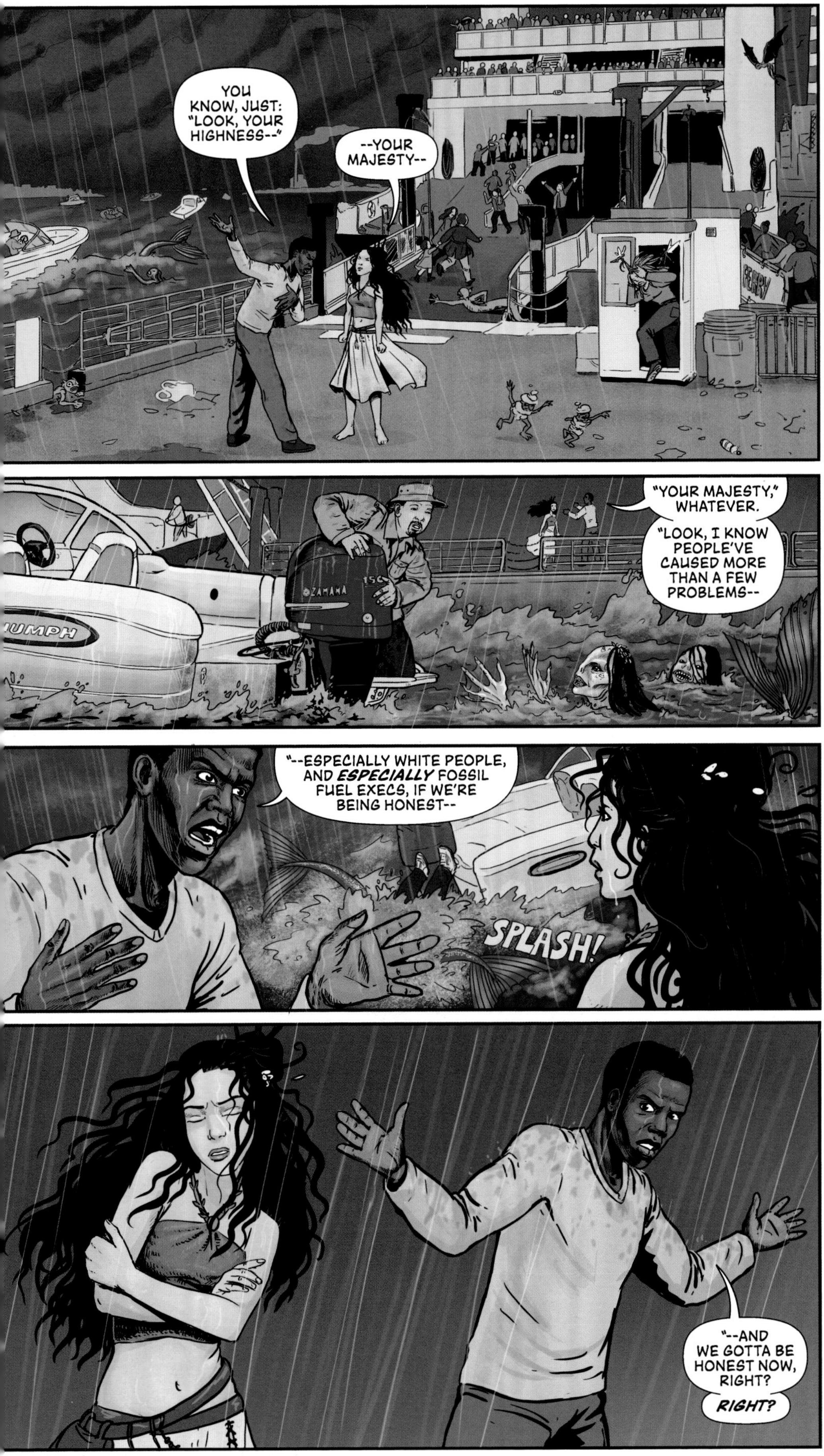
YOU KNOW, JUST: "LOOK, YOUR HIGHNESS--"
--YOUR MAJESTY--
FERRY
"YOUR MAJESTY," WHATEVER.
"LOOK, I KNOW PEOPLE'VE CAUSED MORE THAN A FEW PROBLEMS--
"--ESPECIALLY WHITE PEOPLE, AND *ESPECIALLY* FOSSIL FUEL EXECS, IF WE'RE BEING HONEST--
SPLASH!
"--AND WE GOTTA BE HONEST NOW, RIGHT?
RIGHT?

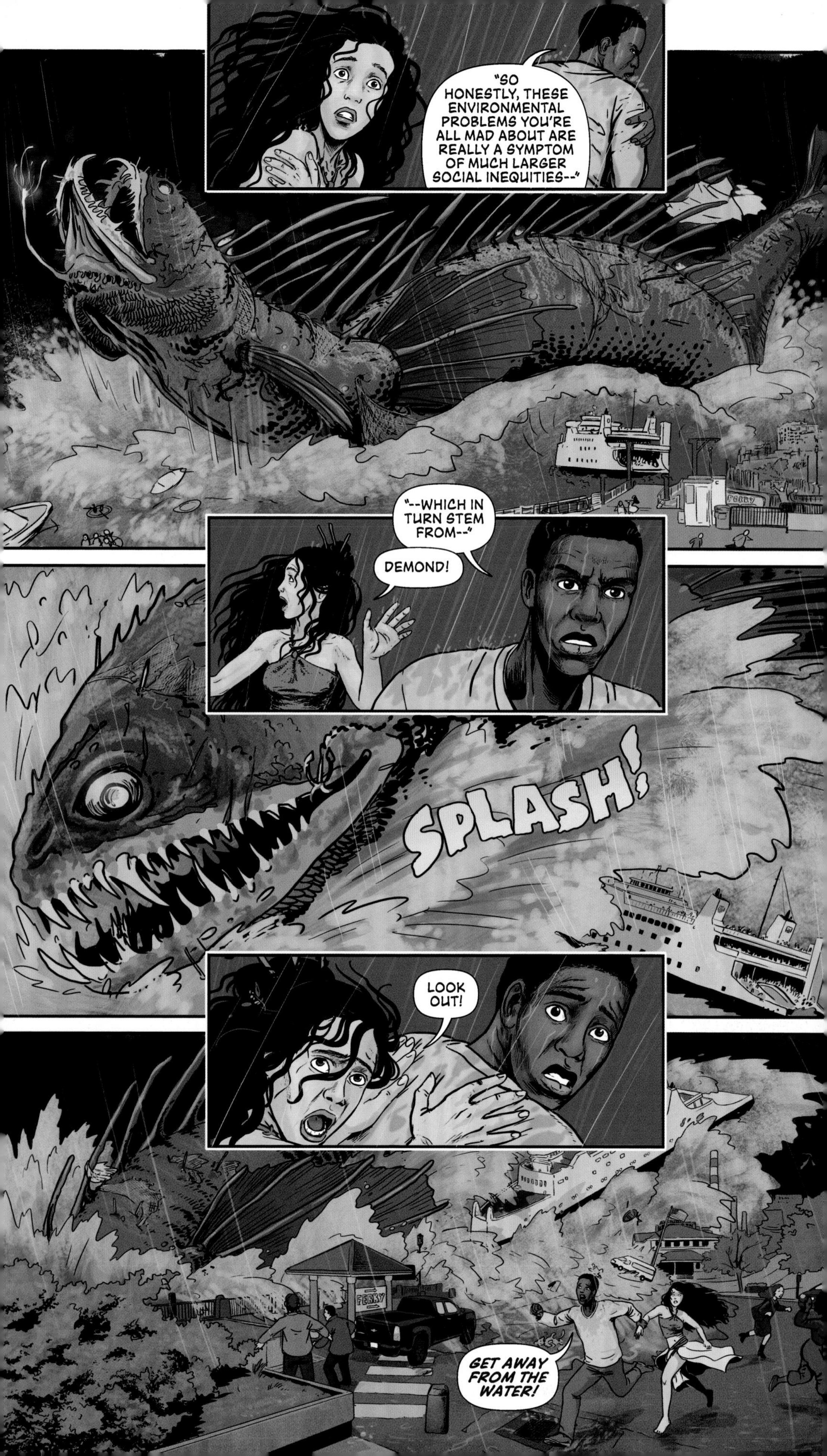
"SO HONESTLY, THESE ENVIRONMENTAL PROBLEMS YOU'RE ALL MAD ABOUT ARE REALLY A SYMPTOM OF MUCH LARGER SOCIAL INEQUITIES--"
FERRY
"--WHICH IN TURN STEM FROM--"
DEMOND!
SPLASH!
LOOK OUT!
FERRY
GET AWAY FROM THE WATER!

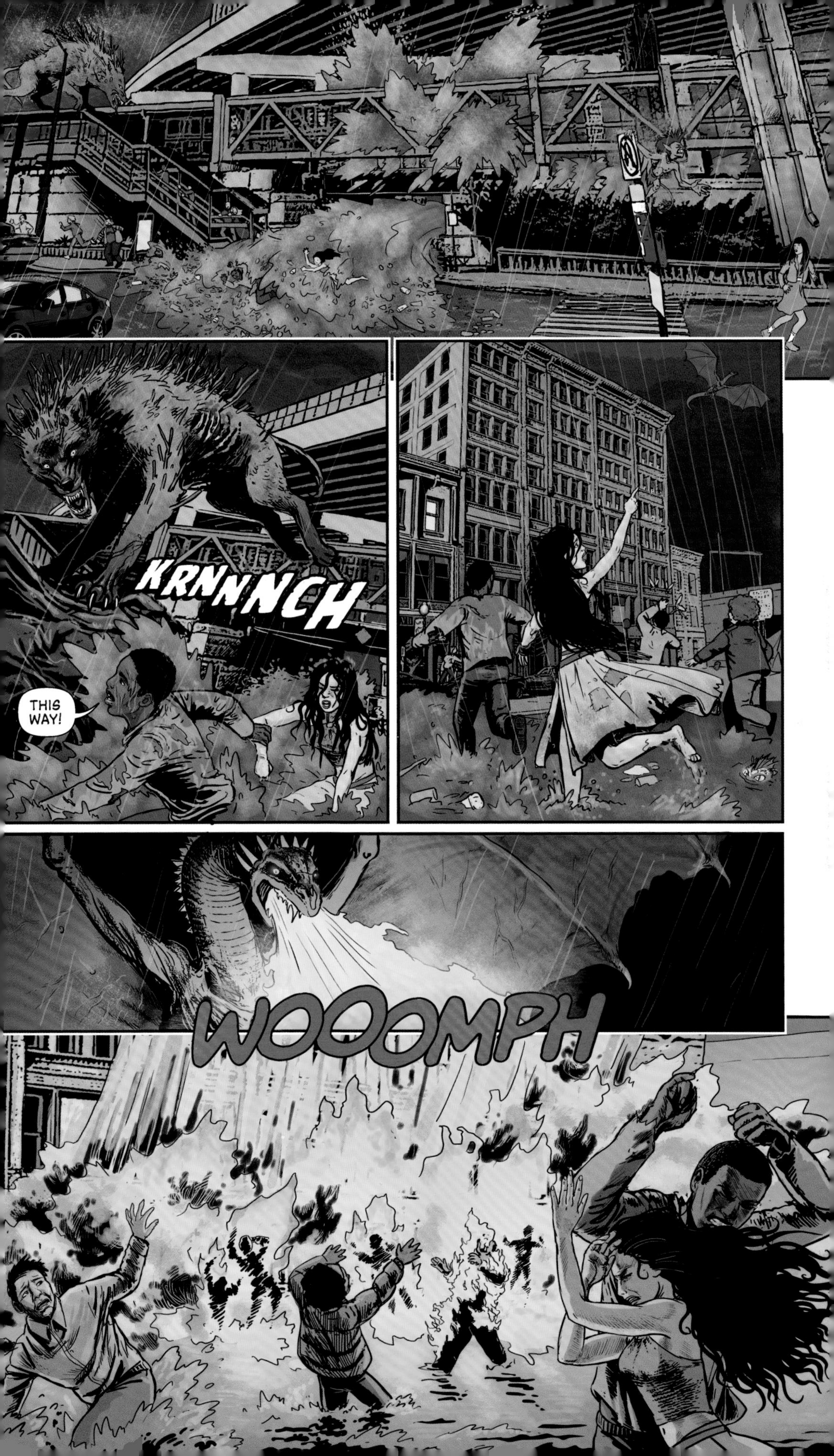
KRNNNCH
THIS WAY!
WOOOMPH

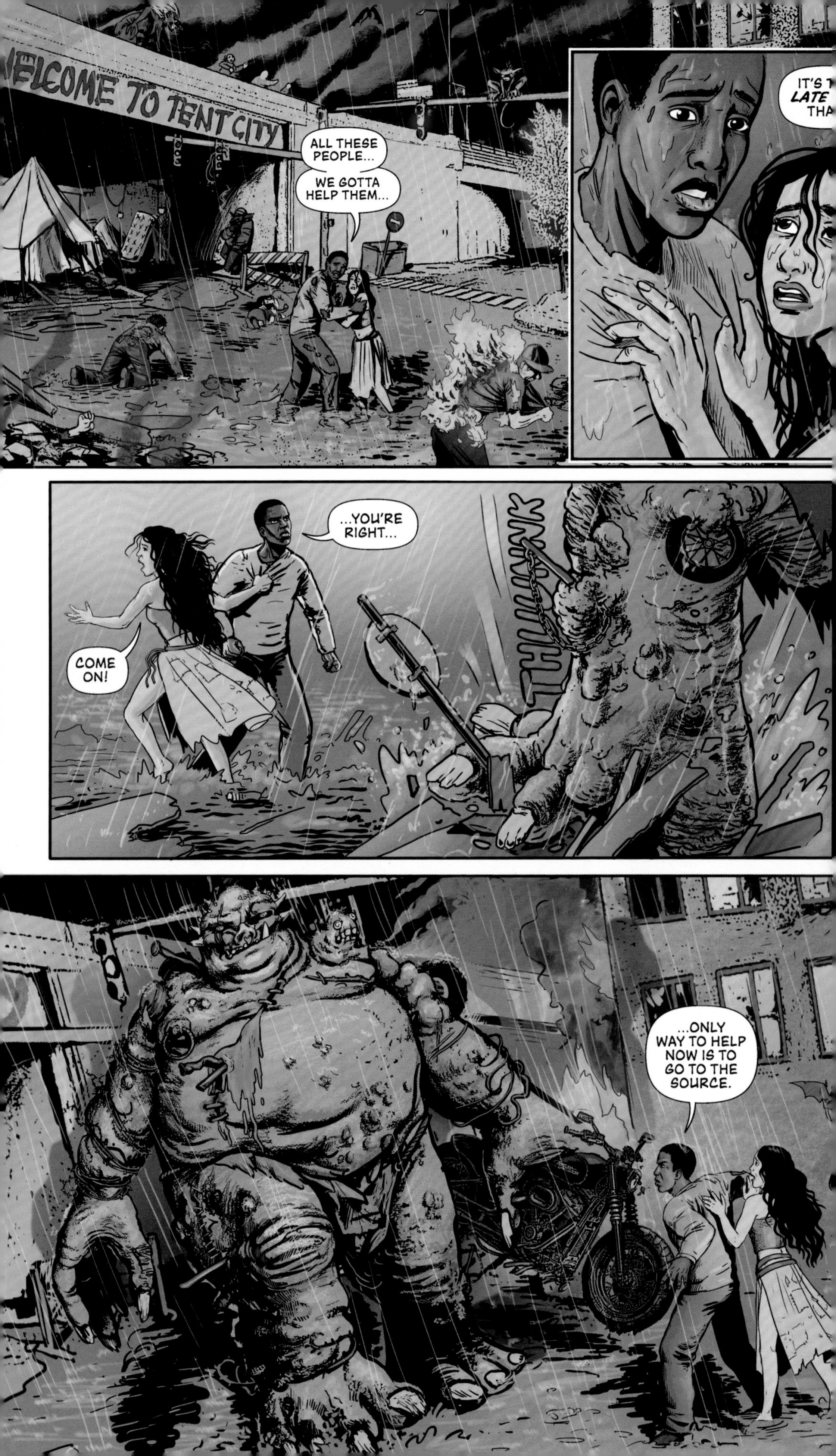
WELCOME TO TENT CITY
ALL THESE PEOPLE...
WE GOTTA HELP THEM...
IT'S T
LATE
THA
...YOU'RE RIGHT...
COME ON!
THHHNK
...ONLY WAY TO HELP NOW IS TO GO TO THE SOURCE.

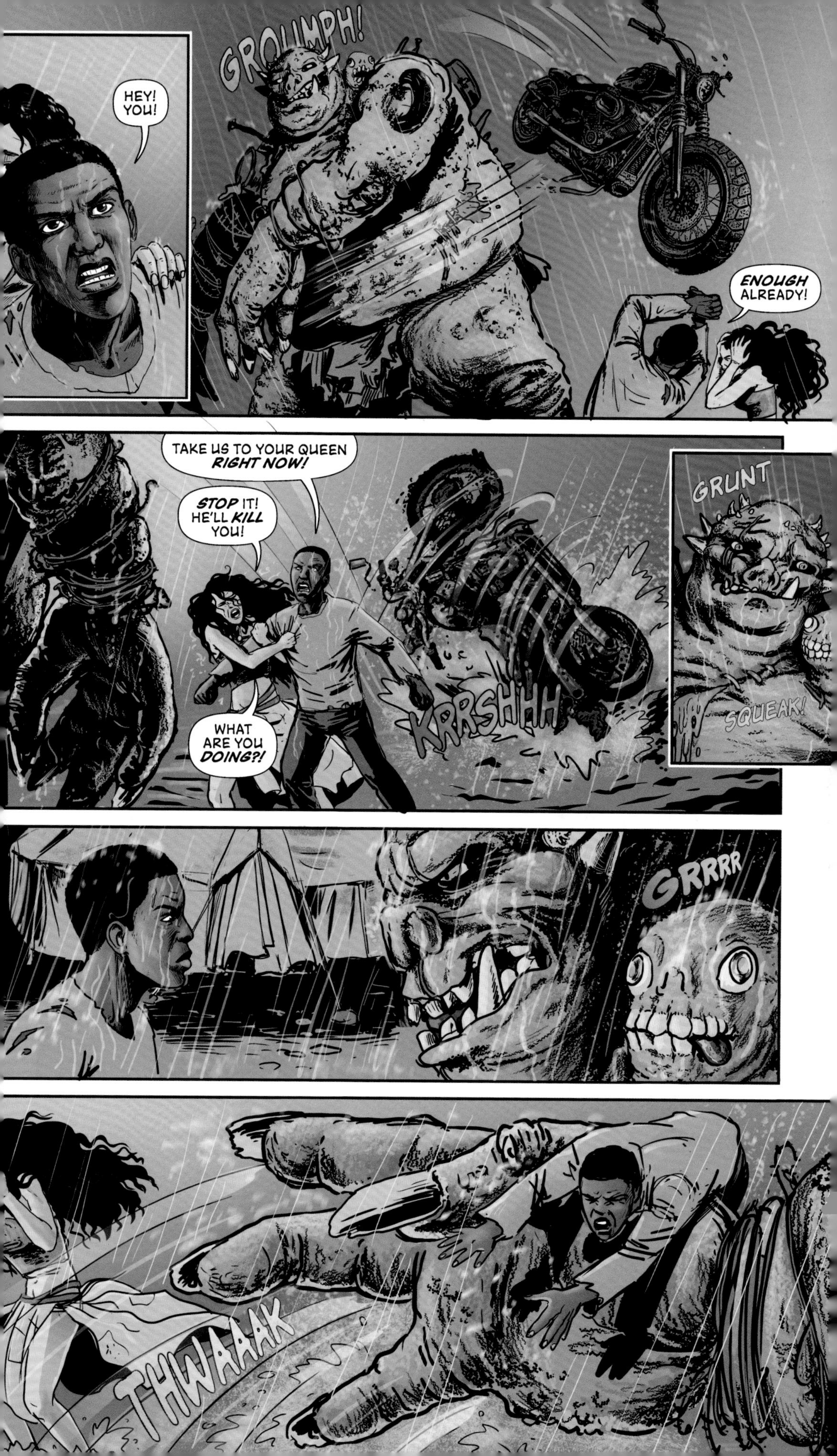
HEY! YOU!
GROUMPH!
ENOUGH ALREADY!
TAKE US TO YOUR QUEEN RIGHT NOW!
STOP IT! HE'LL KILL YOU!
WHAT ARE YOU DOING?!
KRRSHHH
GRUNT
SQUEAK!
GRRRR
THWAAAK

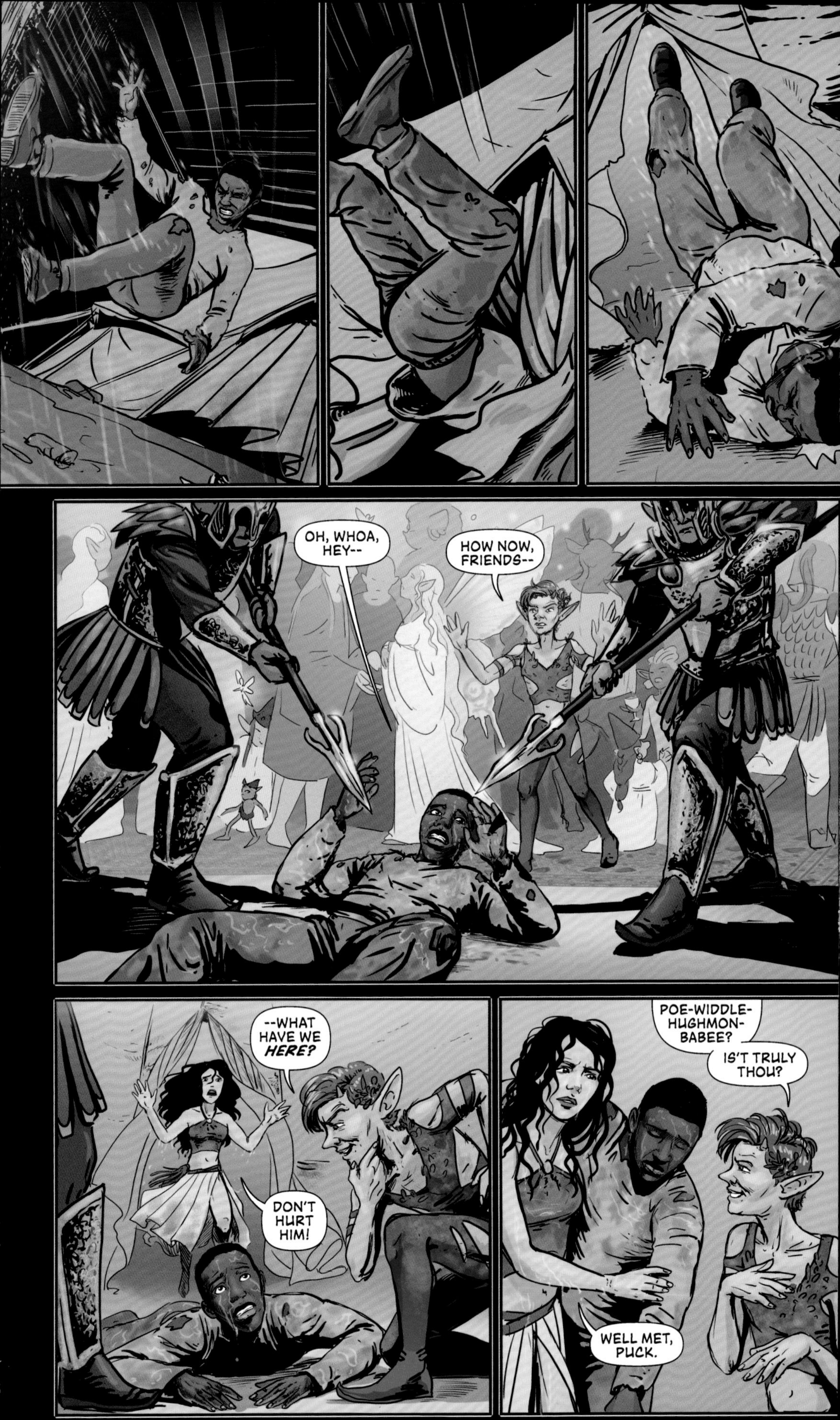
OH, WHOA, HEY--
HOW NOW, FRIENDS--
--WHAT HAVE WE *HERE?*
DON'T HURT HIM!
POE-WIDDLE-HUGHMON-BABEE?
IS'T TRULY THOU?
WELL MET, PUCK.

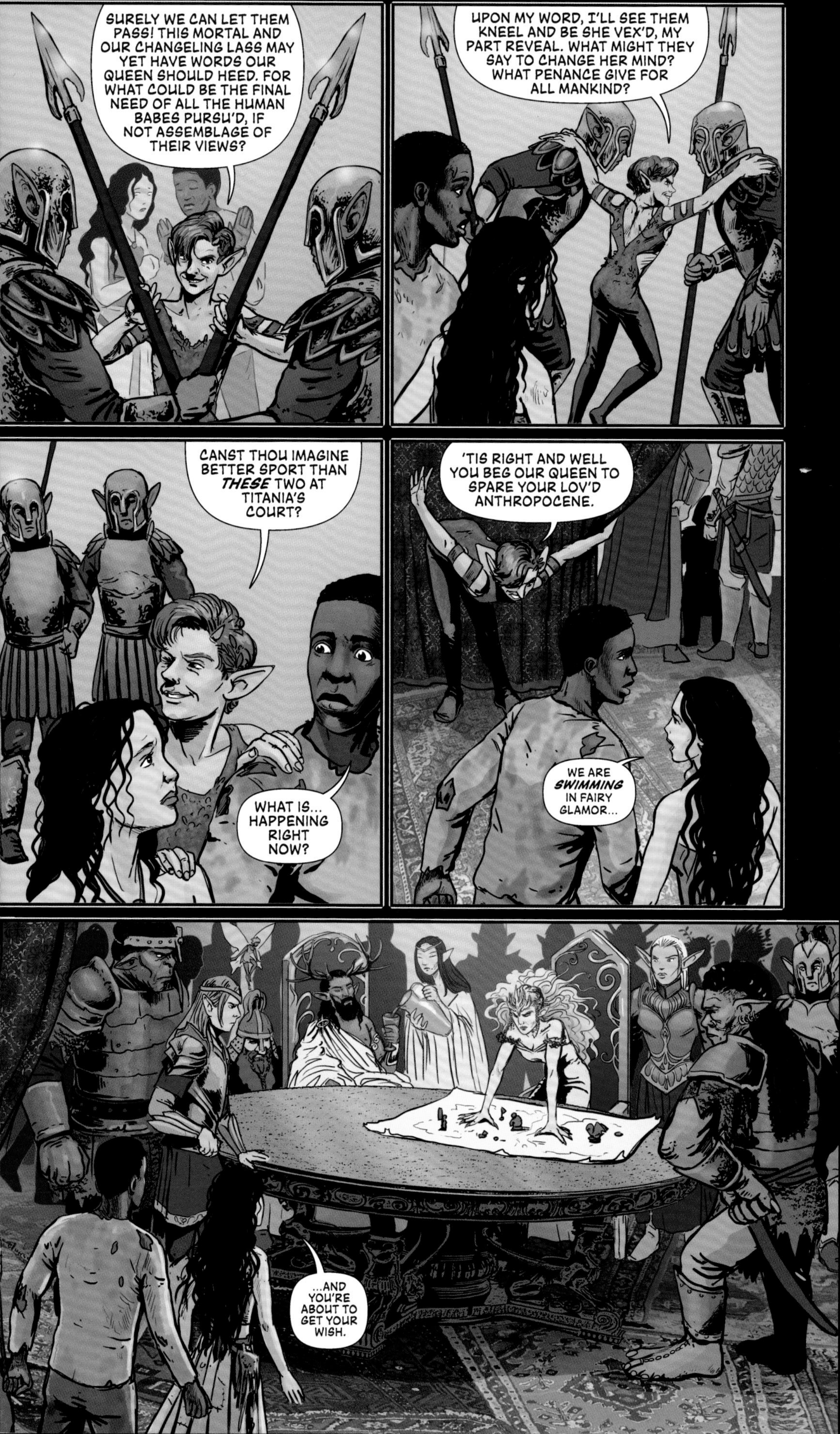
SURELY WE CAN LET THEM PASS! THIS MORTAL AND OUR CHANGELING LASS MAY YET HAVE WORDS OUR QUEEN SHOULD HEED. FOR WHAT COULD BE THE FINAL NEED OF ALL THE HUMAN BABES PURSU'D, IF NOT ASSEMBLAGE OF THEIR VIEWS?
UPON MY WORD, I'LL SEE THEM KNEEL AND BE SHE VEX'D, MY PART REVEAL. WHAT MIGHT THEY SAY TO CHANGE HER MIND? WHAT PENANCE GIVE FOR ALL MANKIND?
CANST THOU IMAGINE BETTER SPORT THAN *THESE* TWO AT TITANIA'S COURT?
WHAT IS... HAPPENING RIGHT NOW?
'TIS RIGHT AND WELL YOU BEG OUR QUEEN TO SPARE YOUR LOV'D ANTHROPOCENE.
WE ARE *SWIMMING* IN FAIRY GLAMOR...
...AND YOU'RE ABOUT TO GET YOUR WISH.

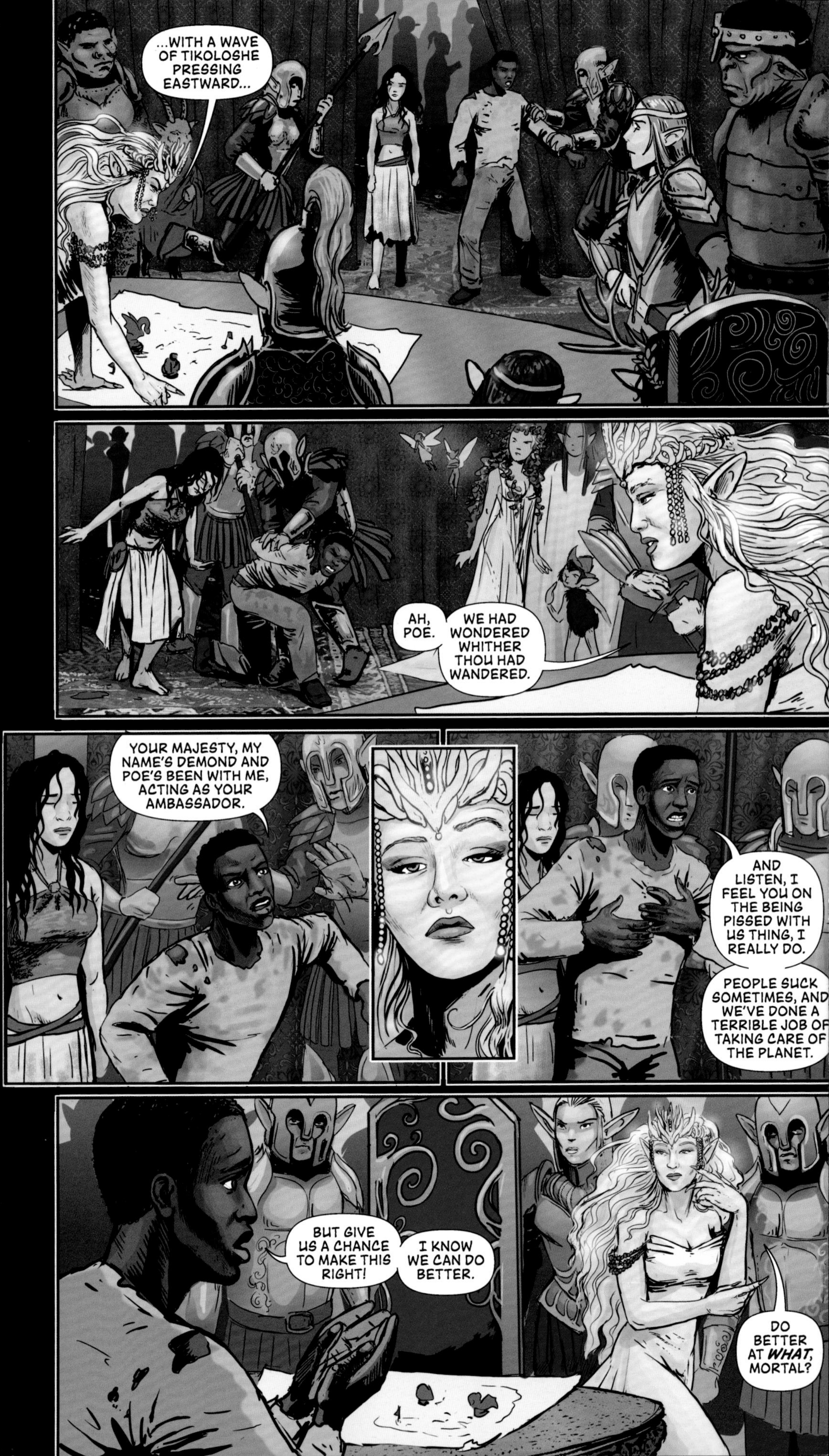
...WITH A WAVE OF TIKOLOSHE PRESSING EASTWARD...
AH, POE.
WE HAD WONDERED WHITHER THOU HAD WANDERED.
YOUR MAJESTY, MY NAME'S DEMOND AND POE'S BEEN WITH ME, ACTING AS YOUR AMBASSADOR.
AND LISTEN, I FEEL YOU ON THE BEING PISSED WITH US THING, I REALLY DO.
PEOPLE SUCK SOMETIMES, AND WE'VE DONE A TERRIBLE JOB OF TAKING CARE OF THE PLANET.
BUT GIVE US A CHANCE TO MAKE THIS RIGHT!
I KNOW WE CAN DO BETTER.
DO BETTER AT ***WHAT***, MORTAL?

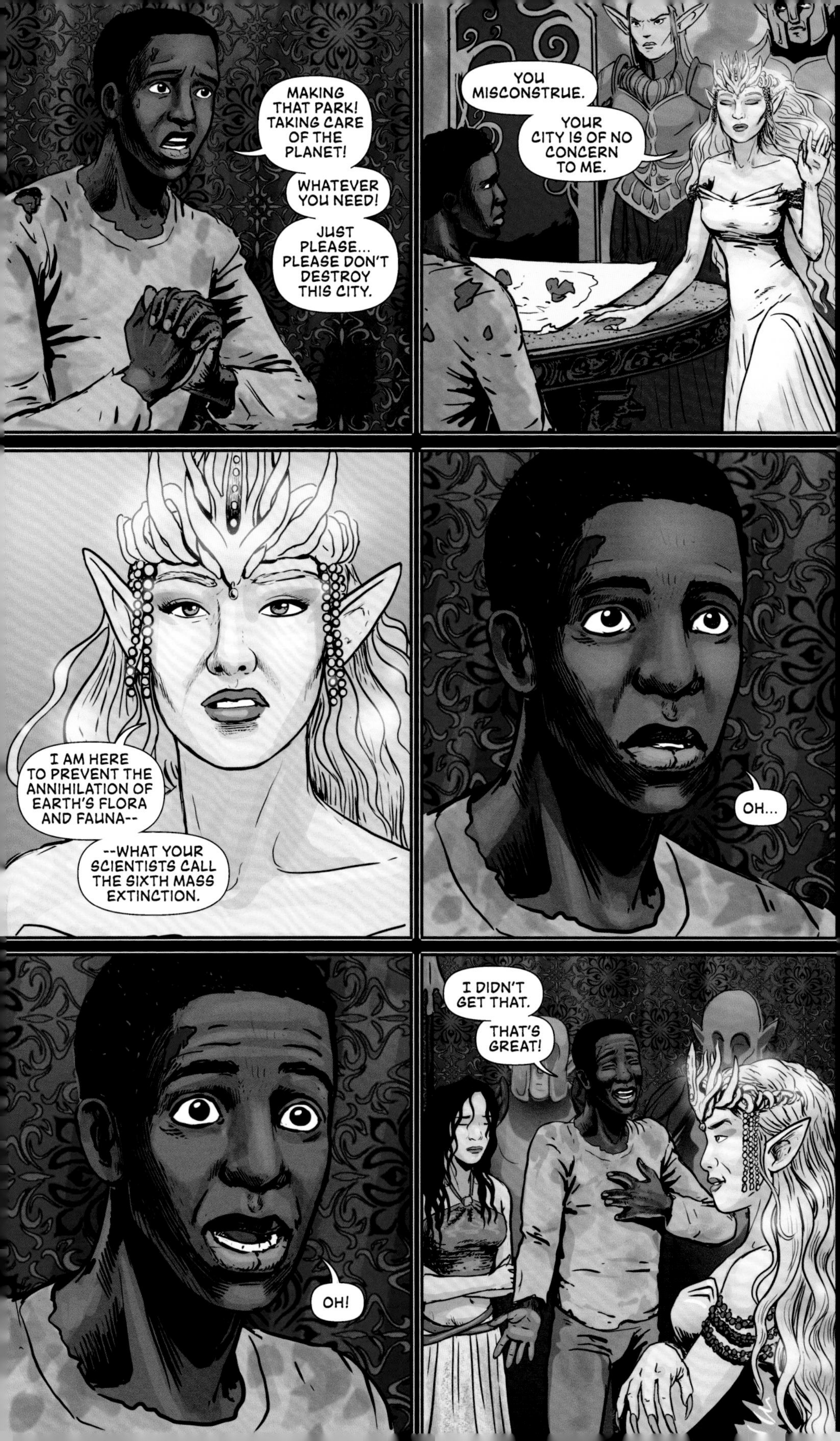
MAKING THAT PARK! TAKING CARE OF THE PLANET!
WHATEVER YOU NEED!
JUST PLEASE... PLEASE DON'T DESTROY THIS CITY.
YOU MISCONSTRUE.
YOUR CITY IS OF NO CONCERN TO ME.
I AM HERE TO PREVENT THE ANNIHILATION OF EARTH'S FLORA AND FAUNA--
--WHAT YOUR SCIENTISTS CALL THE SIXTH MASS EXTINCTION.
OH...
OH!
I DIDN'T GET THAT.
THAT'S GREAT!

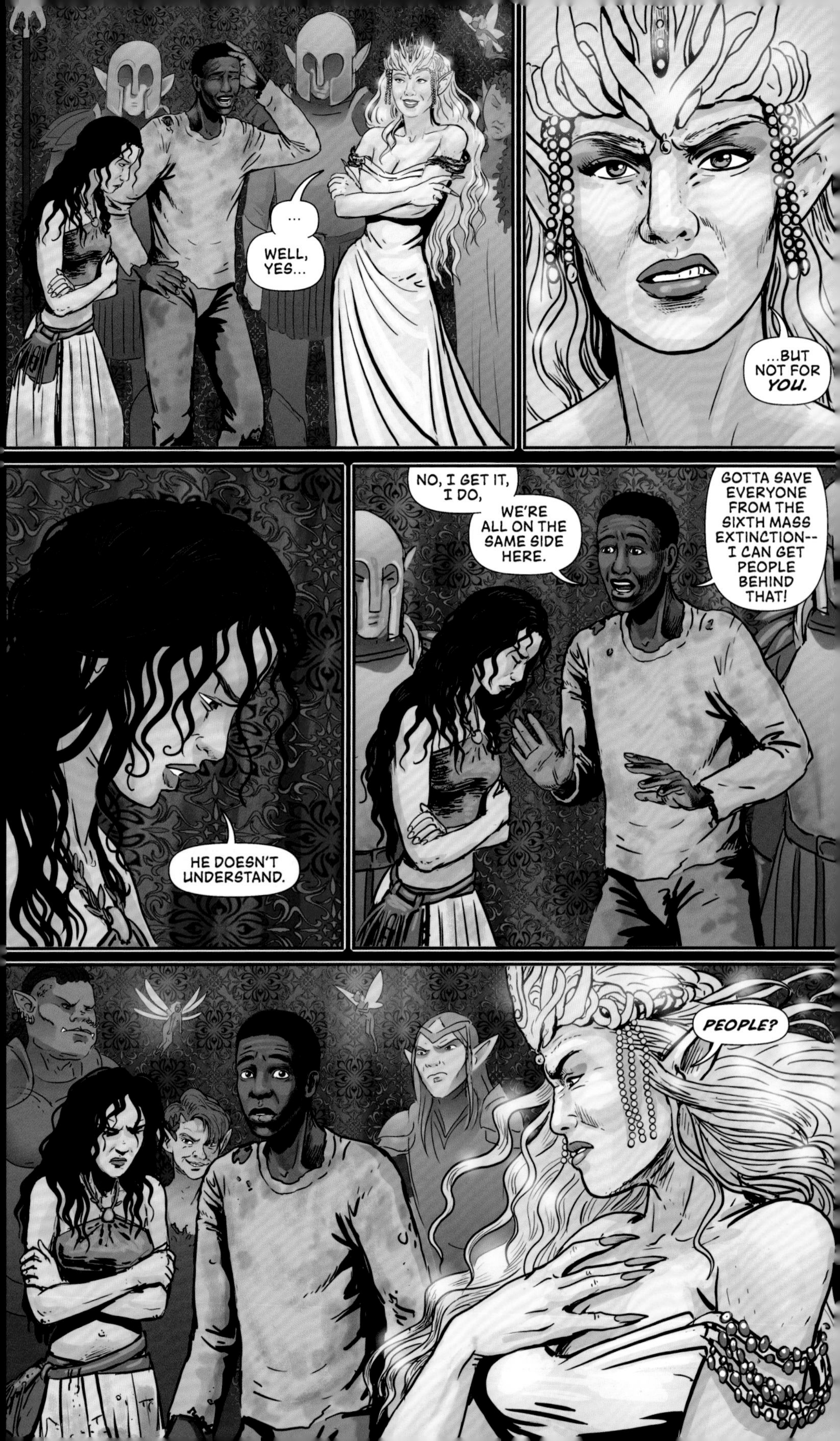
...
WELL, YES...
...BUT NOT FOR *YOU.*
HE DOESN'T UNDERSTAND.
NO, I GET IT, I DO,
WE'RE ALL ON THE SAME SIDE HERE.
GOTTA SAVE EVERYONE FROM THE SIXTH MASS EXTINCTION-- I CAN GET PEOPLE BEHIND THAT!
PEOPLE?

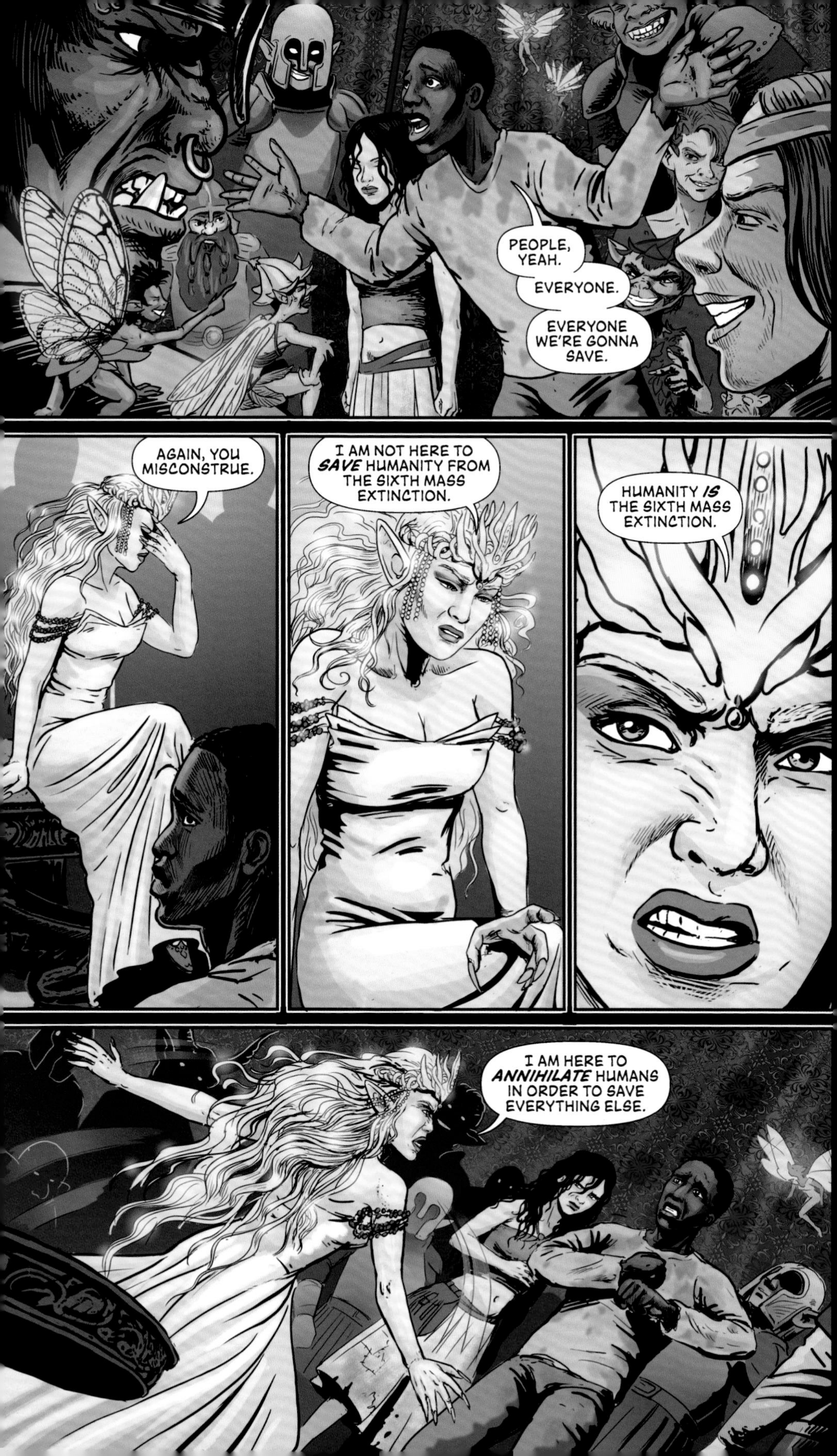
PEOPLE, YEAH.
EVERYONE.
EVERYONE WE'RE GONNA SAVE.
AGAIN, YOU MISCONSTRUE.
I AM NOT HERE TO *SAVE* HUMANITY FROM THE SIXTH MASS EXTINCTION.
HUMANITY *IS* THE SIXTH MASS EXTINCTION.
I AM HERE TO *ANNIHILATE* HUMANS IN ORDER TO SAVE EVERYTHING ELSE.

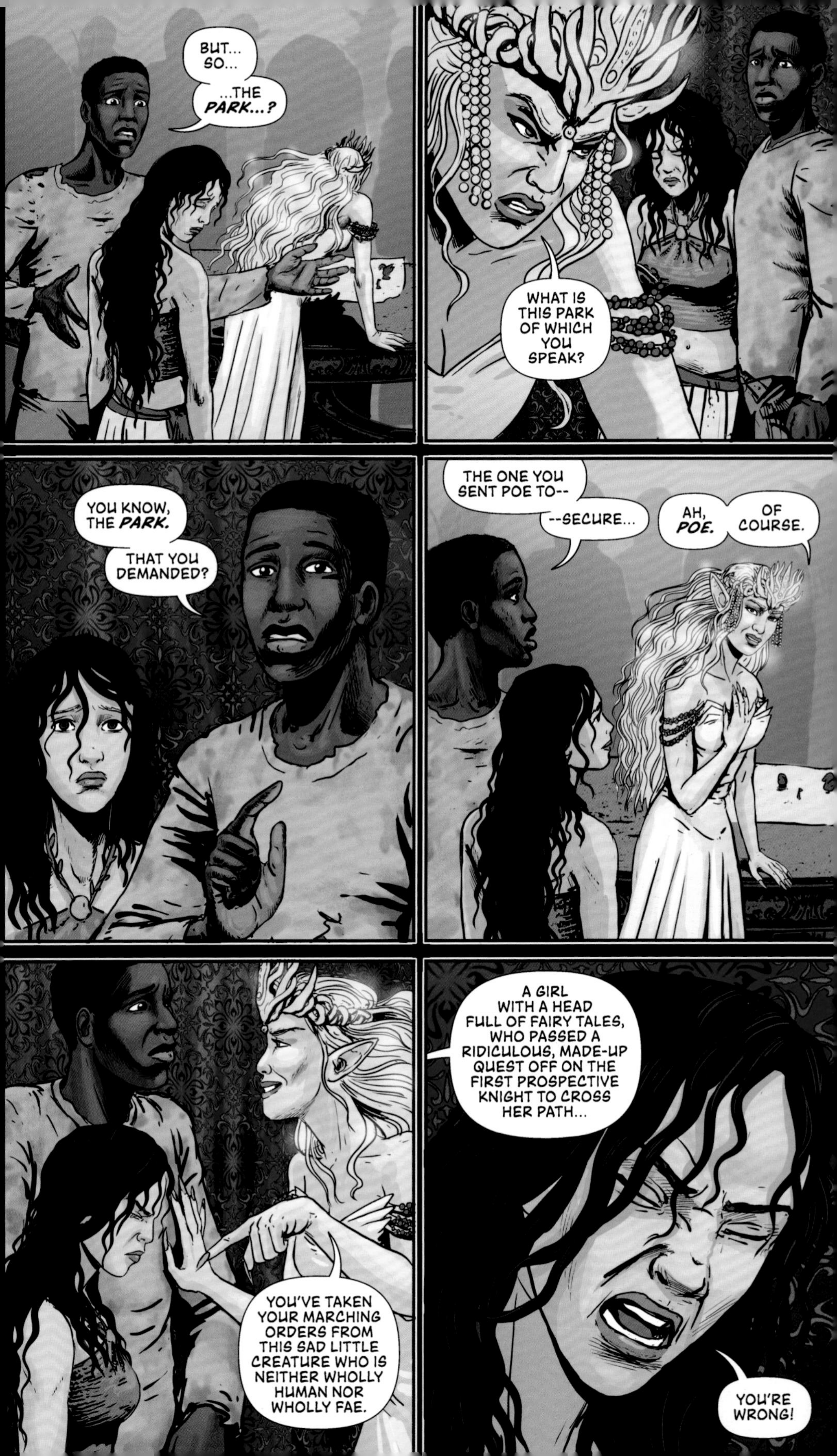
BUT... SO...
...THE PARK...?
WHAT IS THIS PARK OF WHICH YOU SPEAK?
YOU KNOW, THE PARK.
THAT YOU DEMANDED?
THE ONE YOU SENT POE TO--
--SECURE...
AH, POE.
OF COURSE.
YOU'VE TAKEN YOUR MARCHING ORDERS FROM THIS SAD LITTLE CREATURE WHO IS NEITHER WHOLLY HUMAN NOR WHOLLY FAE.
A GIRL WITH A HEAD FULL OF FAIRY TALES, WHO PASSED A RIDICULOUS, MADE-UP QUEST OFF ON THE FIRST PROSPECTIVE KNIGHT TO CROSS HER PATH...
YOU'RE WRONG!

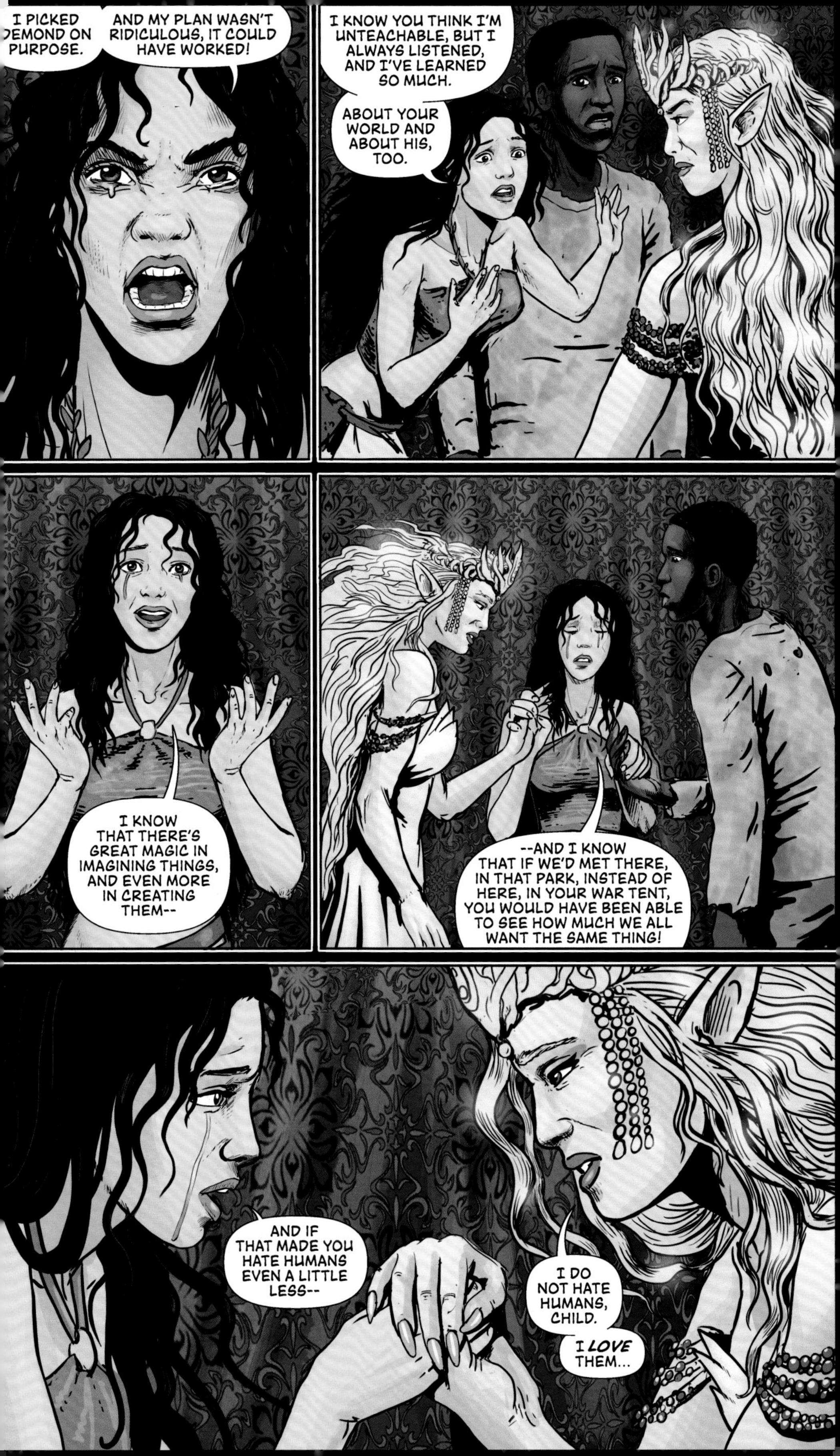

I PICKED DEMOND ON PURPOSE.
AND MY PLAN WASN'T RIDICULOUS, IT COULD HAVE WORKED!
I KNOW YOU THINK I'M UNTEACHABLE, BUT I ALWAYS LISTENED, AND I'VE LEARNED SO MUCH.
ABOUT YOUR WORLD AND ABOUT HIS, TOO.
I KNOW THAT THERE'S GREAT MAGIC IN IMAGINING THINGS, AND EVEN MORE IN CREATING THEM--
--AND I KNOW THAT IF WE'D MET THERE, IN THAT PARK, INSTEAD OF HERE, IN YOUR WAR TENT, YOU WOULD HAVE BEEN ABLE TO SEE HOW MUCH WE ALL WANT THE SAME THING!
AND IF THAT MADE YOU HATE HUMANS EVEN A LITTLE LESS--
I DO NOT HATE HUMANS, CHILD.
I *LOVE* THEM...

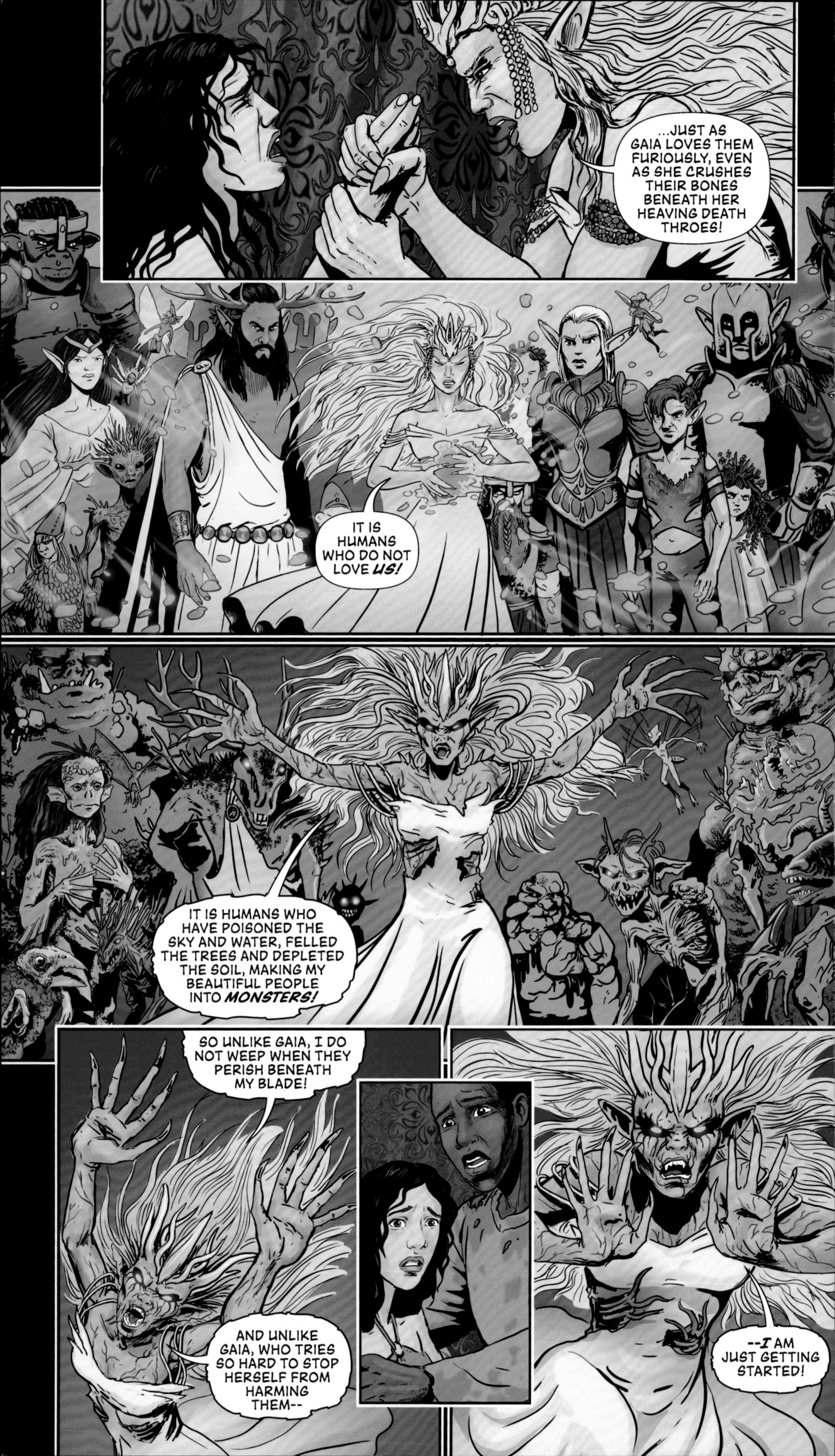
...JUST AS GAIA LOVES THEM FURIOUSLY, EVEN AS SHE CRUSHES THEIR BONES BENEATH HER HEAVING DEATH THROES!
IT IS HUMANS WHO DO NOT LOVE US!
IT IS HUMANS WHO HAVE POISONED THE SKY AND WATER, FELLED THE TREES AND DEPLETED THE SOIL, MAKING MY BEAUTIFUL PEOPLE INTO MONSTERS!
SO UNLIKE GAIA, I DO NOT WEEP WHEN THEY PERISH BENEATH MY BLADE!
AND UNLIKE GAIA, WHO TRIES SO HARD TO STOP HERSELF FROM HARMING THEM--
--I AM JUST GETTING STARTED!

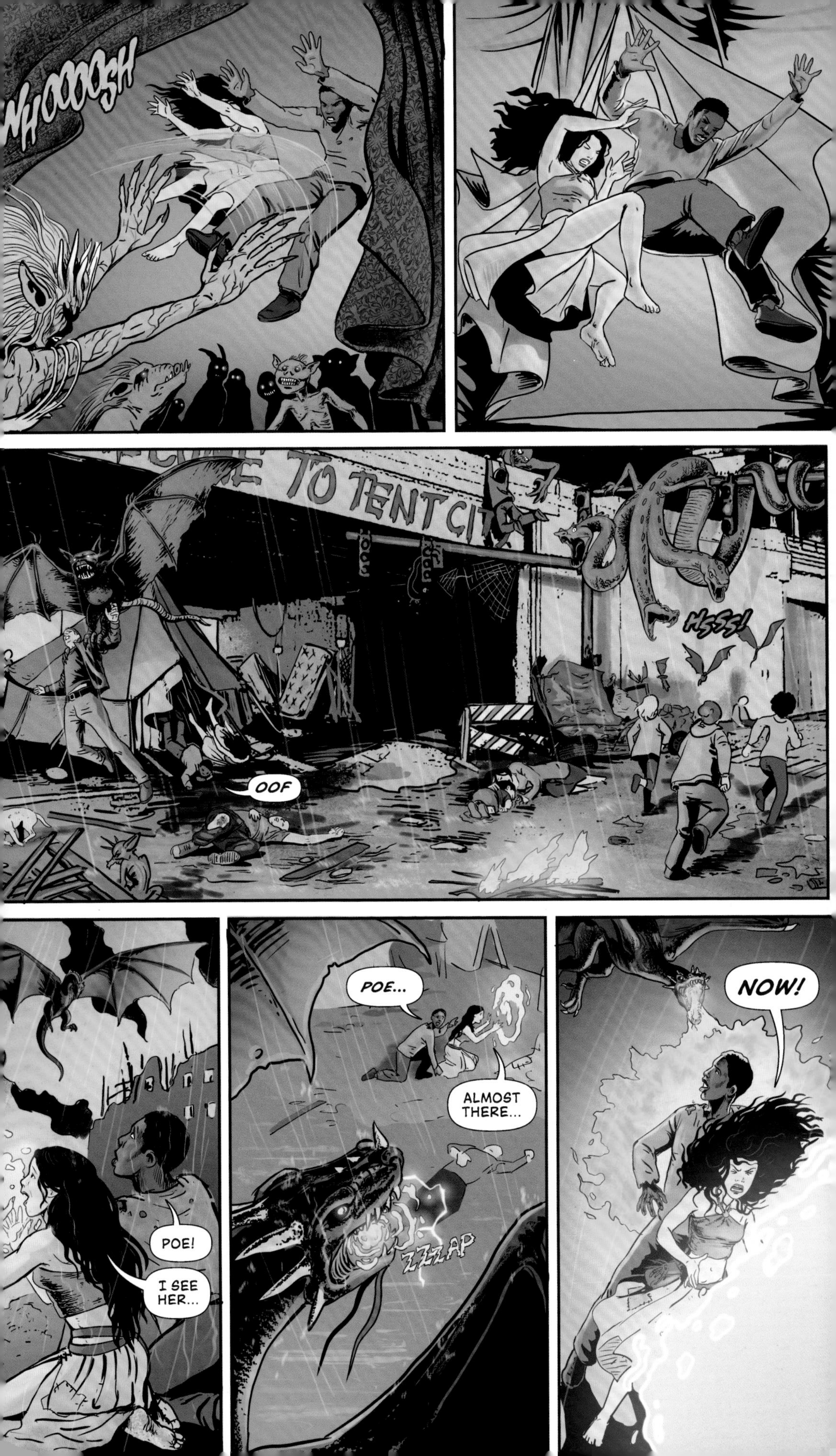
WHOOOOSH
TO TENT CIT
HSSS!
OOF
POE!
I SEE HER...
POE...
ALMOST THERE...
ZZZZAP
NOW!

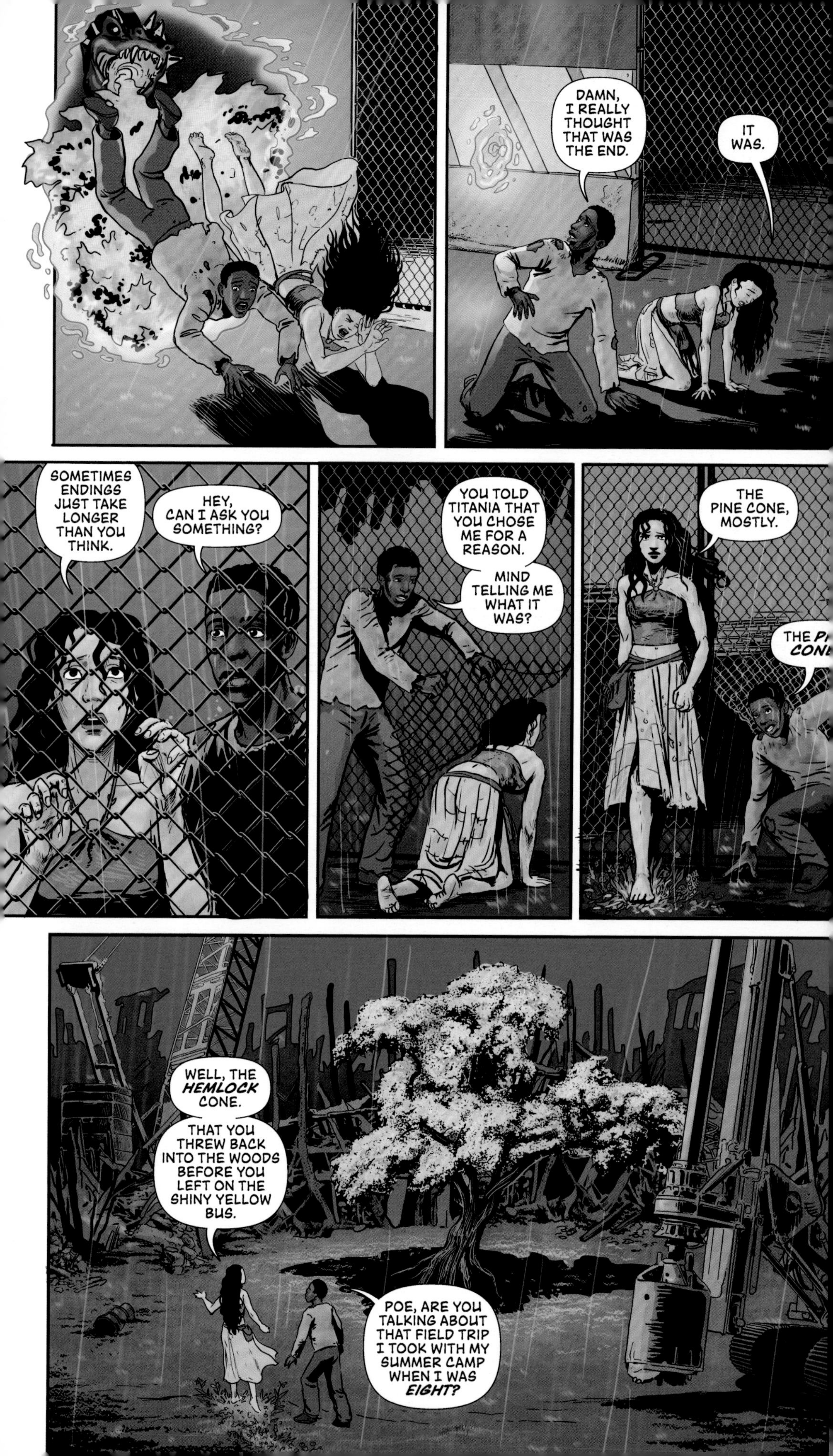
DAMN, I REALLY THOUGHT THAT WAS THE END.
IT WAS.
SOMETIMES ENDINGS JUST TAKE LONGER THAN YOU THINK.
HEY, CAN I ASK YOU SOMETHING?
YOU TOLD TITANIA THAT YOU CHOSE ME FOR A REASON.
MIND TELLING ME WHAT IT WAS?
THE PINE CONE, MOSTLY.
WELL, THE *HEMLOCK* CONE.
THAT YOU THREW BACK INTO THE WOODS BEFORE YOU LEFT ON THE SHINY YELLOW BUS.
POE, ARE YOU TALKING ABOUT THAT FIELD TRIP I TOOK WITH MY SUMMER CAMP WHEN I WAS *EIGHT?*

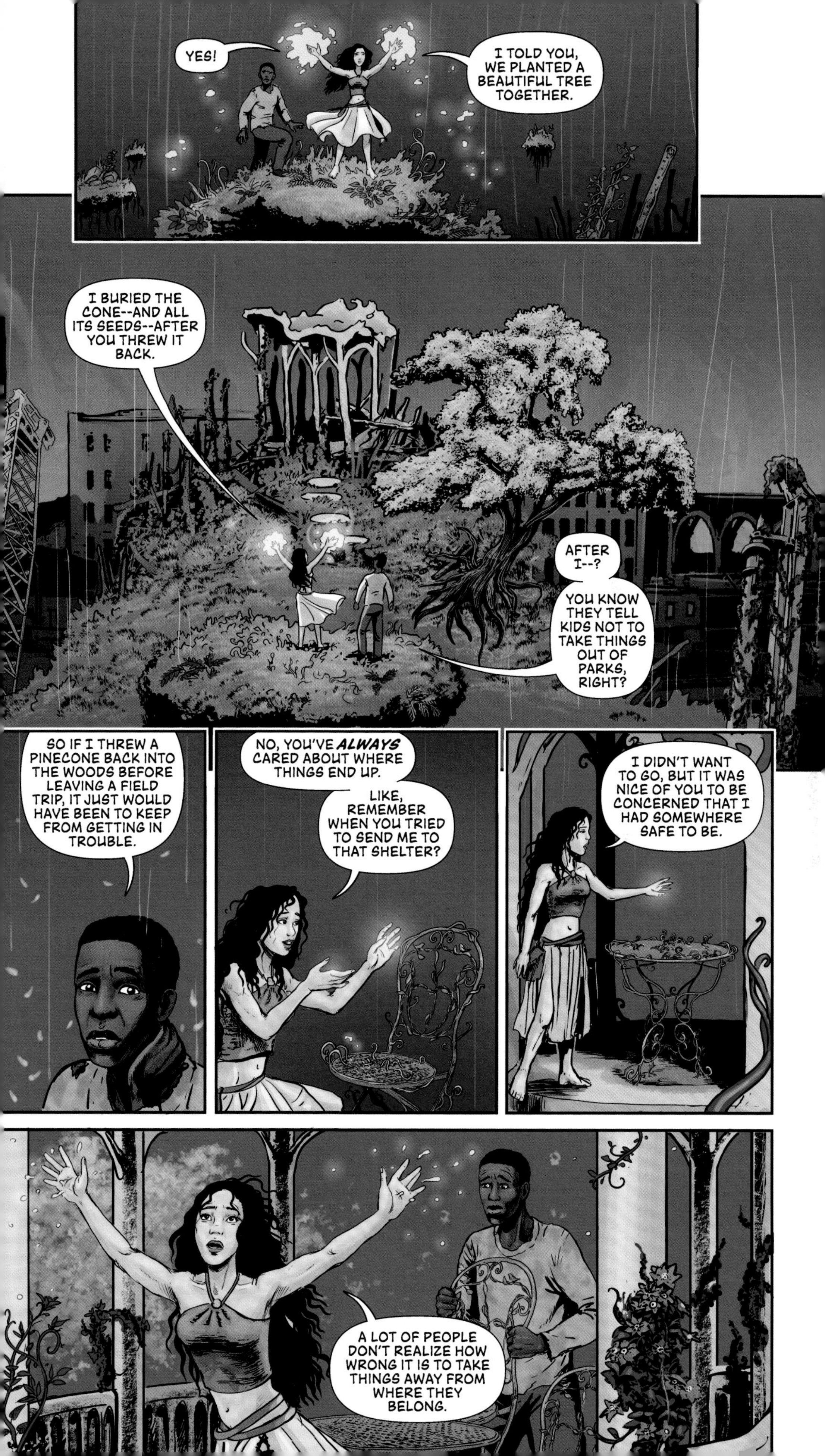
YES!
I TOLD YOU, WE PLANTED A BEAUTIFUL TREE TOGETHER.
I BURIED THE CONE--AND ALL ITS SEEDS--AFTER YOU THREW IT BACK.
AFTER I--?
YOU KNOW THEY TELL KIDS NOT TO TAKE THINGS OUT OF PARKS, RIGHT?
SO IF I THREW A PINECONE BACK INTO THE WOODS BEFORE LEAVING A FIELD TRIP, IT JUST WOULD HAVE BEEN TO KEEP FROM GETTING IN TROUBLE.
NO, YOU'VE *ALWAYS* CARED ABOUT WHERE THINGS END UP.
LIKE, REMEMBER WHEN YOU TRIED TO SEND ME TO THAT SHELTER?
I DIDN'T WANT TO GO, BUT IT WAS NICE OF YOU TO BE CONCERNED THAT I HAD SOMEWHERE SAFE TO BE.
A LOT OF PEOPLE DON'T REALIZE HOW WRONG IT IS TO TAKE THINGS AWAY FROM WHERE THEY BELONG.

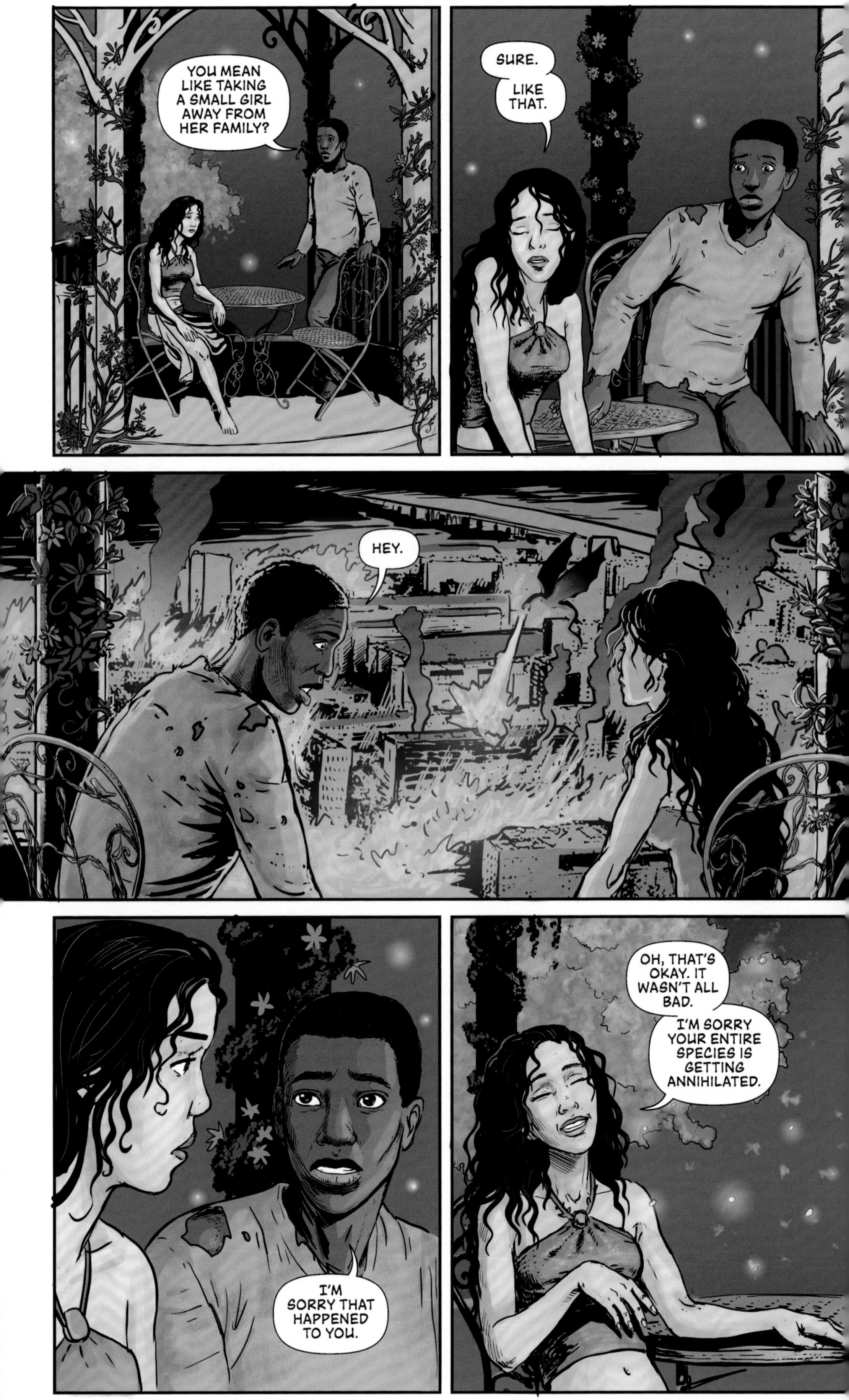
YOU MEAN LIKE TAKING A SMALL GIRL AWAY FROM HER FAMILY?
SURE.
LIKE THAT.
HEY.
I'M SORRY THAT HAPPENED TO YOU.
OH, THAT'S OKAY. IT WASN'T ALL BAD.
I'M SORRY YOUR ENTIRE SPECIES IS GETTING ANNIHILATED.

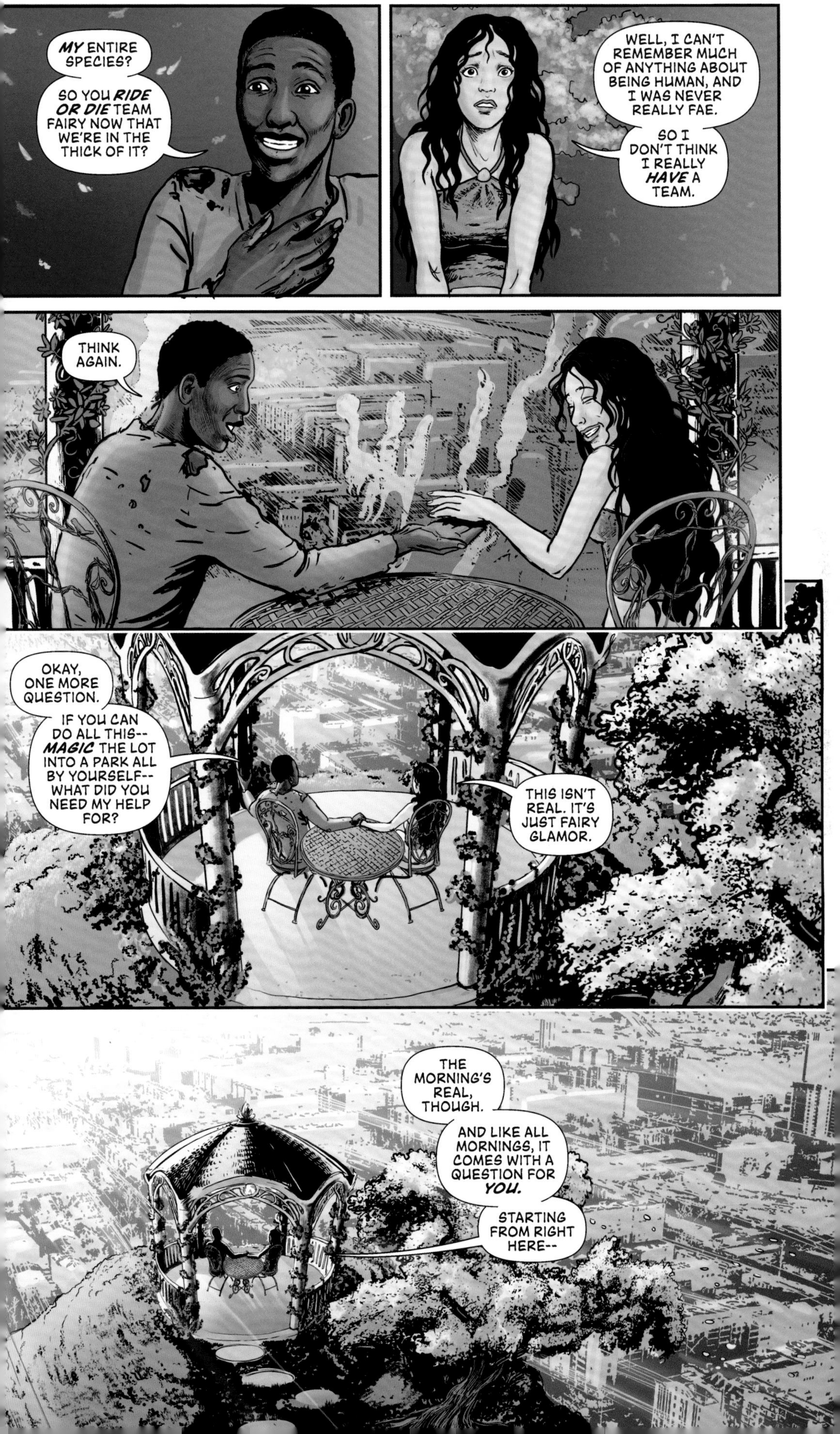
MY ENTIRE SPECIES?
SO YOU RIDE OR DIE TEAM FAIRY NOW THAT WE'RE IN THE THICK OF IT?
WELL, I CAN'T REMEMBER MUCH OF ANYTHING ABOUT BEING HUMAN, AND I WAS NEVER REALLY FAE.
SO I DON'T THINK I REALLY HAVE A TEAM.
THINK AGAIN.
OKAY, ONE MORE QUESTION.
IF YOU CAN DO ALL THIS-- MAGIC THE LOT INTO A PARK ALL BY YOURSELF-- WHAT DID YOU NEED MY HELP FOR?
THIS ISN'T REAL. IT'S JUST FAIRY GLAMOR.
THE MORNING'S REAL, THOUGH.
AND LIKE ALL MORNINGS, IT COMES WITH A QUESTION FOR YOU.
STARTING FROM RIGHT HERE--

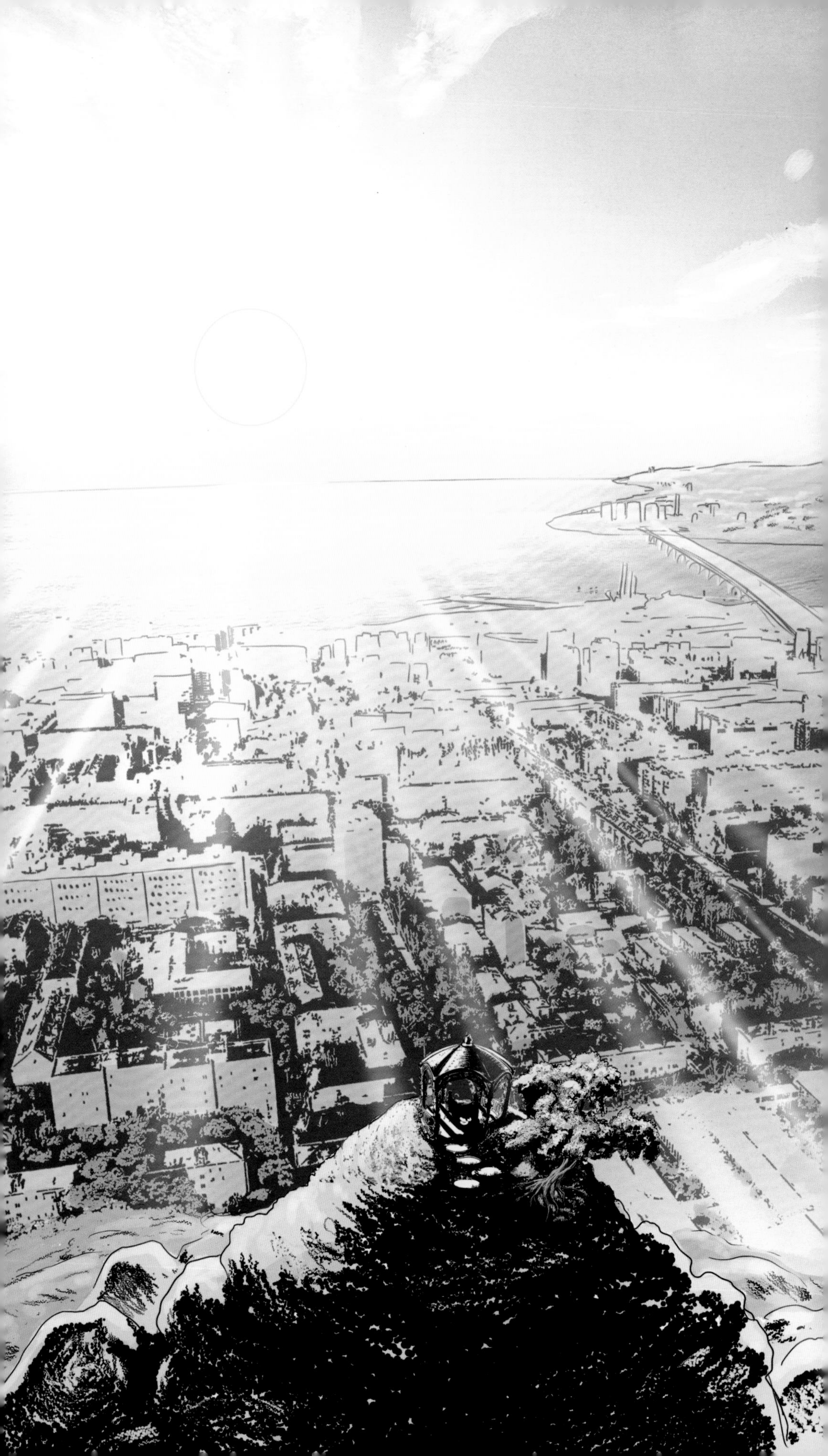

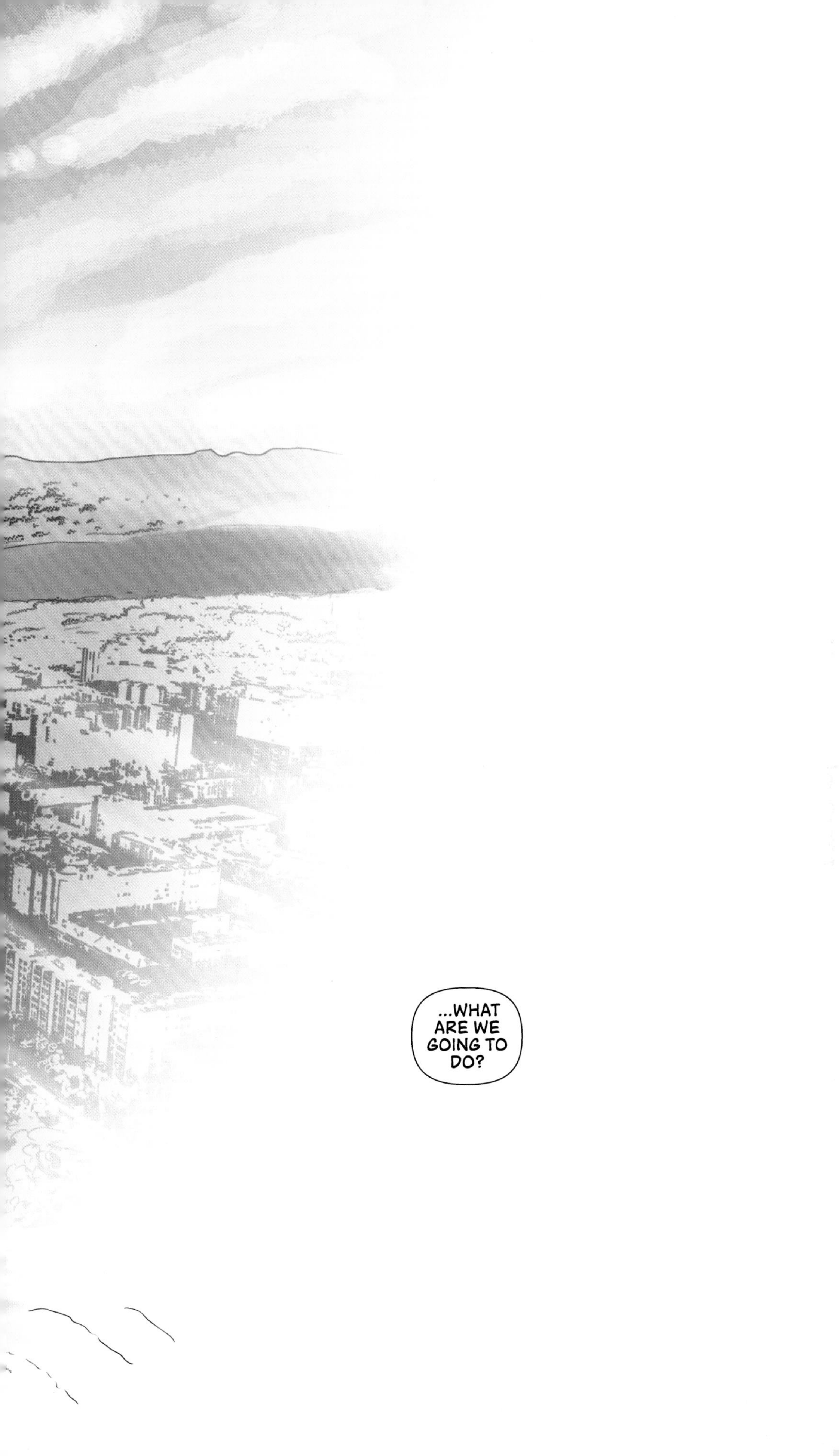
...WHAT ARE WE GOING TO DO?

Afterword

The initial impetus to write *Rewild* was purely emotional.

I live in Northern California, where our annual wildfire season feels like an advanced screening of the end of the world. Locked indoors, nervously eyeing the smoke-darkened sky through drafty, ash-strewn windows, I grieved for my beautiful state and felt tremendously grateful to have a story into which to channel my angst.

As the book began to take shape, though—blossoming into life through Yana's stunning artwork—I started to think about the intention behind it. The last thing I wanted was to put a story out into the world that gave people permission to give up. I felt strongly about that even as I privately questioned our ability to turn things around, a skepticism that did not go unnoticed.

"Where's the hope?" my aunt asked as I described the project to her over the phone. "People need hope in their stories now!"

"Well," I answered tersely, "this isn't that story."

Rewild was always meant to be a fable, a cautionary tale about how much we have to lose if we don't find more immediate and effective ways of addressing the Climate Crisis. Yana and I wanted to reimagine humanity's relationship with nature, create a space to mourn what's been lost, and reconnect readers to their kinship with what can yet be saved. Though the story is fictional, my passion for the subject matter grew as I worked, as did my library of climate-related books, articles, and podcasts. With every new chapter and article I read, I'd find a unique angle to explore or an insight I wanted to share. This proved tricky for two reasons: first, I'd already submitted and gotten a story outline approved. Second, it's rarely a good idea to shove academic lectures into the mouths of fictional characters who aren't academics.

So I promised myself that I could talk to you, the reader, about all of that here, in the afterword. There's so much to discuss, but I'll limit myself to a single observation and a single goal. The observation is that it's challenging to learn about the Climate Crisis without, at some point, getting overwhelmed and losing hope. The goal is to encourage you to move past that.

Consuming the research material I'd collected, I noticed three main postures that people engaging with the Climate Crisis tend to take: optimistic determination, paralyzed despair, and rational hope. I've come to think of them as a progression—an evolution, even—with one stance giving way to the next as your knowledge of and commitment to the cause deepens. If you're able to maintain optimistic determination, then please, continue. I salute you, offer my sincere gratitude, and trust our paths will cross again. But if this story has found you while you're on the cusp of—or possibly already mired in—paralyzed despair, I want to encourage you to keep going. I want to promise you that your actions make a difference. I want to point you in the direction of rational hope.

I first encountered the term "rational hope" in the writings of people who have waded into the fight for humanity's survival with their whole being and managed to sustain their engagement. Key characteristics of their activism often include creative utilization of their unique skill sets and working with lots of social support. I suspect we'd do well to emulate them.

And although I'm not entirely sure that hoping for this is rational, I'd also like to share an epoch-defining creative opportunity I see hidden amid this crisis. To survive as a species, we have to create a better future together. This means we have a chance—an obligation even—to reimagine society from the ground up.

That's daunting, I know. But not without allure. The issues you're passionate about, your skills, concerns, and expertise, even your dreams: all of that can be channeled into action that truly matters. The same characteristics that have gotten us into this mess could still get us out: no other animal is as adept as we are at transforming our environment. We've made many bad decisions and built many political, social, and physical infrastructures that are neither just nor viable. It is absolutely within us to make different choices and build better things. The time to do that was yesterday, but now is what we've got.

You don't need me to run you through all the ways you could be getting involved. The internet is full of solution-oriented lists, and every major environmental nonprofit has one. There are books, articles, podcasts, and thousands of people committed to seeing you engage with the movement. However you find it, there is absolutely something you can do. You just need to believe it matters.

So I promise you, it does.

There's no one here but us. What happens next is in our hands.

Devin Grayson
June 2021

REWILD

**Concept Designs & Notes
by Yana**

MERMAIDS

Once beautiful and colorful, mermaids had to flee from man into deeper waters, becoming more gray, more like the deep-sea creatures. Their long hair has become dead and oily, their skin prone to sickness.

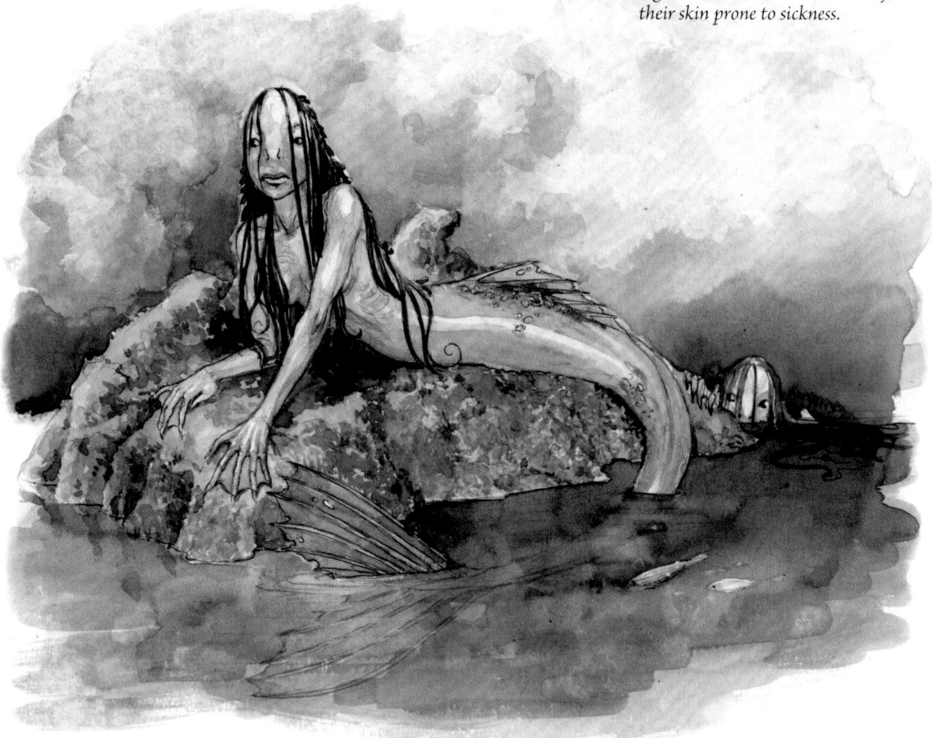

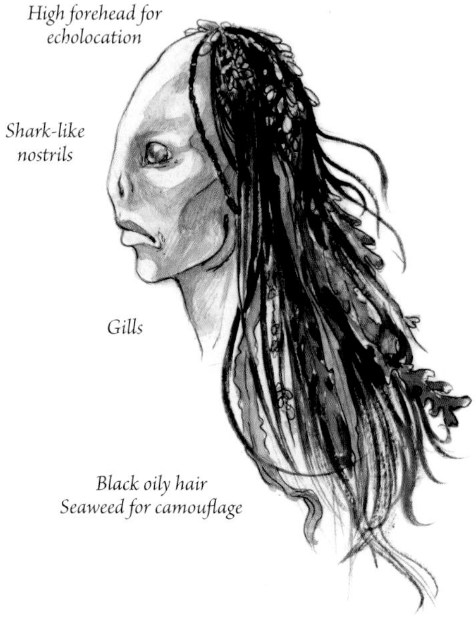
High forehead for echolocation
Shark-like nostrils
Gills
Black oily hair
Seaweed for camouflage

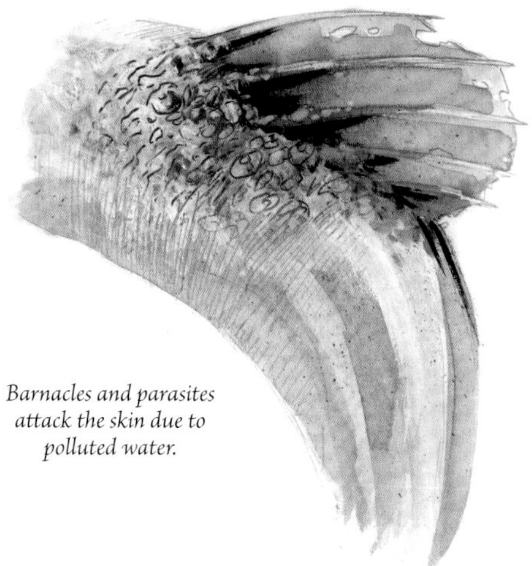
Barnacles and parasites attack the skin due to polluted water.

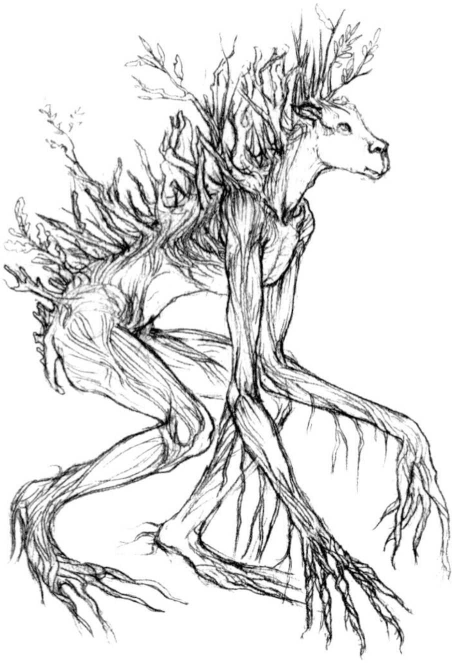

DEFORESTATION DRYAD

This gentle giant is one with the forests it inhabits. Like plants, it feeds on sunlight, rain and soil. As the forests are disappearing, the vegetation that is the dryad's body is drying up, leaving the dryads undernourished and fragile. With lack of energy they have lost the power to take up the human form.

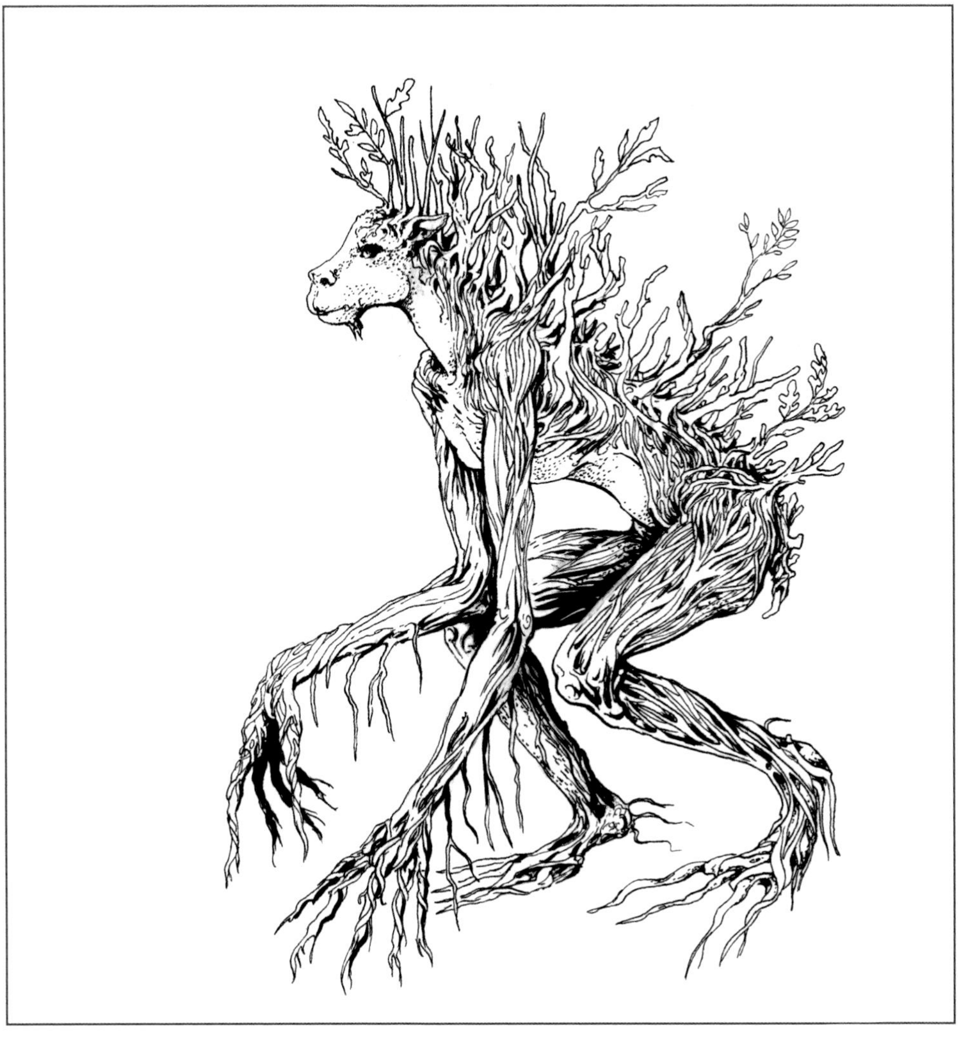

URBAN CREATURES

Some magical creatures had to adapt to life in urban environments. They linger in alleys, abandoned places and rundown parks.

FRACKING GNOME

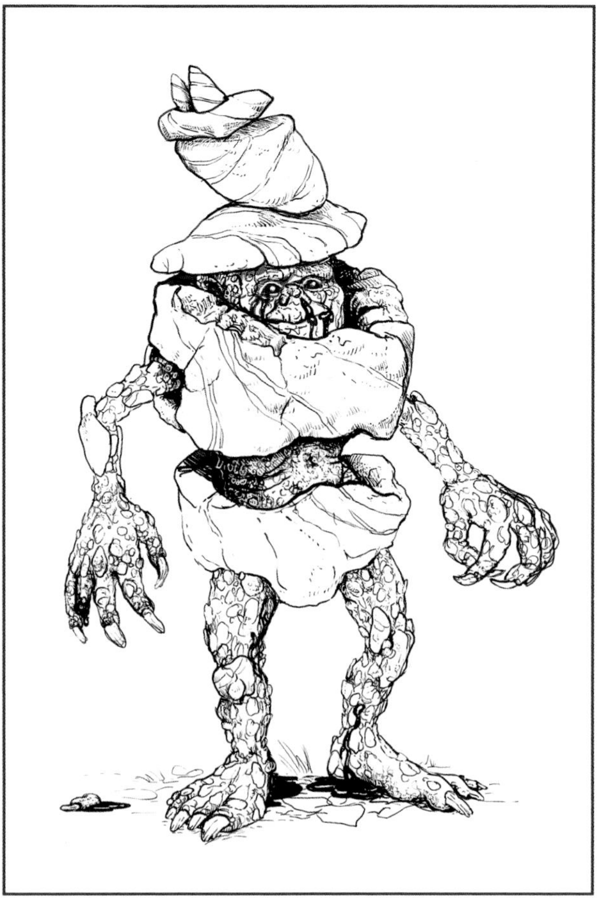

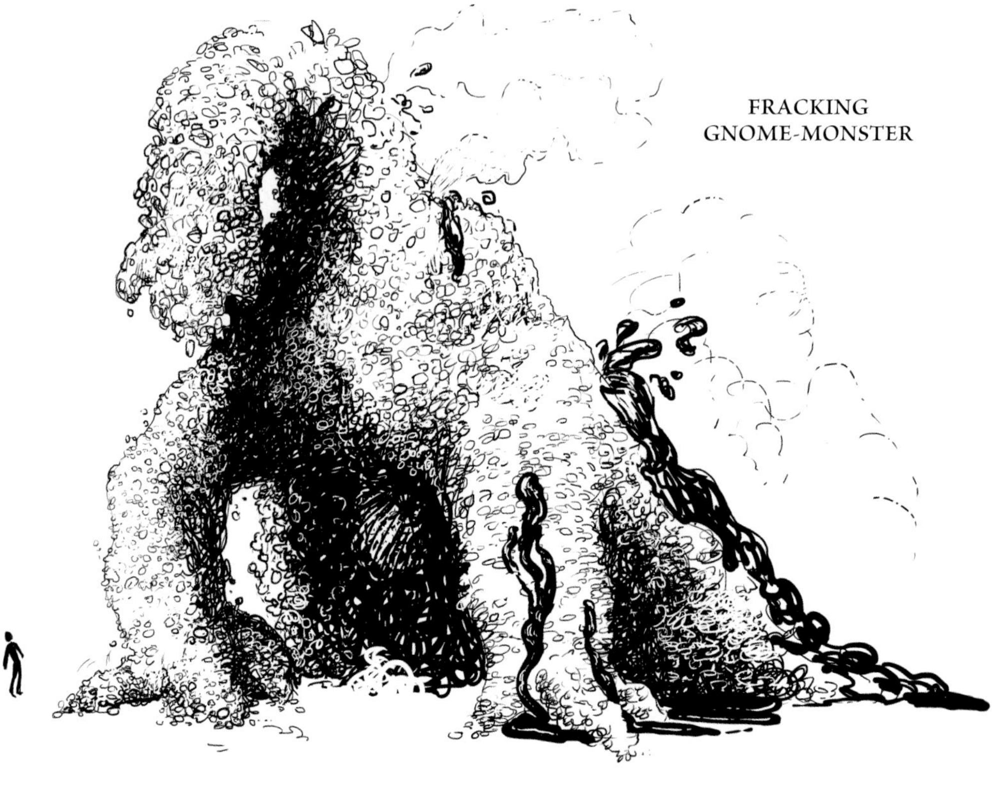

FRACKING GNOME-MONSTER

GARDEN GNOME

Garden gnomes are forced to live in public parks. It has become more and more difficult for them to disappear, so they carry turf and litter on their backs as camouflage.

TINKER-TRASH FAIRIES

Some fairies, the tinkering kind, choose to live near humans, tinkering with garbage people leave lying around in alleyways. They sometimes use food packaging as clothes, since they can't find suitable plants.

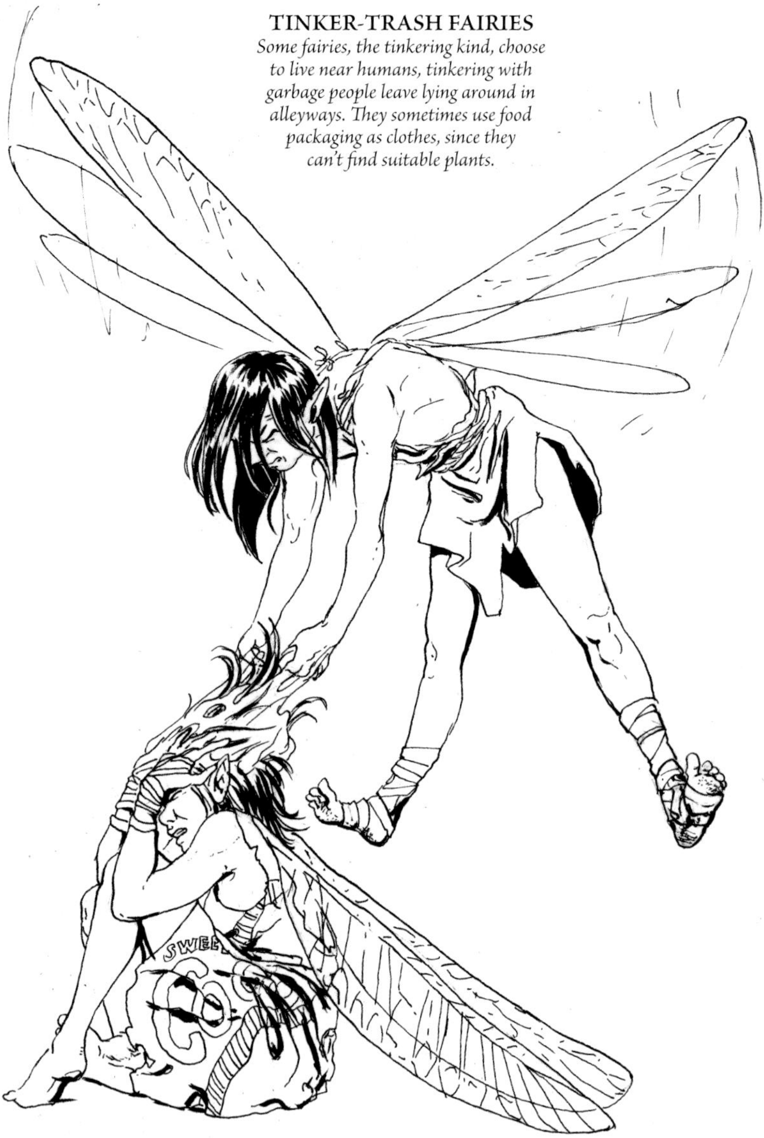

PIGEON PIXIE

Some pixies used their shape-shifting powers to take the forms of urban animals like pigeons and rodents. But because their powers are fading, the forms are often bizarre.

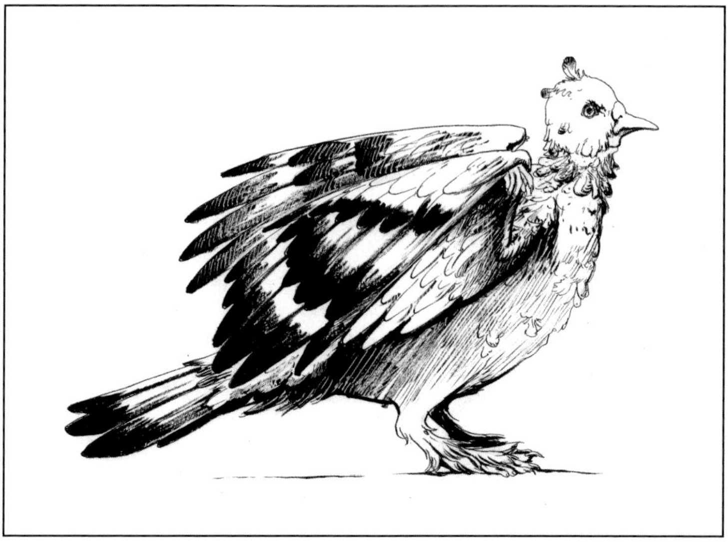

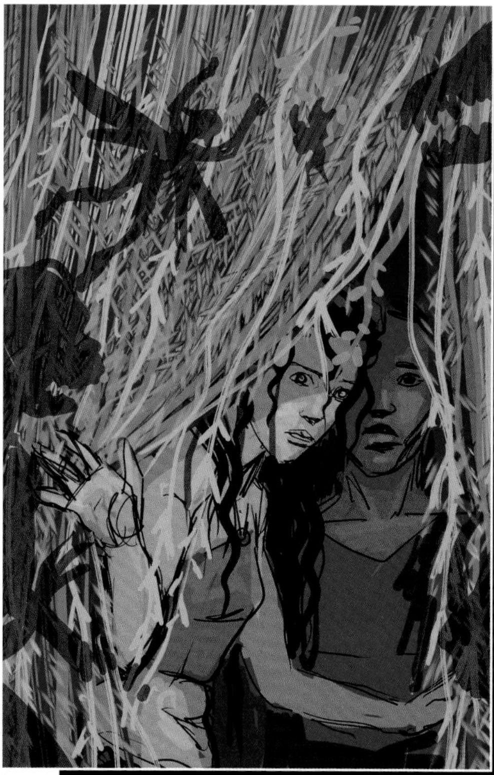

COVER CONCEPTS

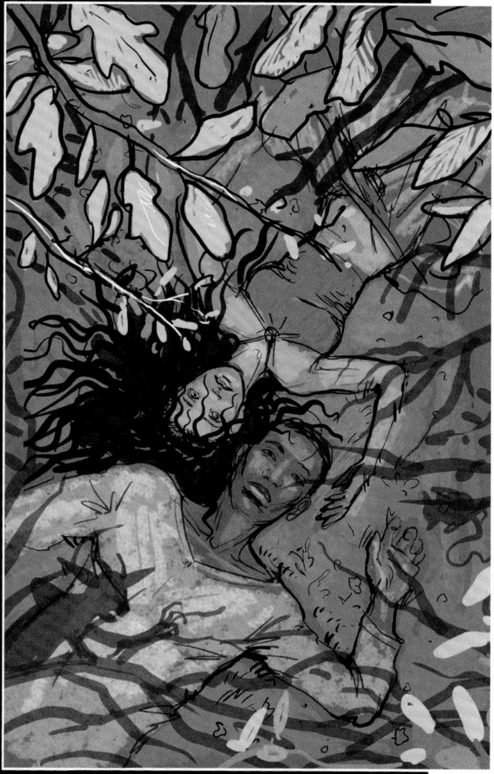

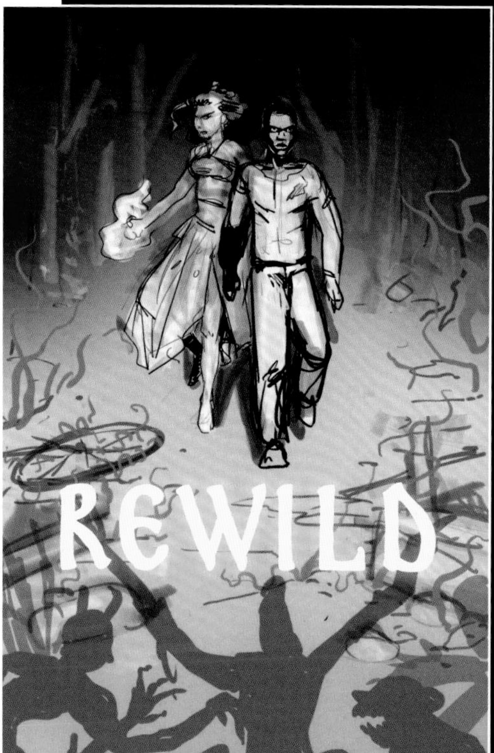
REWILD

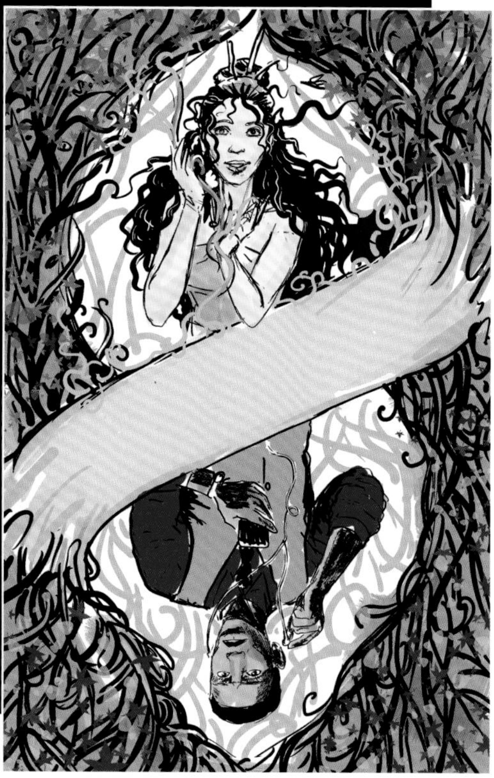

BERGER BOOKS

ANTHONY BOURDAIN'S HUNGRY GHOSTS

One night, chefs gather to outscare each other with tantalizing tales of fear and food—but will they survive?

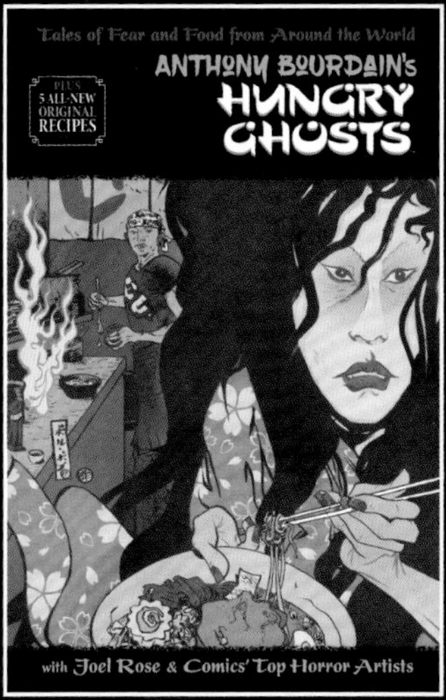
Tales of Fear and Food from Around the World
ANTHONY BOURDAIN'S
HUNGRY GHOSTS
PLUS 5 ALL-NEW ORIGINAL RECIPES
with Joel Rose & Comics' Top Horror Artists

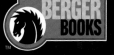

POST YORK

In a New York City drowned in its past, Crosby fights not just to survive... but to fully live. When he meets mysterious Ivy, the way he lives will change forever—but will it be for the better?

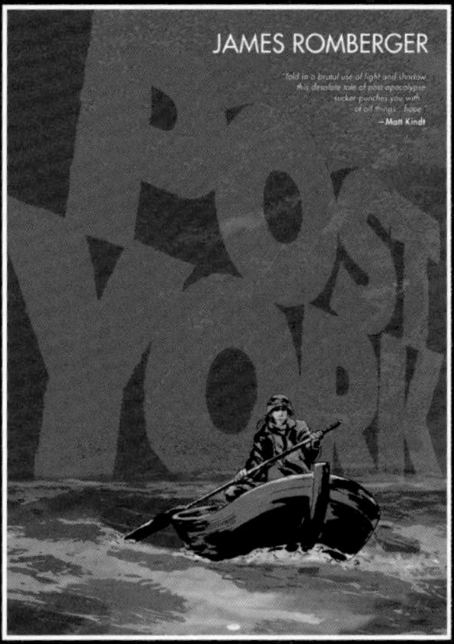
JAMES ROMBERGER
POST YORK

SHE COULD FLY Vol. One

A fantastic, unknown flying woman suddenly explodes mid-air—and crashes into the life of disturbed teen Luna Brewster.

SHE COULD FLY Vol. Two

Luna follows the flying woman's broken trail to find the truth—and to save herself. But is she too far gone?

SHE COULD FLY Vol. Three

In the shocking conclusion of the series, a new, dangerous Flying Woman has come to terrorize Chicago–and it's Luna's turn to take control.

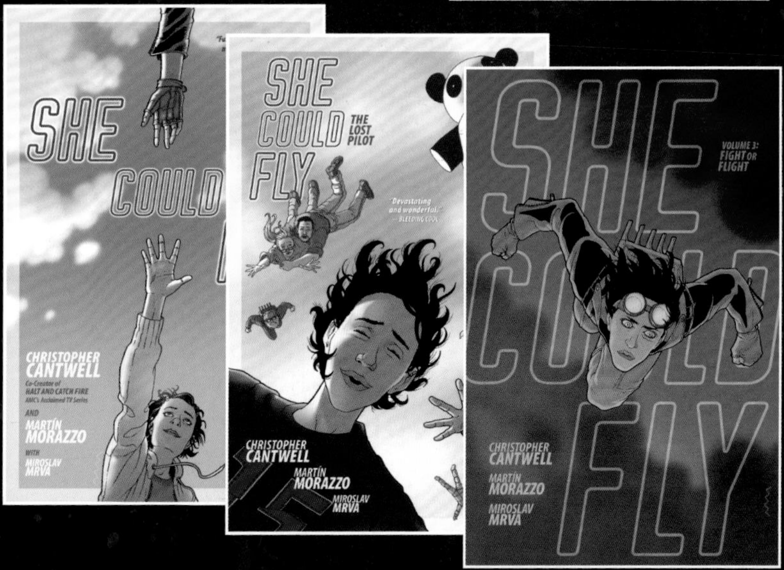
SHE COULD FLY
CHRISTOPHER CANTWELL
AND
MARTÍN MORAZZO
WITH
MIROSLAV MRVA
SHE COULD FLY
THE LOST PILOT
"Devastating and wonderful."
CHRISTOPHER CANTWELL
MARTÍN MORAZZO
MIROSLAV MRVA
SHE COULD FLY
VOLUME 3: FIGHT OR FLIGHT
CHRISTOPHER CANTWELL
MARTÍN MORAZZO
MIROSLAV MRVA

RUBY FALLS

Unlikely detective Lana Blake juggles murder, memory, a love triangle... and three generations of deadly small-town secrets.

EVERYTHING Vol. One

A mysterious superstore arrives in a small town... and catalyzes a horrifying pursuit of happiness.

EVERYTHING Vol. Two

As the Everything store gains power, so do its renegade opponents—but only one side can win this battle for The American Dream.

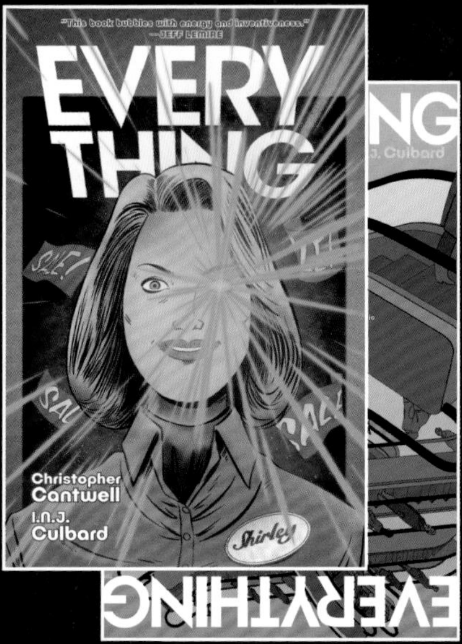
"This book bubbles with energy and inventiveness." —JEFF LEMIRE
EVERY THING
Christopher Cantwell
I.N.J. Culbard
EVERYTHING

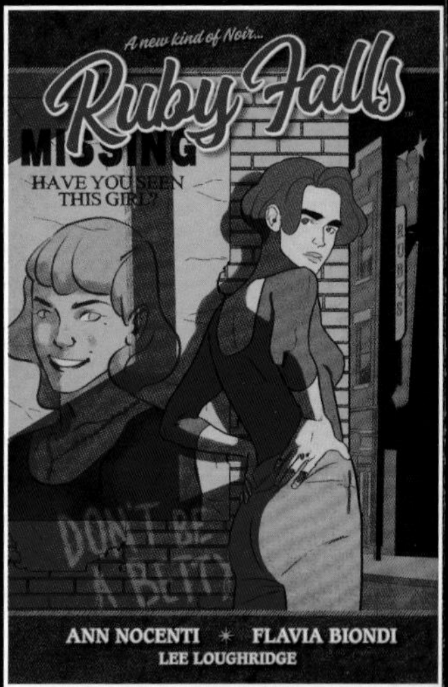
A new kind of Noir...
Ruby Falls
MISSING
HAVE YOU SEEN THIS GIRL?
ANN NOCENTI
FLAVIA BIONDI
LEE LOUGHRIDGE

THE SEEDS
hen an alien falls in love with a human, a journalist stumbles into
story of a lifetime, but reporting it just might destroy planet Earth.

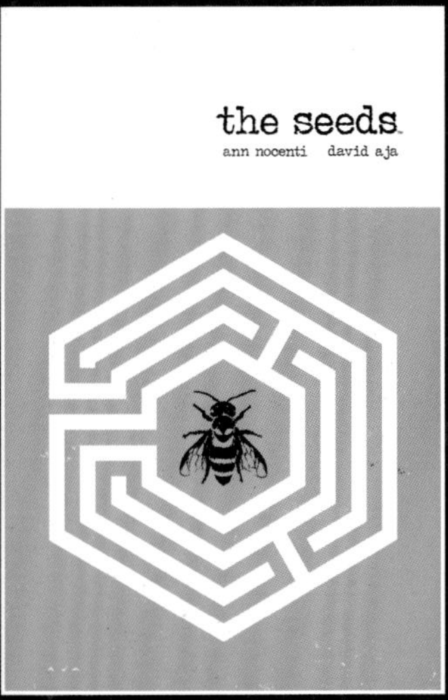
the seeds
ann nocenti david aja

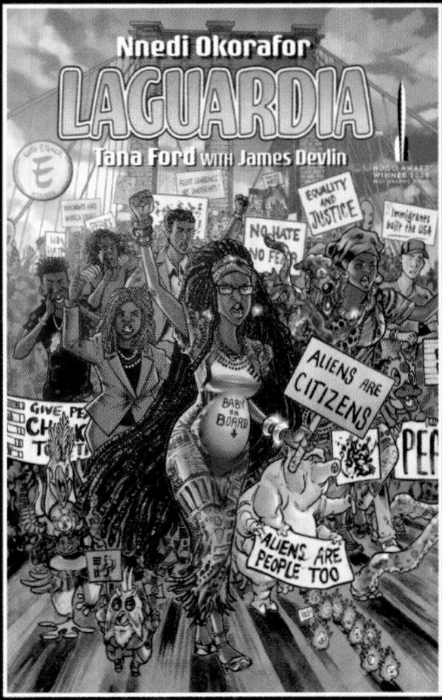
Nnedi Okorafor
LAGUARDIA
Tana Ford WITH James Devlin
ALIENS ARE CITIZENS
ALIENS ARE PEOPLE TOO

EISNER & HUGO AWARD WINNER

LAGUARDIA
In an alien-integrated world, a very pregnant doctor named Future Nwafor Chukwuebuka smuggles an illegal, sentient plant through LaGuardia International and Interstellar Airport, and their arrival in New York marks the abrupt start of an amazing new life—for everyone!

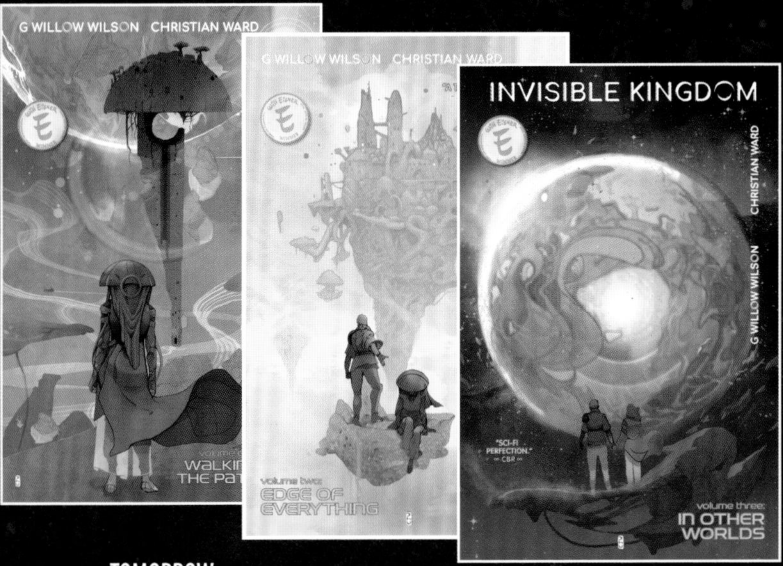
G WILLOW WILSON CHRISTIAN WARD
INVISIBLE KINGDOM
CHRISTIAN WARD
G WILLOW WILSON
"SCI-FI PERFECTION." CBR
volume two: EDGE OF EVERYTHING
volume three: IN OTHER WORLDS

EISNER AWARD WINNER

INVISIBLE KINGDOM Vol. One
A young religious acolyte and a dogged freighter pilot uncover an inconceivable conspiracy between a world's major religion and the mega corporation that controls society.

INVISIBLE KINGDOM Vol. Two
With only part of the truth blown open and bigger secrets looming, will Vess and Grix become stronger —or shatter apart?

INVISIBLE KINGDOM Vol. Three
The breathtaking tale of the *Sundog* concludes, and Vess and Grix are faced with a new choice: love...or destruction.

TOMORROW
esperate twins Oscar and Cira must find their way home
ter a species-jumping computer virus wipes out all adults.

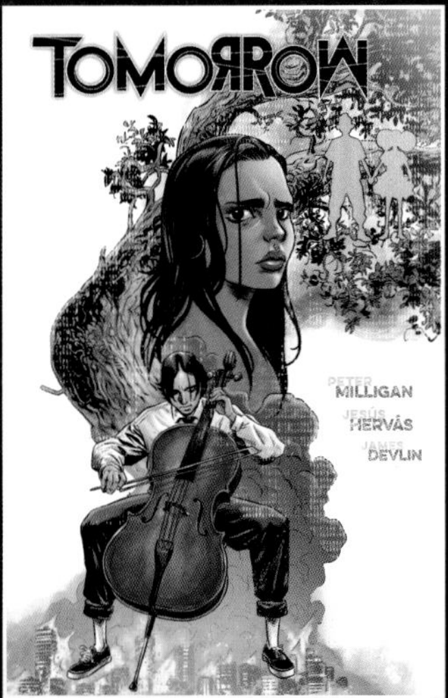
TOMORROW
PETER MILLIGAN
JESÚS HERVÁS
JAMES DEVLIN

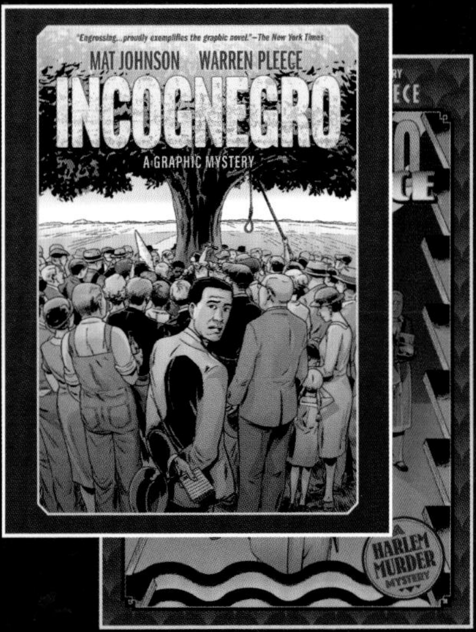
"Engrossing...proudly exemplifies the graphic novel."—The New York Times
MAT JOHNSON WARREN PLEECE
INCOGNEGRO
A GRAPHIC MYSTERY
HARLEM MURDER MYSTERY

INCOGNEGRO: A GRAPHIC MYSTERY
Zane Pinchback goes "incognegro" to investigate his brother's arrest in a fast-paced exploration of race and identity.

INCOGNEGRO: RENAISSANCE
Our race-bending protagonist penetrates a world where he feels stranger than ever before.

ACKNOWLEDGMENTS

~ Devin ~

So many unique projects inspired me as I worked on this. I would love to share just a tiny handful. Richard Powers' compelling novel *The Overstory* showed me how potently fiction could shift our perspective. Dr. Ayana Elizabeth Johnson and Alex Blumberg's *How to Save a Planet* podcast, along with Drs. Johnson and Katharine K. Wilkinson's gorgeous climate anthology, *All We Can Save*, consistently stoked my ardor while illuminating new corners of the Climate Crisis and offering concrete steps for engagement.

On a more personal note, there are no words to express how much I've enjoyed working with Yana and how grateful I am to Karen Berger for believing in our vision and helping us bring this story to life. Thanks, too, to Rae Boyadjis, Richard Bruning, and Sal Cipriano for lending their talent and enthusiasm to this book. Additionally, I remain forever indebted to Scott Peterson and Doselle Young for reading, rereading, and re-rereading everything I send them, usually without complaint. Love and eternal gratitude to my brilliant aunt Bree and my beloved husband Arnold for, well, everything. And finally, the warmest thanks to my dad, Bob, and my stepmom, Linda, for always providing shelter and support.

~ Yana ~

First of all, to Devin Grayson, thank you for inviting me to join you on this splendid adventure and for being such a wonderful friend. My gratitude goes out to Karen Berger, Rae Boyadjis, and the rest of the Berger Books team for helping this story find its way into the light. Thank you to TKV, a talented Serbian street artist, for allowing me to use her work and bring a piece of Belgrade into *Rewild*. And lastly, to my amazing partner Igor Kordey, thank you for all of your love and support.

Karen Berger – Editor
Rae Boyadjis – Associate Editor
Richard Bruning – Book Designer
Mike Richardson – President & Publisher

First Edition: November 2021
ISBN: 978-1-50672-263-4
Digital ISBN: 978-1-50672-264-1

1 3 5 7 9 10 8 6 4 2
Printed in China

Published by Dark Horse Books
A division of Dark Horse Comics LLC
10956 SE Main Street, Milwaukie, OR 97222

Names: Grayson, Devin K., author. | Adamovic, Yana, artist.
Title: Rewild / script, Devin Grayson; art, Yana Adamovic.
Description: First edition. | Milwaukie, OR : Dark Horse Books, 2021 |
Identifiers: LCCN 2021021427 (print) | LCCN 2021021428 (ebook) |
ISBN 9781506722634 (paperback) | ISBN 9781506722641 (ebook)
Subjects: LCSH: Animals, Mythical—Comic books, strips, etc. |
Changelings—Comic books, strips, etc. | Graphic novels. |
LCGFT: Horror comics. | Fantasy comics. | Graphic novels.
Classification: LCC PN6727.G723 R49 2021 (print) |
LCC PN6727.G723 (ebook) | DDC 741.5/973—dc23
LC record available at https://lccn.loc.gov/2021021427
LC ebook record available at https://lccn.loc.gov/2021021428